THE AMERICAN INSTITUTE OF ARCHITECTS
DESIGN FOR AGING CENTER

DESIGN FOR AGING REVIEW

First published in Australia in 2004 by
The Images Publishing Group Pty Ltd
ABN 89 059 734 431
6 Bastow Place, Mulgrave, Victoria, 3170, Australia
Telephone: + 61 3 9561 5544 Facsimile: + 61 3 9561 4860
Email: books@images.com.au
Website: www.imagespublishinggroup.com
Copyright © The Images Publishing Group Pty Ltd

Previous editions of this book are:
Design for Aging: 1992 Review (AIA Press)
Design for Aging: 1994 Review (AIA Press)
Design for Aging: 1996–97 Review (AIA Press)
Design for Aging: Four (published online at www.aia.org)
Design for Aging Review, 5th edition (The Images Publishing Group)

The Images Publishing Group Reference Number: 437

National Library of Australia Cataloguing-in-Publication Data

Design for Aging Review, 6th edition.

Includes indexes.

ISBN 1 920744 17 7.

1. Aged - Dwellings - United States - Design and construction.
2. Architecture - Awards - United States.
3. Old age homes - United States - Design and construction.
4. Architecture and the aged - United States.
I. The American Institute of Architects Design for Aging Center.

725.560222

Designed by The Graphic Image Studio Pty Ltd
Mulgrave, Australia

Film by Mission Production Limited
Printed by Everbest Printing Co. Ltd, in Hong Kong/China

CONTENTS

Nursing

JURY

JURY

Glen A. Tipton, FAIA, Jury Chair

Glen A. Tipton, FAIA, is senior vice president of Cochran, Stephenson & Donkervoet, with offices in Baltimore and Dallas. The 100-person firm provides a range of specialized studio practices, including its largest, the design of senior living communities. Mr Tipton has led the development of CSD's senior living practice over the past 30 years, during which time it has grown to be internationally recognized. Having led the design of more than 100 senior living communities, from full continuing care to assisted living, nursing, and Alzheimer's care, Mr Tipton was recognized in 2002 for his career-long commitment to the betterment of this specialized practice by elevation to the AIA College of Fellows.

Mr Tipton has shared his expertise in dozens of educational seminars for various senior living industry groups, as well as at the AIA, the Urban Land Institute, and related venues. His projects have received 32 design awards, and he has served on several design juries, including jury chair for the 2001 Design for Aging program. Mr Tipton now serves as chair of the AIA's Design for Aging knowledge community.

Kate Kwiecinski

Kate Kwiecinski is the president and CEO of Arbor Glen, a Quaker-affiliated continuing care retirement community (CCRC) located in Bridgewater, N.J. Prior to her current position she served as the assistant executive director at Medford Leas, another New Jersey CCRC.

A graduate of Pennsylvania State University, Ms Kwiecinski also holds a master's degree in health care administration from St Joseph's University in Philadelphia and is a licensed nursing home administrator. Before coming to the long-term care profession, she worked in acute care. Ms Kwiecinski has been an evaluator for the Continuing Care Accreditation Commission (CCAC) since 1987. She was a member of the CCAC Standards Revision Task Force in 1991, and was part of the faculty for evaluator training from 1991 to 1992, and again from 1995 through 1999. She served on AAHSA's CCRC Committee for four years, as a member of the CCRC Advisory Panel, and has been a contributing author to the CCAC Resources Manual and the RHP CCRC module. Ms Kwiecinski is a member of the Nursing Advisory Committee of the State of New Jersey's Department of Health and Senior Services, and she chairs the Registered Nurse Selection Committee for the New Jersey Governor's Nursing Merit Awards.

William (Bill) E. Ruff, AIA

Bill Ruff, principal and cofounder of LRS Architects, Inc., has over 30 years of architectural design and planning experience on more than 100 senior housing projects in 19 states. His clear strategic vision and development experience have helped LRS Architects pioneer numerous successful "firsts" in housing applications and receive national recognition. He designed and developed the first assisted living facility (ALF) and first Medicaid-eligible ALF in Oregon, the first licensed ALF in Iowa, and the first specialty design dementia facilities for Alzheimer's disease, among others. Mr Ruff is also a hands-on architect who has been instrumental in the success of two other "firsts" in the country: High Lookee Lodge for the Confederated Tribes in Warm Springs, Oregon, is the first ALF devoted solely to tribal elders, and Chestnut Lane in Gresham, Oregon, is the first new facility constructed specifically for the needs of deaf and deaf/blind seniors.

Gary B. Selmeczi

Gary B. Selmeczi is executive director of the Goodwin House in Alexandria, Va. Mr Selmeczi is a licensed nursing home administrator, a certified preceptor, and has served as an evaluator for the Continuing Care Accreditation Commission. He has also served on the boards of the Virginia Health Care Association and the Virginia Association of Nonprofit Homes for the Aging. He is a member of the Alexandria Rotary Club and currently serves on the board of Senior Services of Alexandria. Mr Selmeczi is a graduate of Westminster College in New Wilmington, Pa., and earned a master's of health services administration from George Washington University in Washington, D.C. He has completed postgraduate work in nonprofit management at Harvard Business School.

INTRODUCTION

The American Institute of Architects (AIA) Design for Aging Center (DAC), in affiliation with the American Association of Homes and Services for the Aging (AAHSA), is proud to present the *Design for Aging Review*, 6th edition. This beautiful and informative book presents the finest designs for senior living facilities submitted in the 2001–2002 cycle and is the second edition of the review published by The Images Publishing Group.

The AIA Design for Aging Center comprises a multidisciplinary group of professionals with a common bond of concern for our aging adults and the environments in which they live. Although most DAC members are architects, the center also includes gerontologists, interior designers, and other professionals whose efforts affect senior living environments. Anyone interested in assisting the DAC is encouraged to contact the AIA or AAHSA.

Every two years, the DAC sends a Call for Entries to architects and owners for this biannual review. Due to the interdisciplinary nature of this program, input ideally comes from both architects and owners/providers. In 2001 the DAC received and categorized 73 submissions, of which a jury of four (two architects and two providers of senior housing or services) selected 68 projects for publication, 44 for exhibition, and seven to receive an AIA/AAHSA Citation for design excellence.

The submissions represented 48 architects and projects in 30 states (eight projects in Ohio alone). For the first time this year, a European project (from Belgium) was submitted, attesting to the growing awareness of seniors' needs around the world. In fact, AAHSA continues to explore this growing global phenomenon through the International Association of Homes and Services for the Aging (IAHSA).

The Design for Aging exhibit was displayed three times: at the AAHSA Annual Meetings in 2001 and 2002 and at the AIA National Convention in 2002. In addition, jurors conducted post-occupancy evaluations of two of the seven Citation projects, the results of which were presented at the AAHSA 2002 Annual Meeting. Audiotapes of the jury's overview of this cycle's review (presented at the AAHSA 2002 Annual Meeting) are available from AAHSA, which also offers a CD-ROM of the entire 2002 AAHSA Annual Meeting that includes the post-occupancy evaluations.

Categories of Submissions

Perhaps the single most telling trend in the field of senior living facility design is reflected by the proliferation of project categories. No longer do projects fall neatly into categories such as Continuing Care Retirement Community (CCRC), Nursing Home, or Independent Senior Living Apartment. (A CCRC typically includes facilities that serve multiple levels of need, from fully independent living through assisted living and finally to nursing care.) For this cycle, DAC members categorized the projects as follows, often as combinations of project types:

- *New CCRCs*
- *Renovated/Expanded CCRCs*
- *Nursing*
- *Nursing/Assisted Living*
- *Assisted Living/Alzheimer's Care*
- *Independent Living*
- *Independent Living/Assisted Living*
- *Community Outreach/Wellness.*

Clearly, owners/providers are housing and serving seniors in an expanding variety of ways, as the demands of the consumer and the public dictate. The lines of definition between "independent" and "assisted," and between "assisted" and "nursing," are increasingly blurred as residents receive more and more care in "independent" settings. Meanwhile, increasingly frail assisted living residents are receiving light nursing care in states whose codes mandate an "aging-in-place" standard that prescribes building standards for assisted living building standards that are equivalent to those for nursing homes. In many states, Alzheimer's care can be offered in non-nursing settings, which promote a far less institutional environment.

The inescapable lesson for architects and owners/providers is that the world of design for seniors is changing. Senior consumers are seeking the facilities that suit them best, and the answer to their needs is "choice." Seniors want choices—in both facilities and services—hence the ever-expanding diversity of project types, which ultimately encourages creativity and, ideally, higher-quality design and service. The partnership of architect and provider must continue this exploration!

Trends and Observations

Beyond the overarching trend of increasing project types—and decreasing distinctions between care levels—the jury agreed upon several observations (including further trends) that merit the reader's consideration in this edition of the review.

The owner/provider needs a more powerful voice in this program.
While the Design for Aging program celebrates building design, it also encourages the beneficial partnership of a well-reasoned owner/provider program with a creative, well-considered architectural design. Too often, the jury felt that this cycle's submissions could have articulated more clearly the owner's operational and/or programmatic imperatives. Perhaps this also has been true in the past, but the DAC will endeavor to improve this situation in the next cycle by encouraging a more fully coordinated architect-owner/provider submission.

Over-regulation inhibits creativity.
With a few notable exceptions, the level of creativity from submissions in the Nursing category was disappointing. Few nursing projects ventured far from the strict edicts of nursing home design regulations that most states mandate. The jury lamented a lack of clear explanation of the owner/provider's goals (as opposed to the architect's), which produced the lack of creative explorations in this category.

Perhaps the more creative providers have focused on other project categories. For example, nursing facilities created as part of CCRCs or in conjunction with assisted living exhibited significantly higher levels of creativity.

Assisted living continues to influence the field.
Although apparently overbuilt in many locations, the assisted living facility (either stand-alone or in conjunction with other service and housing components) continues to present a more residential image and more creative programmatic options than its cousin, the nursing home. Perhaps because assisted living facilities were created as an attractive alternative to nursing homes, or perhaps because they are subject to increased marketplace competition (largely due to alleged overbuilding), the assisted living projects generally reflected much greater attention to residents' environmental needs (e.g., lighting and finishes).

In addition, to make assisted living a more attractive alternative to remaining at home (including remaining in an independent living setting in a CCRC), assisted living has become much more similar to independent living than to nursing care. The increasing size of living units, the expanding range of amenities, and the overall residential feel continues to refine the quality of assisted living designs.

Alzheimer's care and design are ever evolving.
Alzheimer's and other forms of dementia are perhaps the least understood of all senior conditions, yet facilities designed specifically for residents with these unique needs reflect a remarkable array of design solutions. A smaller-scale environment dominates all of the submissions in this category. Typically, for example, a household has 12 to 15 beds, and the facilities offer a highly familiar residential environment.

Among the design approaches to the common areas, the "Town Center" or "Main Street Commons" concept achieves a Disneyesque indoor-outdoor environment in many submissions, with varying success. A secure, well-designed garden is also becoming a common therapeutic programmatic element.

Many Alzheimer's facilities are not classified as nursing facilities, as they once were, but rather as Assisted Living. This may be due in part to the residents' needs and to the less restrictive nature of assisted living or similar care categories.

The CCRC remains a trendsetter.
In many ways, the largest number of creative approaches to familiar problems emerged from the CCRC category—perhaps due to a higher level of consumer competition. Another factor may be the greater willingness of the CCRC owner/provider to eschew the cookie-cutter approach that many stand-alone independent living and, especially, assisted living or nursing projects often take. Arguably, the CCRC also enjoys an economy of scale that permits greater creativity.

In any event, the CCRC submissions exhibited unique site-planning solutions; a diverse array of building and unit types; and a general increase in the size of, and amenities within, living units. Similarly, the number of program and dining spaces, as well as the inclusion of indoor pools and fitness facilities, reflect the demand for choice and wellness. Sociologists, anthropologists, and market demographers have observed a generational shift in the expectations of the new CCRC consumer—a shift that clearly has motivated much of the exploration of new paradigms within the CCRC building type.

Older CCRCs deserve attention.
Surprisingly few submissions involved upgrades of existing CCRCs. Surely, existing CCRCs
are being renovated and expanded. If not, the DAC expects a tremendous surge soon in the
Renovated/Expanded CCRCs category. CCRCs will be forced to renew themselves as they age and
competitive new communities are built. Though few in number, the Renovated/Expanded CCRC
submissions exhibited highly aggressive approaches.

DAC members hope that these submissions will encourage more owners/providers to address
the environmental needs of their aging CCRCs.

More affordable housing and care options are encouraged.
Most of the submitted projects had quite ample budgets. In many cases, the jury wished for a
clearer explanation of the budgetary parameters, which would enable the jury to correlate the
cost of construction with the market's expectations and needs. The jury also would like to have
seen more creatively affordable projects. Only on a limited basis did some submissions celebrate
affordability. Again, a better integration of owner/provider goals with the architect's solution
would be beneficial.

Regionalism and vernacular design benefit residents and the community.
Many successful submissions clearly exhibited an architectural and interior design that celebrates
the region in which the facility is located or the heritage of the sponsoring owner/provider. All of
the Citation recipients and the vast majority of the exhibited submissions embraced the local
architectural vernacular in one way or another.

This approach is important to the residents because familiar surroundings reassure seniors who
are making the transition to a new home. It also makes such facilities or communities welcome
additions to their environs. So often, facilities for seniors are misunderstood by community groups
and planning and zoning authorities. Many of the submissions exemplified the positive impact
that such developments can have within a neighborhood.

This is not to say that regionalism and vernacular design should slavishly follow or shallowly
reflect the popular image of "traditional" architecture. Rather, they should demonstrate, as in most
successful cases herein, a sympathetic understanding of the regional design influences in
massing, fenestration, materials, details, and so on. In fact, the jury encourages fresh approaches
that intelligently explore new directions—rooted in, and respectful of, the environment in which
the facility is built.

Community outreach enhances quality of life.
Increasingly, owners/providers are building health, fitness, and cultural facilities to reach a much
broader range of constituents. Typically, these facilities are on the sites of existing senior
campuses, but many are stand-alone community resources, fully integrated within the larger
communities. They are among the responses to the demands of the new generation of seniors,
many of whom want far more options than facilities provided in the past.

These community outreach approaches include wellness and fitness centers focused on the
unique needs of the elderly—the wellness concept addressing physical, mental, spiritual,
psychological, emotional, and other aspects of wellbeing. Integration of a community resource
(such as a child care center or a performing arts center) within a senior campus is another form
of community outreach that enhances senior adults' quality of life.

"Thinking outside the box" advances the field.
The submissions included many excellent examples of what the jury called "thinking outside
the box"—several of which received a Citation. The unique, innovative approaches featured
throughout this edition of the *Design for Aging Review* include the following:

- *Adaptive reuse of existing buildings to create new senior-oriented uses*
- *More contemporary design solutions both inside and out, especially in the European and West Coast examples*
- *Redefinition of the classic double-loaded corridor nursing environment*
- *Juxtaposition of child daycare with Alzheimer's care*
- *Integration of an entire CCRC into a larger residential development plan*
- *Blending of "nursing households" within residential neighborhoods as a site-planning concept.*

The jury encourages all architects and owners/providers in this field to explore new collaborative
directions to ensure the continued positive growth of senior living communities.

CONTINUING CARE RETIREMENT COMMUNITY

Mary's Woods at Marylhurst

1

ARCHITECT'S STATEMENT

The Sisters of the Holy Names of Jesus and Mary needed to support and nurture their retired Sisters. They took the bold step of creating a nondenominational continuing care retirement community (CCRC) using their historic Provincial House as the heart of the development. The new CCRC:

- celebrates the history of the site, the buildings, and the Sisters
- maintains the site's serenity and botanical beauty
- creates a resident-centered environment that promotes and enhances wellness of mind, body, and spirit
- strengthens connections to the surrounding community and neighboring Marylhurst University.

Major design objectives and responses

Celebrate the history of the building and the Sisterhood.
The historic Provincial House is the heart of the development, renovated as the new commons building. The architectural style of the building acts as a model for all other buildings, which are oriented toward it. The main entry was returned to its original entry facing the Willamette River. The independent apartment buildings, wellness center, and health care building connect to the Provincial House.

Maintain the site's serenity and botanical beauty.
Each building's plan is shaped by how it defines courtyards and saves significant heritage trees. An old apple orchard was restored, as well as mature evergreens from an old Christmas tree farm, an arboretum,

and several 100-foot sequoias. Walking paths connect significant sites for residents to explore.

Provide a state-of-the-art health care center based on a residential model.
The 22-unit Alzheimer's residence is composed of three houses, each for six to eight residents, and each with its own living room, dining room, and kitchen, to help create a familiar, residential scale. Each house is designated by using the unique and basic shapes of the circle, square, and triangle. These shapes are duplicated in signs, art, fabrics, pavements, furniture, and so on, to aid residents' sense of place. Every Alzheimer's house opens onto a protected exterior courtyard. A retaining wall around a saved landmark maple tree encloses the courts.

ARCHITECT	MITHUN
SITE LOCATION	SUBURBAN
SITE AREA	24.3 ACRES/1.059 MILLION SQUARE FEET
CAPACITY	235 APARTMENTS, 33 COTTAGES, 40 ASSISTED LIVING UNITS, 22 DEMENTIA-SPECIFIC UNITS, 23 SKILLED NURSING UNITS
TOTAL PROJECT COST	$57.2 M

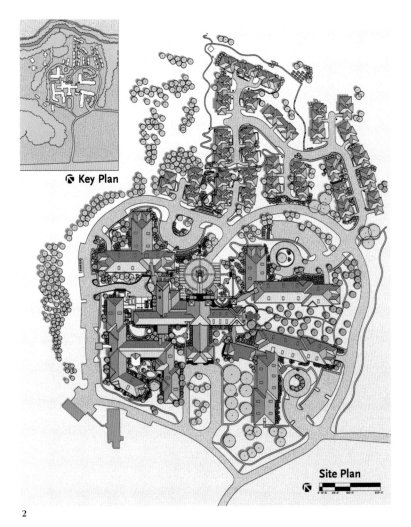

Key Plan

Site Plan

2

3

4

The 23-bed skilled nursing residence is divided into two houses, each with its own living room, dining room, and serving pantry. Resident rooms are designed to allow flexibility as to bed position and the inclusion of personal belongings.

The 40-unit assisted living residence was purposely not broken into smaller 'homes' in order to foster a larger sense of community among those living on the floor (many of them Sisters) who would not be as adversely affected by larger common spaces as those in Alzheimer's or skilled nursing. In addition, a lounge and direct connection to the shared spaces of the commons building were included both to encourage residents to take part in the activities of the larger community and to encourage others to visit the assisted living residence.

Provide adequate resident orientation.
Residents have a view of the Provincial House at each elevator lobby. This view reinforces the concept of the Provincial House as the heart of the project and helps to orient residents within the large building complex.

Maximize residential units.
The layouts were designed to break up the typical box feeling and expand the sense of space within the units by connecting spaces and using perspective techniques. Residents are allowed some degree of customization.

1 Commons building, lobby
2 Site plan
3 Attached villas
4 Exterior, commons building
Photography: Eckert & Eckert

5

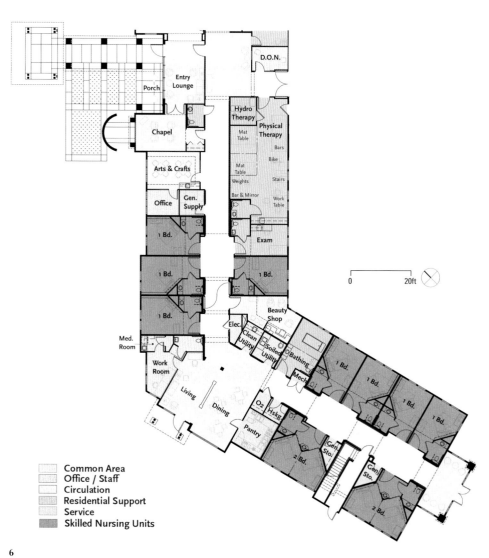

6

Common Area
Office / Staff
Circulation
Residential Support
Service
Skilled Nursing Units

5 Bridge between independent apartments and commons building
6 Floor plan, health care center and skilled nursing household
7 Existing wood doors in commons building preserved as fixed panels
8 Main dining room, commons building
9 Health care center, resident room
10 Alzheimer's dining room
Photography: Eckert & Eckert

7

8

9

10

ALDERSGATE
CHARLOTTE, NORTH CAROLINA

ARCHITECT'S STATEMENT

When the board of directors of this 56-year-old continuing care retirement community first contacted FreemanWhite Senior Living, it was understood that numerous changes were necessary for the facility to remain competitive in the next millennium. Aldersgate was finding it increasingly difficult to compete against newer facilities, and the board wanted to evaluate whether the facility should remain at its current location—a beautiful 225-acre site in a declining neighborhood—or move to a new site.

Faced with this challenge, the board began with a planning workshop. Such workshops, organized by the firm, are designed to bring financial consultants, market researchers, the board of directors, and key staff members together with the project designers and master planning team to discuss the various project components.

The workshops assist with smart decision making and help the team understand the project's mission and how it can be incorporated into the world of daily operations and financial accountability. For this project, the planning workshop assisted in making numerous decisions, the most pressing one being to remain at the current site.

Major design objectives and responses
Reinvent the campus.
A new entrance into the community would route residents and visitors away from the adjacent neighborhood. In addition, one of the oldest buildings would need to be demolished because renovation was not a viable option. Much of the site's acreage was undeveloped, including a lovely lake area. By renovating some of the existing buildings, demolishing others, and

incorporating the overlooked lake views into the facility expansion plans, a dynamic new campus plan was born.

New memory support unit incorporates the Eden Alternative and Main Street USA concepts of Alzheimer's and dementia care. The design includes three 15-resident households with resident rooms clustered around traditional homelike spaces: living room, dining room, kitchen, laundry, den/study, and back porch. All these spaces connect to the outside, allowing residents to freely wander inside and out. Natural light filters through these spaces and into a large atrium in the Town Square. Dogs, cats, and birds will live throughout the home, with their needs discreetly provided for, to allow ease of contact for the residents, staff, and visitors.

ARCHITECT	FREEMANWHITE SENIOR LIVING
SITE LOCATION	SUBURBAN
SITE AREA	225 ACRES
CAPACITY	63 APARTMENT UNITS, 15 COTTAGES, 45 SPECIAL CARE BEDS
TOTAL PROJECT COST	$23.8 M (ESTIMATED)

5

6

1   Household living room
2   Apartment building
3   Community building
4   Town Square
5   Commons living room
6   Pool
7   Site plan

The Town Square will have a general store, movie theater, pet store, café with sidewalk dining, hair salon, and plant shop—all surrounding a central garden area with a walking path, goldfish pond, and aviary. Residents will be able to wander from their homes to the outside garden areas to the Town Square and back, and engage in activities and stimulating environments throughout.

The design's framework creates the foundation to promote positive interaction between the residents and staff, families, and the outside community, enhancing residents' quality of life. Other project components include a new 63-unit apartment building, a new community building with wellness center and indoor pool, and a 15-unit cottage community.

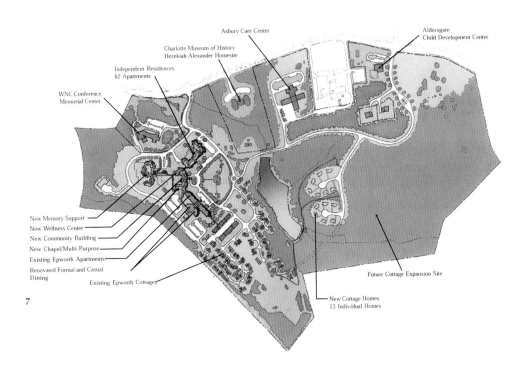

7

BRISTOL GLEN
NEWTON, NEW JERSEY

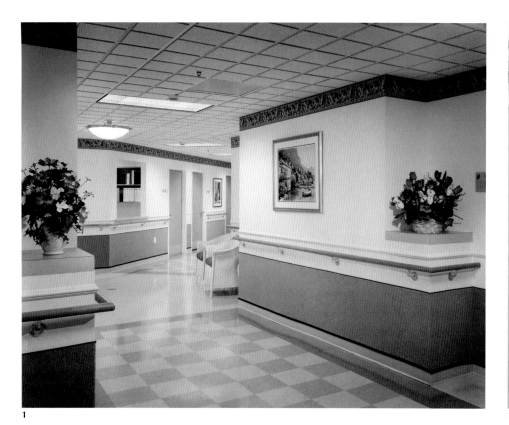

1

2

ARCHITECT'S STATEMENT

The client's mission is to provide high levels of service and amenity to low- to moderate-income seniors. The challenge was to provide three distinctly separate yet related buildings, one for each level of care, internally linked to share as much service and common space as possible, while also keeping the public and private functions separated.

The solution was to place the common and service spaces on the ground level of the central assisted living building. A service courtyard at the center of the complex provides private access away from the three separate public building entrances, located on the outside edges of the facility. The common spaces, shared by residents of all three buildings, are separated along two corridors. The more private garden corridor

contains offices, therapy, medical, and personal care functions. The public main street corridor includes gathering and activity spaces with a general store, post office, and bank.

The site, though quite large, was limited in its use by a power line easement that cut the site approximately in half and by a split between two townships, with one piece having no access to utilities. The steep, forested grades and large rock outcroppings, some as high as 40 feet, further limited the site's 'buildable' area. The remaining area had to be grouted before construction due to large voids in the ground. The site's beauty and potential for future cottage development made the extra work worthwhile.

Major design objectives and responses
Reduce apparent scale of a large complex of buildings.
The buildings step down a sloped site, from one-story nursing at the upper end down to four-story apartments at the lower end. The buildings are visually separated, and the site features elements to screen buildings from each other. A mansard roof is used on the fourth floor of apartments.

Include separate yet unified buildings.
Buildings are related by their colors and materials. Synthetic stucco, brick, and vinyl siding are used differently on each building but provide a unifying effect.

Balance privacy and costs in nursing rooms.
Nursing care rooms are developed as two 'rooms,' each with its own window and

ARCHITECT · DONNELLY WAGNER NELSON REBILAS ARCHITECTS, LLC

SITE LOCATION · RURAL

SITE AREA · 74 ACRES/3,223,440 SQUARE FEET

CAPACITY · 88 APARTMENT UNITS, 40 SENIOR LIVING/ASSISTED LIVING/PERSONAL CARE UNITS, 60 SKILLED NURSING CARE BEDS

TOTAL PROJECT COST · $26.7 M

3

4

5

1   Health care center corridor
2   Town Center Main Street
3   Assisted living (left), independent living (right)
4   Formal dining room
5   Independent living building with garage entrance
6   Site plan
Photography: Ernest Duck (3,5);
Barry Halkin (1,2,4)

6

closet, off a shared vestibule and bathroom, providing most of the privacy associated with fully private rooms while controlling costs and shortening corridors.

Facilitate nursing staff management.
The health care center is divided into three 20-bed neighborhoods, each with its own staff station, bath, and utility rooms, visually linked to the center core. This allows for flexibility in staffing based on the time of day.

Create a sense of place for residents who seldom leave the building.
There is a two-story atrium and stair in the assisted living building and a skylit rotunda in nursing.

7

9

10

8

7 Atrium rotunda
8 Garden corridor
9 Typical assisted living unit
10 Typical assisted living tea kitchen
11 Main Street corridor
12 Apartment plans, independent living units
Photography: Barry Halkin

11

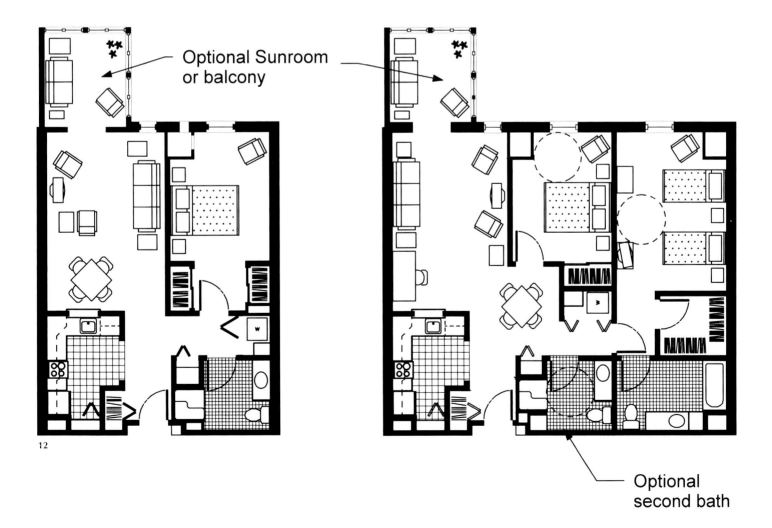

Optional Sunroom or balcony

12

Optional second bath

BUCKINGHAM'S CHOICE

FREDERICK, MARYLAND

1

ARCHITECT'S STATEMENT

This community is situated in a rural setting on a hilltop with panoramic views of a river valley and the mountains beyond. The site slopes down to the east and south to the river valley, which gives the main dining room a view of a mountain peak. The main building steps down to the south, conforming to the natural slope of the site, so that the main level and the terrace level are easily accessible to both residents and visitors. Architectural elements remind residents of neighboring structures, such as antebellum plantations and farmhouses.

Major design objectives and responses

Create a vital arrival/entry space that is sensitive to pedestrian traffic patterns and includes places to sit.
The entrances to the assisted living facility and to independent living apartments and

cottages (via the covered walkway) are distinguished from one another and surround the circular entry drive and porte-cochère, making this a vital social area. The porte-cochère leads directly to the heart of the community: the two-story main lobby with its views to the mountains beyond.

Create familiar architectural forms inspired by rural Maryland.
The central masonry portion of the main building—with its higher central roof form, flanking white columns, balcony railings, and masonry chimneys—recalls the antebellum plantations in nearby Buckeystown. The smaller-scaled courtyard cottages, with a classically rural four-columned porch, are at the center of a larger asymmetrical composition that recalls Maryland farm structures.

Maximize views of the farmland and river valley from the inside and outside.
From the outside, cottages frame long views from within the community. In the main building, windows are positioned in common spaces, such as the living room, main dining room, pool, and library, to capture views of the surrounding countryside.

Create an exciting assisted living entrance with its own identity but one that is integral to the larger community.
An exciting entry and curving two-story lobby have been created by using a unique geometric form off the main entrance to the community.

ARCHITECT	PERKINS EASTMAN ARCHITECTS
SITE LOCATION	SUBURBAN
SITE AREA	34 ACRES
CAPACITY	80 APARTMENTS, 130 COTTAGES, 45 SENIOR LIVING UNITS, 42 SKILLED NURSING CARE BEDS
TOTAL PROJECT COST	$36.1 M

1 Exterior, independent living apartments
2 Main building, independent living apartments
3 Main building, assisted living lobby
4 Main building, assisted living entry
5 Conference room
Photography: Chuck Choi

Create a site plan that has variety and complexity that speak to both the individual resident and the community as a whole.

The loop road was used as a unifying element for the rhythms of repeating cottages, punctuated by the openness of the pond and the south lawn outside the main dining room. The cottage clusters inside the loop road were designed to provide intimate public spaces close to the main building.

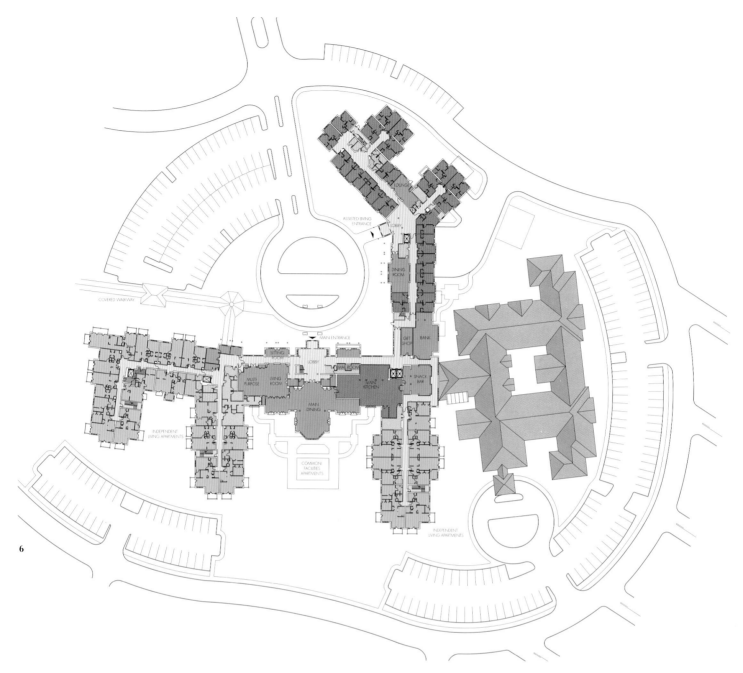

6

7

8

6   Site plan
7   Main building, dining room
8   Main building, pool
9   Main building, assisted living entry
10 Main building, resident corridor
11 Main building, lobby
Photography: Chuck Choi

9

10

11

1

2

3

ARCHITECT'S STATEMENT

The Cedars of Chapel Hill is a continuing care retirement community in a university town. The project is part of Meadowmont, a 435-acre planned neighborhood that includes single-family homes, townhouses, apartments, shops, restaurants, offices, a bank, a hotel, an elementary school, a wellness center, parks, bike and pedestrian paths, and an easement for a regional mass transit system.

The classical style of the Cedars reflects two cherished aspects of the town of Chapel Hill, which are the university campus and the older residential neighborhoods. The central feature of the site plan is the Great Lawn, with its proportions modeled after similar spaces on the university campus. The site plan for cottages is designed to replicate the streetscape that is so appealing in the older

parts of the town. Twelve different cottage plans with multiple options for exterior materials and colors ensure that no two cottages are identical.

Major design objectives and responses

In the larger buildings of the community, evoke the character of the nearby university campus.
The site plan's central feature, defined by apartment buildings and the clubhouse, is the Great Lawn. Its proportions are modeled after similar spaces on the university campus. All of the buildings on the lawn are designed in the Georgian style of the campus. Subtle differences in the classical detailing give each building its own character.

In the cottage development, evoke the character of the charming older residential neighborhoods of Chapel Hill.
All cottages have front porches and are close to the street, which is lined with sidewalks, trees, and traditional lampposts. Garages are hidden at the back; this arrangement keeps the cars out of sight and allows the houses to be close together, minimizing walking distances and creating a pedestrian-friendly streetscape.

Maximize the use of the site while minimizing the impervious surface area and meeting strict requirements for storm water management.
Much of the parking for the project is located under the apartment buildings, which makes more land available for gardens and recreation and allows higher density within impervious area restrictions.

ARCHITECT	CALLOWAY JOHNSON MOORE & WEST, PA
SITE LOCATION	SMALL TOWN
SITE AREA	47 ACRES/2,047,409 SQUARE FEET
CAPACITY	300 RESIDENTIAL UNITS, 24 ASSISTED LIVING UNITS, 52 SKILLED NURSING BEDS
TOTAL PROJECT COST	$91.8 M

4

5

6

The cottage driveways consist of two strips of concrete with a grass median. This design reduces impervious surface area and is reminiscent of the design of driveways in older neighborhoods. The decorative ponds and waterfall are part of the storm water management system.

Maximize the light and views in all residential units.
'Villa' buildings were designed to maximize the number of corner and end apartments to bring in natural light from more than one direction and to minimize corridor length. The 'H' shape of the 'Veranda' buildings allows each unit to have windows on three sides.

Design the health care center for flexibility in the future.
Phase 1 of the health care center is licensed for skilled nursing but it is also designed for future use for dementia care. Rooms are intended for single occupancy but can be double occupancy in an emergency. The master plan allows for significant future expansion of the health care center.

1 Typical veranda apartment
2 Veranda apartments, rendering
3 Villa apartments, rendering
4 Site plan
5 Cottage streetscape, rendering
6 Clubhouse, rendering

COVENANT MANOR COURTYARD, ADDITION

1

ARCHITECT'S STATEMENT

The Covenant Manor Courtyard addition and renovation adds 125 larger, more varied apartments to the 126 apartments built in 1980 and 1986. This work also creates three guest apartments. The horseshoe-shaped design on a landlocked, 2-acre parcel of land is six and seven stories tall and maximizes views to the south and the courtyard. Underground parking is provided below the building and accessed through the existing parking.

The Village Center provides focus with its library, beauty shop, game room, gift shop, café, computer center, health clinic, and business rental offices for the residents. The Village Street extends into the existing building, to the dining and activity spaces. Dining remains in its original location to maintain its picturesque creekside location.

The courtyard addition is constructed on 65-foot piles bearing on rock. The site also has a high water table, which creates the need for an extensive under-floor drainage system in the parking level. The density (64 units per acre) on this 2-acre site requires the detention ponding to be designed in three different locations with three different concepts. The pond in the courtyard serves the courtyard area. Special roof drains allow the roof to act as a detention pond for the building area itself. Large detention culverts beneath the perimeter drive around the building, satisfying the detention requirements for the drive and parking areas.

Major design objectives and responses

Maximize sun and view orientation.
Eliminate north-facing apartments with a single loaded corridor. The U-shaped building allows sun to penetrate the courtyard and the apartments.

Provide campus focus.
The Village Center and courtyard give a campus focus.

Ensure an updated, more residential image.
Gable roofs and a more varied traditional-style interior palette, using more wood for warmth, enhance the residential feeling.

Unify image with existing structure.
Gable roofs and the interior palette are extended to the existing structure.

ARCHITECT	HORTY ELVING & ASSOCIATES, INC.
SITE LOCATION	SUBURBAN
SITE AREA	2 ACRES
CAPACITY	125 NEW APARTMENTS ADDED TO EXISTING 126 APARTMENTS
TOTAL PROJECT COST	$21 M

1 Village Center
2 First floor plan
3 View of courtyard from north
Photography: courtesy Horty Elving & Associates, Inc.

CYPRESS COVE AT HEALTHPARK FLORIDA

FORT MYERS, FLORIDA

1

2

ARCHITECT'S STATEMENT

Cypress Cove is located on the 400-acre campus of HealthPark Florida. The housing and care facilities are clustered around a commons building featuring an outdoor courtyard with pools and fountains and a main dining room facing a large lake. Focus on indoor/outdoor connections was provided through courtyards, gardens, and gaming lawn areas.

The design solution creates a residential environment with an elegant yet comfortable feel. Incorporating plantation shutters, lattice, and trellis elements both inside and outside helped to create the residential scale and grounded the project within the imagery of Florida's west coast.

The wellness center—containing the pool, aerobics, free weights, and a resistance-training program—is adjacent to the main entrance as an expression of its importance.

The health center uses a 32:16:8 neighborhood design concept within a two-story structure. The one-bedroom assisted living units include kitchenettes and walk-in closets. Both facilities enjoy courtyard and garden views.

Major design objectives and responses

To create a building that felt comfortable in South Florida.
The use of concrete tile, hip roofs, trellis, lattice, and louvers, combined with the yellow stucco, accomplished this objective.

To keep walking distances to a minimum—less than 700 feet.
The architect created a fairly dense four-story apartment building that feeds directly into the community center, with parking around the perimeter.

To create a sense of place as you enter the community center.
A lush courtyard with water features was located on an axis with the entry and the access halls that wrap it.

ARCHITECT	REESE, LOWER, PATRICK & SCOTT, LTD.
SITE LOCATION	SUBURBAN
SITE AREA	50 ACRES
CAPACITY	212 APARTMENTS, 30 COTTAGES, 42 SENIOR LIVING UNITS, 64 SKILLED NURSING CARE BEDS
TOTAL PROJECT COST	$54.4 M

3

1 Courtyard, commons building
2 Lounge at main dining room, commons building
3 Swimming/therapy pool, commons building
4 Apartment building
Photography: Larry Lefever

4

HILLSIDE COMMUNITIES

1

ARCHITECT'S STATEMENT

This 20-year-old continuing care retirement community revitalized its image and repositioned itself in the market by developing a master plan that:

- adds 44 new two- and three-bedroom cottages and 64 apartments to become more financially stable
- presents an updated, fresh image consistent with its rural Willamette Valley surroundings
- meets its commitment to address the middle-income market
- increases site density without the feeling of a dense site
- optimizes a contiguous building plan on a sloping site

- creates a state-of-the-art residential health care center with 40 assisted living apartments, 20 Alzheimer's units in two clusters, and 20 skilled nursing beds
- offers home health care and adult day care services.

Major design objectives and responses
Present an updated, fresh image consistent with the community's rural surroundings.
A new main entrance to the community is closer to town. A new 'town square' greets visitors as they enter the community. The building appears as a series of connected farmhouses, barns, and country inns. Light meals and snacks are available at a country store off the town square.

Increase site density without the feeling of a dense site.
New four-plex homes are designed so that cars are hidden. Four-plexes are built to order so that initial residents can select two- or three-bedroom units. All cottages have their own garden.

Create a state-of-the-art health care center.
Skilled care, Alzheimer's care, and assisted living environments are designed to be as flexible as possible to adapt to changing market demands. All of the corridors are wide enough to allow the skilled care facilities to be expanded, if required. In addition, all of the units are identical to allow flexibility in the use of each unit.

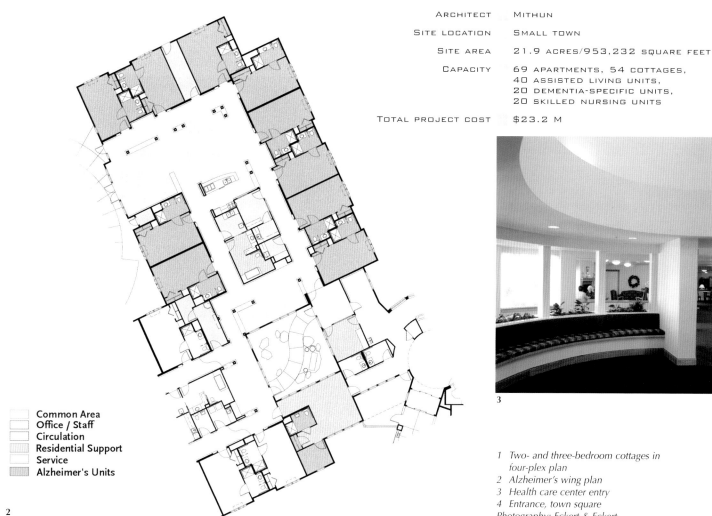

ARCHITECT	MITHUN
SITE LOCATION	SMALL TOWN
SITE AREA	21.9 ACRES/953,232 SQUARE FEET
CAPACITY	69 APARTMENTS, 54 COTTAGES, 40 ASSISTED LIVING UNITS, 20 DEMENTIA-SPECIFIC UNITS, 20 SKILLED NURSING UNITS
TOTAL PROJECT COST	$23.2 M

Common Area
Office / Staff
Circulation
Residential Support
Service
Alzheimer's Units

2

3

1 Two- and three-bedroom cottages in
   four-plex plan
2 Alzheimer's wing plan
3 Health care center entry
4 Entrance, town square
Photography: Eckert & Eckert

4

5

6

7

8

5 Country store in Alzheimer's wing
6 Entry lobby connecting living room (foreground)
  with country store
7 Living room
8 Country store
Photography: Eckert & Eckert

PEABODY MANOR

APPLETON, WISCONSIN

1

ARCHITECT'S STATEMENT

The challenge was to design a replacement 68-bed, multiple-licensed care facility that is resident-centered and operationally efficient. The process engaged all project stakeholders and resulted in a design that established a clear hierarchy of space from public to private, and a scale that is appropriate to a residential context.

A true 'aging in place' model requires an overlay licensing of several care models. Up to now, the state of Wisconsin allowed only separate buildings or occupancy compartmentalization whereby a resident would be moved to the appropriate care level needed. Unfortunately, this is very disruptive to the residents, family, and support staff, as it breaks down the relationships that have been formed.

Negotiations with regulators from Health and Family Services resulted in a compromise solution that appears to

be unique. The facility is designed and constructed for the most stringent life-safety, building, and operational codes, which allows each resident room to carry a multiple license. Although simple in concept, this solution had never been achieved before this project. With this variance, residents can maintain personal and social interactions with their fellow residents, regardless of the level of care they require.

Major design objectives and responses

Coordinate with current and transitional staff training, resident expectations, and organizational culture.
A dynamic and interactive process engaged all project stakeholders. The programming process sought input from residents, their families, the existing nursing home staff, the sponsoring health care organization,

and regulatory officials. Preliminary design concepts were tested with actual and virtual mockups. Ongoing communication through focus groups and interactive participation throughout the process encouraged holistic and synergistic solutions.

Provide facilities designed around services that are resident-centered and adaptable to persons with varying and continually changing levels of cognitive, sensory, and mobile activity.
The plan encourages movement and mobility. Distances to all activities of daily living are within 30 feet of each private resident's room. This includes shared living spaces, activity spaces, dining, and passive and active interior and exterior recreation elements. Visual cuing, a residential scale of space and form, and an interconnected

ARCHITECT	HOFFMAN CORPORATION
SITE LOCATION	URBAN
SITE AREA	68,935 SQUARE FEET
CAPACITY	10 ASSISTED LIVING UNITS, 48 SKILLED NURSING BEDS, 10 HOSPICE CARE UNITS
TOTAL PROJECT COST	$9.4 M

3

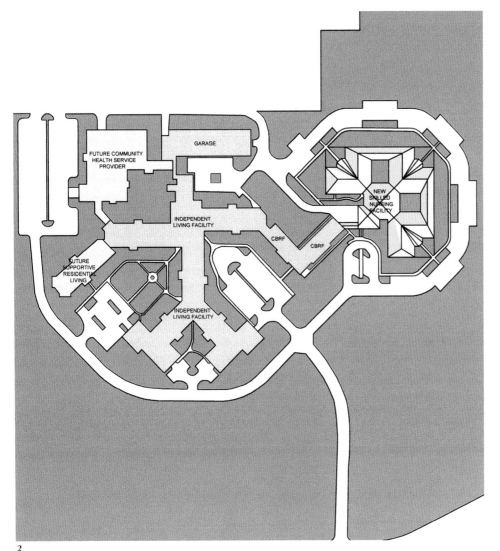

2

4

5

household circulation system unobtrusively assist residents with various forms of cognitive impairment.

Ensure that the outside is 'brought in' whenever practical through visual and physical access to exterior activity space.
Access to nature and a link to the community are important environmental and social experiences. The campus had no large community gathering space. Peabody Hall now serves this function as a central anchoring element for the resident households. Although it is at the core center of the building, it is surrounded by natural light from the interior winter gardens. Wayfinding is grounded in the interior winter garden views. Resident rooms use projected window bays to provide abundant daylight, views, and access to the exterior patio and courtyards.

Ensure that the design focuses on atmosphere and the practicality of operational requirements.
Small-scale living spaces and a hierarchy of space are core design elements. Spaces progress from public to private. Households are organized around 10 or 11 private-resident units. This size provides for supportive living and dining functions that are smaller and more residential in scale. Interconnecting households provide better staff utilization and service-delivery accommodation.

Accommodate both current and future resident care and support needs.
'Aging in place' was an idealistic concept that became a realistic deliverable of this project. As the building responded to the form and function of a residential environment, it encouraged individual

choice, independence, and a supportive and nurturing environment. The final licensing of the facility combines a community-based residential facility and a skilled nursing facility overlay. One household is a separately licensed hospice facility.

1 Winter garden
2 Master plan
3 Dining room
4 Exterior, resident rooms
5 Peabody Hall
Photography: Bob Freund (3,5);
Tom Lemkuil and Chad Ulman (1,4)

PEABODY RETIREMENT COMMUNITY

1

ARCHITECT'S STATEMENT

Peabody Retirement Community is the reinvention of a 70-year-old senior community in North Manchester, Indiana. New programs include a 126-bed health center, a 48-bed memory enhancement center, a health promotion center, and renovations to existing residential care services.

The new health center, consisting of 126 private rooms, is organized into three houses of 42 beds each, with six clusters of seven rooms per house. Each neighborhood is organized into 21 rooms around community spaces, including living and dining rooms, parlors, therapeutic spas, and coffee nooks. All resident rooms have views of gardens, courtyards, and walkways.

The memory enhancement center, which consists of 48 private rooms, is organized into four neighborhoods of 12 rooms each.

The cluster concept supports the use of Montessori principles to reduce resident anxiety and increase resident participation in activities and programs. Each neighborhood includes life task stations, including sports, business, housework, shopping, grooming, music, and nature.

The health promotion center will include physical fitness and educational facilities to promote healthy, successful aging. Aquatic therapy and exercise are provided through warm-water therapy, while cardiovascular fitness, muscle strength, and balance programs are provided in a state-of-the-art fitness center. The center also includes an auditorium to support educational programs, including gerontology experts, as well as art and entertainment. Additional amenities include a day spa, gift shop, bistro, rehabilitation center, meditation chapel, and child day care.

The North House is an assisted living facility with many amenities associated with independent living. The building is adjacent to and linked to the campus commons (phase 2), providing easy access to activities and services.

Ground-level dining, bistro, and clubrooms offer additional social life options. From larger unit plans to interior detailing, the design reinforces the social model and supports a seamless level of care for assisted living residents.

Major design objectives and responses
Empower older adults.
Sensitive design and effective programming enhance opportunities for choice, independence, and control.

1 Fitness center
2 First floor plan, health center
3 Health care unit, Plan B
4 Health care unit, Plan A
5 Entry court perspective
6 Health care unit, Unit B

ARCHITECT   REESE, LOWER, PATRICK & SCOTT, LTD.

SITE LOCATION   RURAL

SITE AREA   11.46 ACRES/499,200 SQUARE FEET

CAPACITY   48 DEMENTIA-SPECIFIC ASSISTED LIVING
UNITS, 144 SKILLED NURSING BEDS

TOTAL PROJECT COST $41.5 M

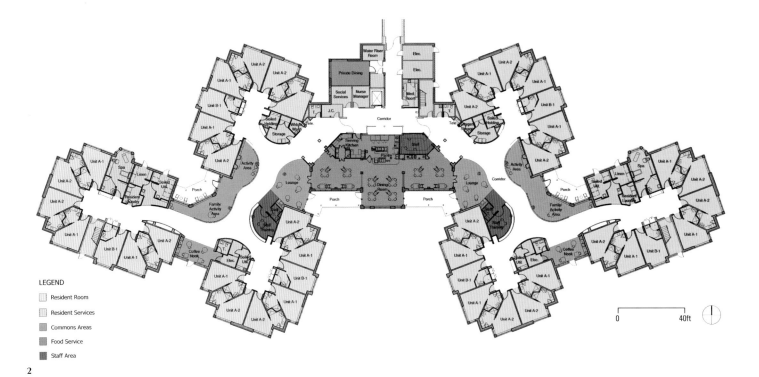

2

LEGEND

Resident Room
Resident Services
Commons Areas
Food Service
Staff Area

0   40ft

3   4   5

Provide shorter walking distances.
Clustered, decentralized design concepts
improve resident mobility and access to
programming.

Increase staff time with residents.
Clusters of seven and 12 rooms permit
caregivers to attend to the needs of
residents effectively and efficiently.

Increase access to outdoors.
All rooms and public spaces have generous
views and access to courtyards, gardens,
and walking paths.

Improve staff productivity.
Staff receive an on-site child day care
program, use of the marketplace and bistro,
and access to education and fitness
facilities on the campus.

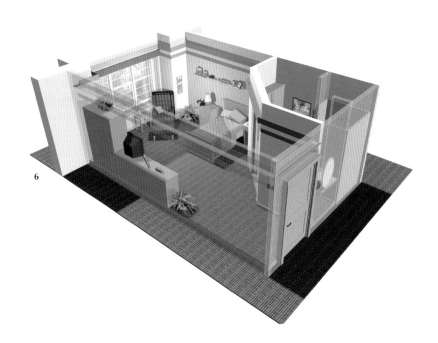

6

PECONIC LANDING

SOUTHOLD, NEW YORK

1

2

ARCHITECT'S STATEMENT

Peconic Landing is a continuing care retirement community designed to meet the needs and satisfy the preferences of the next generation of retirees. Located on the east end of Long Island with a half-mile bluff overlooking Long Island Sound, this community is a true retirement 'destination.'

The community center is centrally sited to minimize walking distances and enhance access from apartments and cottages. The design responds to a desire for choice and an emphasis on wellness and fitness by offering:

- a variety of gathering spaces, ranging from residentially scaled to large-scaled ballroom/auditorium
- intimately scaled dining rooms, each with varied and distinctive décor
- a library emphasizing computer workstations, electronic media, and internet access

- generously sized fitness facilities, designed for proactive wellness programs, including exercise equipment, aerobics, and a pool configured for lap swimming, aqua-aerobics, and a spa.

The wellness center balances the benefits of connection to the community center with a non-institutional appearance and a scale that blends seamlessly into the residential image of the campus.

Major design objectives and responses

Create a campus development that will be recognized as a welcome addition to the local community.
Only 70 acres of the 140-acre site are being developed, to preserve the bluff and the indigenous coastal woodland character of the site. This environmentally sensitive community will enhance the naturally occurring ponds, helping to preserve wildlife habitats. The site includes a historic house that will be restored for

use by the local community to encourage connections between the residents and the community of Southold.

Develop a CCRC that reflects the character of the North Fork of Long Island.
The architecture and scale of the community reflect the venerable yet contemporary Shingle style of the local area, with dramatic roof forms; long, open wraparound porches; and large areas of fenestration. The 118 cottages are sited to take advantage of the site's unique feature, creating an image of private individual houses by preserving the natural vegetation between home lots.

The three-story apartment buildings are arranged to maximize views of the bluff and pond and to provide a convenient connection with community facilities. Parking is located at the lower level, below-grade, for maximum resident convenience and accessibility, and to help preserve the open space of the site.

ARCHITECT	EWING COLE CHERRY BROTT
SITE LOCATION	SMALL TOWN
SITE AREA	140 ACRES
CAPACITY	26 ASSISTED LIVING UNITS, 44 SKILLED NURSING BEDS, 250 INDEPENDENT LIVING UNITS
TOTAL PROJECT COST	$124.5 M

PECONIC LANDING

Long Island Sound

3

4

5

1   Community center, rendering
2   Cottages and gazebo, rendering
3   Site plan
4   Community center lounge, rendering
5   Dining room, rendering

Maximize choice for residents and provide for changing lifestyles of the next generation of seniors.
The 139 apartments include 12 different plans, and any cottage plan can be accommodated on any of the 111 cottage lots. Residents can choose from a variety of models designed for the way seniors live, in response to different retirement lifestyles identified in focus groups with prospective residents. Each model offers an extensive list of options and upgrades so residents can customize their units.

Encourage residents' fitness, wellness, and overall vitality.
The 140-acre site has extensive walking paths, including paths along the bluff with 'rest stop' gazebos conveniently located at key lookout points for view and wildlife observation. The fitness facilities and indoor pool are located and designed to be highly visible and accessible elements of the campus.

Provide a wellness program that is flexible to adapt to the changing health care needs and expectations of next-generation seniors.
The lower level of the nursing care center is arranged in four clusters of nine private and semiprivate rooms to accommodate 44 residents requiring different levels of nursing and memory support care. Staff support areas are unobtrusively integrated into the resident living areas and are adjacent to dining and activity areas to enhance staff and resident interaction. Secure outdoor garden areas are freely accessible from cluster living rooms and the dining rooms. The wellness center connects the care center to the community center, providing the potential for healthy connection and community interaction.

Create an assisted living program that encourages an active lifestyle and offers a meaningful transition from independent living.
A separate elevator lobby/entry and distinct dining rooms serve the 26 one-bedroom assisted living apartments. These apartments are conveniently located near the community clinic, the fitness center/pool, and other community amenities to encourage wellness and participation in community life. The assisted living apartments range in size from 550 to 750 square feet and offer kitchen and bathroom designs that encourage independence and safety for the physically frail.

RIVER TERRACE ESTATES

BLUFFTON, INDIANA

1

ARCHITECT'S STATEMENT

This continuing care retirement community is designed to be similar in scale to the neighboring residential communities throughout this rural locale. The concept is to provide residents with a comfortable neighborhood environment that will meet their needs as they age.

Services will be in place to provide maintenance for the residents in independent housing, allowing them to enjoy their leisure time and participate in community activities. As the residents age and their abilities to live alone diminish, the community will provide housing that includes personal care assistance, such as help with housekeeping tasks, bathing, food service, and medications. The facility will also provide dementia care and skilled nursing units.

2

ARCHITECT	COLLINS GORDON BOSTWICK ARCHITECTS
SITE LOCATION	SUBURBAN
CAPACITY	12 COTTAGES, 58 ASSISTED LIVING UNITS, 30 SKILLED NURSING UNITS
TOTAL PROJECT COST	$11.59 M

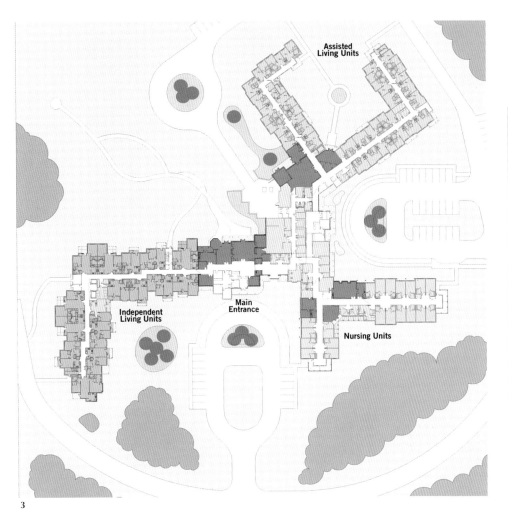

1 Entrance
2 Exterior, nursing units
3 Site plan
4 Dining room
5 Lounge
Photography: William H. Webb, Infinity Studio

Sumner on Ridgewood

1

2

Architect's statement

The design philosophy of this new continuing care retirement community is to create a living community—not a retirement community—integrating nature throughout the architecture. A holistic wellness philosophy emphasizes a comprehensive approach rooted in Eden Alternative™ principles. The entry boulevard highlights a formal garden and focuses on the manor house, which offers a variety of activity and dining options. A lap pool and spa provide for the residents' physical wellness. An auditorium for lectures, a library, and a cyber-lounge promote intellectual wellness. Garden apartments are attached directly to the manor house to minimize walking distances. Green Houses provide for residents who require catered assistance or enriched care. These houses are interconnected structures with residentially

scaled spaces and full-amenity suites. The focus of each Green House is a light-filled courtyard.

Major design objectives and responses

To create a new and progressive community that is not a retirement community but a living community.
This independent lifestyle is translated into the site planning and architecture. The architecture connects residents to nature and the many gardens.

Site planning uses town-planning design standards.
Eden Villas are arranged into neighborhoods, along with the bungalow-style Green Houses. 'Neighborliness' was designed into the Eden Villas by organizing them into duet and quartet arrangements that frame courtyards. All the villas have gracious front or side porches that face the street and

courtyards to encourage casual conversations with passersby. Garages are tucked behind the buildings to avoid creating a streetscape of prominent garage doors.

Provide for the upcoming multiple-choice generation.
A variety of dining options was programmed into the manor house, including formal, bistro, and patio. Options for independence include multistory garden apartments, which are connected to the manor house by the gateway arch, or single-story Eden Villas, which feature attached garages.

Provide care that is gracefully given as an art.
The architecture of the Green Houses features a residential center hall design, with interconnected parlor, living room,

ARCHITECT	DORSKY HODGSON + PARTNERS
SITE LOCATION	SUBURBAN
SITE AREA	64 ACRES/279,936 SQUARE FEET
CAPACITY	79 APARTMENTS, 22 COTTAGES, 40 SENIOR LIVING UNITS, 48 SKILLED NURSING CARE BEDS
TOTAL PROJECT COST	$42 M

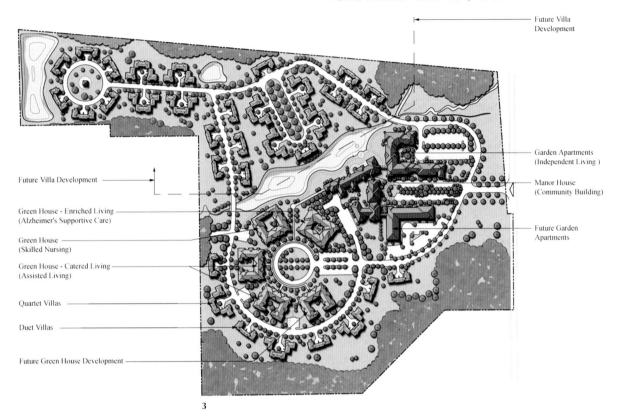

Future Villa Development

Garden Apartments (Independent Living)

Manor House (Community Building)

Future Garden Apartments

Future Villa Development

Green House - Enriched Living (Alzheimer's Supportive Care)

Green House (Skilled Nursing)

Green House - Catered Living (Assisted Living)

Quartet Villas

Duet Villas

Future Green House Development

3

4

and dining room with a view and access to the garden courtyard. The resident suites are accessed from a private hallway, much as bedrooms are accessed in a house. The service areas of the Green Houses are located as they would be in a house; the kitchen is the center of caring activity. There is also a utility room with washer and dryer, and a pantry that functions as a serving and preparation area. The front door has a foyer, not a reception desk.

The resident suites are more than bedrooms. They are large, gracious sitting and living rooms, with kitchenettes and complete private bathrooms. The honor and dignity that are the cornerstones of the Eden Alternative™ are evident in the design of the Green Houses, where the art of giving care focuses on a homelike ambiance and resident convenience.

Medication carts have been replaced by individual medicine cabinets in each private bathroom.

Translate the graciousness of the sponsor's original historic Tudor mansion.
A Tudor Revival style of architecture throughout the community blends with the architecture of the sponsor's original campus.

1   Manor house perspective (community building)
2   Villa-quartet perspective
3   Site plan
4   Garden apartment elevation

VILLAGE SHALOM
OVERLAND PARK, KANSAS

1

2

ARCHITECT'S STATEMENT

Village Shalom is a new continuing care retirement community developed by the Jewish community of Kansas City. A major design goal was to provide a safe continuing care environment for the residents while inviting in the outside community. The commons includes a full-service kosher bistro, elder fitness center, museum-quality art gallery, and a social hall, all open to the public. Indoor and outdoor play spaces provide interest for younger visitors.

Village Shalom provides a number of living options, from cottages to skilled nursing units, which are designed to appeal to people of various ages. Gardens and patio spaces extend the living and therapeutic spaces to the outdoors. Art is integrated throughout the interior and exterior of the

facility. Interior finishes were selected to embody a contemporary design aesthetic. An emphasis on wellness and quality of life is reflected in the warm-water pool, exercise equipment rooms, beauty spas, and restaurant-quality food service.

Major design objectives and responses

Involve the larger community in the life of the campus.
Visitors are encouraged to use the campus amenities. The bistro, store, playroom, fitness center, art gallery, and social hall are open to residents and members of the community outside the campus.

Create a residential character in living spaces.
Social areas are varied in size and distributed throughout the facility. Dining rooms are broken into smaller spaces. The

residential areas are separated from the more public zones of the upper and lower commons to provide residents with more privacy.

Offer a full range of housing and care options within the campus.
The cottages provide the most independent living option. The assisted living apartments serve residents who require more supportive services. Shalom suites and the nursing home are options for people with severe health and cognitive problems. Dementia day care and frail adult day care programs serve people both inside and outside the campus.

Provide a high-quality food service.
Resident dining occurs in small dining rooms throughout the campus. Pantries with commercial kitchen equipment allow

ARCHITECT	NELSON-TREMAIN PARTNERSHIP
SITE LOCATION	SUBURBAN
SITE AREA	25 ACRES/1.09 MILLION SQUARE FEET
CAPACITY	64 INDEPENDENT LIVING UNITS, 54 ASSISTED LIVING UNITS, 64 SKILLED NURSING BEDS, 36 DEMENTIA-SPECIFIC UNITS
TOTAL PROJECT COST	$25.9 M

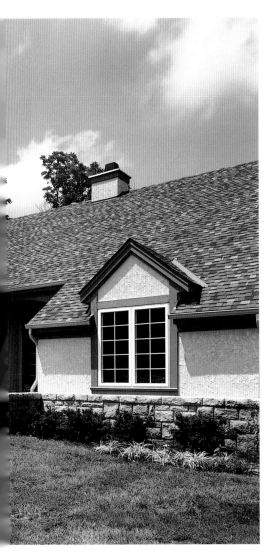

3

preparation and reheating of food prepared in the main kitchen. Food is served restaurant-style from the pantries. The kosher bistro offers an alternative for residents and visitors.

Improve wellness.
The ElderSpa wellness center provides warm-water exercise in the fitness pool, equipment, weight training, and exercise classes.

1 *Assisted living apartments and pool, exterior*
2 *Single-family villa*
3 *Children's play space*
4 *Second floor overall plan*
Photography: Architectural Fotographics

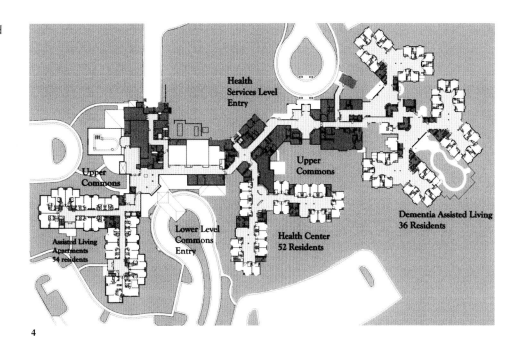

4

5

6

7

WESTMINSTER VILLAGE, ADDITION

1

ARCHITECT'S STATEMENT

With the addition of this 42-unit assisted living and 17-unit dementia facility to the Westminster Village Campus, Presbyterian Homes, Inc., now offers a continuing care retirement community for the mid-Atlantic region.

The building has three assisted living neighborhoods and one dementia neighborhood. Units range from alcove units to three-room units. Standard units are furnished by the resident and typically offer a kitchenette (assisted units only), accessible bathroom with built-ins, excellent natural light, and a residential feeling. A large, accessible walk-in/roll-in closet allows for a complete wardrobe and at least 120 cubic feet of in-room storage for the resident's personal items.

Multiple dining options are available, ranging from the formal dining room to three community kitchens. Residents can socialize with other residents in 16 public lounges, libraries, beauty parlors, laundry rooms, parlors, terraces, bars, and solariums. The monumental stair lobby has a baby grand piano and is home to Sunday's religious services.

Major design objectives and responses

High occupancy on site and high occupancy of building:
- required two separate zoning variances
- required extensive reworking of campus master plan, pedestrian, and vehicular circulation patterns due to larger building footprint

- required site modifications in order to provide 100 percent perimeter emergency access to the fire department at each domicile structure on the campus due to increased density.

Maintain a low construction budget.
Art niches were set into stud cavities with the painted surface tinted darker to help exaggerate their depth. The formal dining room has 8-foot painted 'paneled' wainscoting on the walls composed entirely out of drywall with ogee wood trim. Stained oak trim was limited to surfaces where residents' hands would come into contact with it, such as stair and corridor rails.

ARCHITECT	BECKER MORGAN GROUP, INC.
SITE LOCATION	SUBURBAN
SITE AREA	3.38 ACRES/147,103 SQUARE FEET
CAPACITY	42 ASSISTED LIVING UNITS, 17 DEMENTIA-SPECIFIC UNITS
TOTAL PROJECT COST	$4.87 M

2

Validate intensive site preparation demands and location of work area inside fully occupied, active site.

In order to validate resident interaction with construction, a crew of residents was hired, given hard hats and T-shirts, and assigned to shifts to monitor construction and then present progress reports to the entire community. These 'sidewalk superintendents' were a huge public relations success with the resident community.

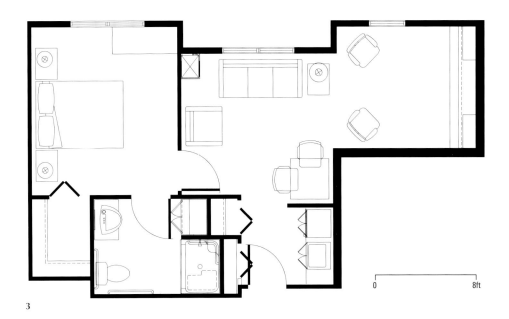

1   Public terrace and balcony
2   Vehicular building approach
3   Resident unit plan
Photography: Wayne Lyons Photography

3

0   8ft

THE WINDROWS AT PRINCETON,
FORRESTAL APARTMENT BUILDING

2

1

3

1 Main entry and porte-cochère
2 Resident towers
3 Community center, rear entry
4 Main entry, with view of resident wing
5 View from main entry
6 Villa residences and park
Photography: Rob Karosis

ARCHITECT'S STATEMENT

This 192-unit, senior living apartment building is one component of an age-restricted community that offers a distinctive lifestyle for senior adults who seek the benefits of home ownership without the associated burdens. The independent living apartment building also houses the shared community center (42,000 square feet), which includes a woodshop, computer/media center, arts and crafts, club/billiard room, tennis court, bank, greenhouse, library, spa, and parlor/bridge room. As residents' needs change, a continuum of care is provided on campus in the form of an 86-unit assisted living residence and a 190-bed skilled nursing and rehabilitation facility.

The community is located on a 45-acre site that is 4.5 miles from the gates of a prestigious university campus. The natural setting is rolling farmland lined with windrows of majestic evergreens. The high quality incorporated into this community is reflected in its architecture and landscaping. Through a range of style elements, a variety of massing and rooflines, and high-quality detailing and use of materials, the image of housing that might have been built 50 years ago has been evoked.

Major design objectives and responses

Provide benefits of ownership to residents.
The community has a condominium ownership plan.

Provide a continuum of care to residents.
Assisted living and skilled nursing are offered on campus.

Foster an independent lifestyle for residents.
Maintenance and home security are provided, as well as a linen service and meal plans.

Maintain natural site amenities.
Tree lines are preserved.

Create a community with pride of place.
Sensitive attention has been paid to community planning, architecture, and site amenities.

ARCHITECT	WILMOT/SANZ, INC.
SITE LOCATION	SUBURBAN
SITE AREA	12 ACRES/530,000 SQUARE FEET
CAPACITY	192 APARTMENTS, 86 ASSISTED LIVING UNITS, 190 SKILLED NURSING CARE BEDS
TOTAL PROJECT COST	$55.6 M

4

5

6

7

8

9

7   Atrium lobby view
8   Atrium lobby
9&12 Community center dining room
10   Atrium lobby lounge
11   Community center living room
13   Lobby seating nook
14   Lobby seating area
Photography: Rob Karosis

10

11

12

13

14

DESIGN for AGING REVIEW

AS

ASSISTED LIVING

1

ARCHITECT'S STATEMENT

The Rebecca Residence is a nonprofit charitable organization founded more than 100 years ago in Wilkinsburg, Pennsylvania, and is dedicated exclusively to the care of the elderly. The new building is conceived as a residence, which is non-institutional in appearance and atmosphere. The goal is not only to address medical needs but also to maximize opportunities for physical activity and social interaction. Independence, self-management, and privacy are emphasized.

The Rebecca Residence provides 40 assisted living apartments, 20 assisted living dementia bedrooms, 45 private and semiprivate nursing bedrooms, and 15 private and semiprivate nursing dementia bedrooms. Common public rooms, dining rooms, and activity rooms are provided for the residents.

Major design objectives and responses
Create residential building in scale and expression.
A two-story building nestles into and steps down the hillside to architecturally complement the rural site. Small-scale wings with enclosed courtyards are carefully integrated into the surroundings of the site. Visitor and staff parking and load areas are screened from view and landscaped to intrude as little as possible.

Encourage residents to experience the outdoors.
Each floor of the multistory building has at least one exit directly to grade. Enclosed courtyards for less mobile residents provide a secure outdoor experience while a lit, nonskid cement walk meanders around the ponds for more active residents.

Design a non-institutional setting.
The comfortably furnished interiors feature small, clustered living areas and larger common rooms for dining, gatherings, activities, and informal socializing. In the bedrooms, large windows with generous sills hold personal items, while the low windows allow residents to see the outdoors from their beds or chairs. Each room has a tea kitchen with a small refrigerator, sink, and microwave, which allows residents to prepare snacks at 'home.' Building services are physically and visually separated from the resident portions of the building.

Maintain historical continuity.
The original Rebecca Residence provided shelter for Civil War widows, and the client wanted to maintain the historical continuity

ARCHITECT	PERKINS EASTMAN ARCHITECTS, PC
SITE LOCATION	RURAL
SITE AREA	13.7 ACRES/98,500 SQUARE FEET
CAPACITY	58 ASSISTED LIVING UNITS, 40 SKILLED NURSING CARE UNITS
TOTAL PROJECT COST	$14 M

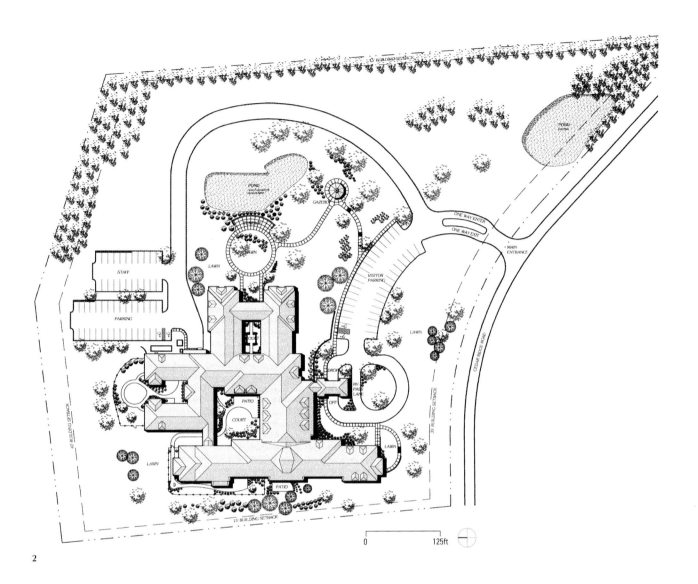

2

by furnishing the new Rebecca Residence with the antique furnishings, art, and accessories from the original facility. The elegant antiques contribute to the facility's homelike interior and maintain a strong connection with the organization's past.

1 South façade
2 Site plan
3 Assisted living country kitchen
Photography: Bob Ruschak

3

4 Library
5 Nursing private room
6 Courtyard
7 Entry parlor
8 First floor plan
Photography: Bob Ruschak

4

5

6

7

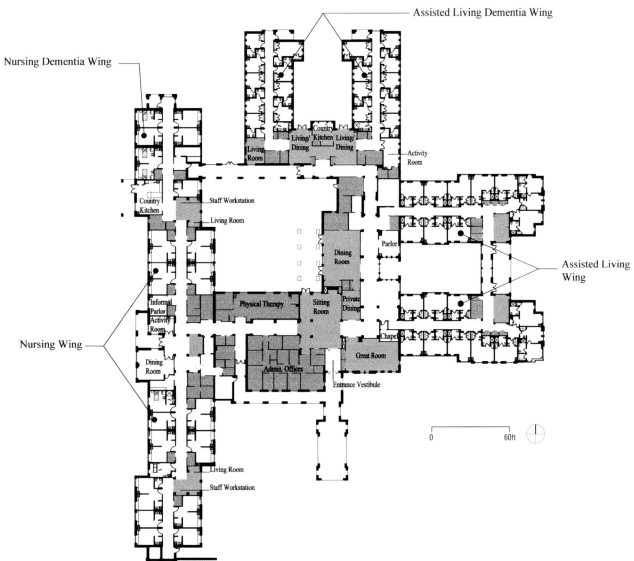

Assisted Living Dementia Wing

Nursing Dementia Wing

Country Kitchen

Living/ Dining

Living/ Dining

Living Room

Activity Room

Country Kitchen

Staff Workstation

Living Room

Parlor

Dining Room

Assisted Living Wing

Physical Therapy

Sitting Room

Private Dining

Informal Parlor

Activity Room

Chapel

Nursing Wing

Dining Room

Great Room

Admin. Offices

Entrance Vestibule

0   60ft

Living Room

Staff Workstation

8

CHASE POINT

DAMARISCOTTA, MAINE

1

2

3

ARCHITECT'S STATEMENT

Overlooking a tidal estuary in a coastal Maine community, this assisted living facility includes 42 assisted living units, 18 of which are specifically designed for dementia and Alzheimer's residents. The overall design integrates a turn-of-the-century architectural style with sweeping views of the landscape, which imparts a sense of living in a shingle-style seaside estate.

Interior Victorian references permeate the facility as purposeful reminders of an earlier time—ornately patterned carpeting, decorative wall sconces, and wood wainscoting are supplemented by rich, historical paint colors. Beadboard, alcoves with seating, and porch rockers further evoke the seaside cottage theme. The gambrel roof design is a special feature of this facility. It blends well with the shingle-style seaside theme.

Another unique element is the layout of the lower level, which is a public area. The lower level, although technically a walkout basement, is an open area with glass windows along one side, ushering in the daylight and thus defying the typical notion of a basement. Outside the windows is a beautiful garden, a popular place among the residents.

Major design objectives and responses
Integrate the site.
The assisted living area of this facility continues the residential theme, and its design emphasizes social areas—the living room, sunroom, and clubroom offer living spaces similar to those found in shingle-style seaside residences.

Create a sense of community.
An adult day care program within the facility fosters greater social interaction by enabling seniors in the surrounding community to spend each day with peers at the facility. Studies have shown that 'buddy' support can be highly therapeutic, and the integration of the adult day care unit is a valuable enhancement to the outlying community.

Maintain a sense of independence.
Designing an assisted living facility that can accommodate a range of health care necessitates a delicate balance. The notion of independence should resonate within a senior living facility, embracing and encouraging those residents who are able to live somewhat independently. At the same time, a comprehensive senior living

ARCHITECT	JSA INC.
SITE LOCATION	SMALL TOWN
SITE AREA	5,540 ACRES/241,320 SQUARE FEET
CAPACITY	24 ASSISTED LIVING UNITS, 18 DEMENTIA-SPECIFIC UNITS
TOTAL PROJECT COST	$3.5 M

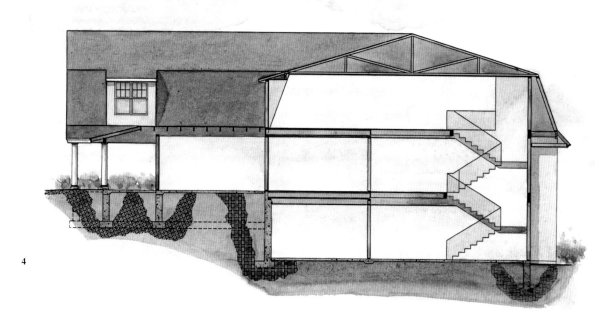

4

facility must provide maximum care for residents who require more supervision. This facility addresses this challenge through an architectural design that keeps the Alzheimer's area separate from the assisted living area while also being cohesive enough to unify the entire community.

Provide therapeutic environments.
Two secure, highly supervised Alzheimer's 'neighborhoods' are designed around a central kitchen. The country kitchen serves both as a gathering spot for residents of the two Alzheimer's areas and as a workplace for staff. The staff's presence in the country kitchen results in a more interactive environment, and incorporating staff work areas with social spaces for the residents makes the facility seem less institutional and more like a large residence.

Facilitate privacy.
The library illustrates the privacy afforded to residents. It provides opportunities for social interaction, as well as cozy spaces designed for quiet reflection and solitude. The emphasis on social areas such as the clubroom, sunroom, and living room provides designated spaces for gathering, which help to ensure that the residents' rooms are private, quiet places.

1 Front entrance
2 Sunroom
3 Lobby
4 Sectional view with lower level
5 Front entrance
6 Living room
Photography: Dan Gair Photography

5

6

7 Dining room
8 First floor plan
9 Visual cues and circular wandering paths link
   inside and out for Alzheimer's residents
Photography: Dan Gair Photography

7

8

9

THE FOREST AT DUKE, ADDITION

DURHAM, NORTH CAROLINA

ARCHITECT'S STATEMENT

The Forest at Duke, a continuing care retirement community that opened in 1992, is building an addition to its health care center. Scheduled for completion in 2003, the project will create two distinctly different environments for assisted living. On the second floor, there will be residential apartments with common areas and support services. On the ground floor, there will be two special care 'neighborhoods' with homes, streets, and gardens.

A new village center will become the focal point of the entire health care building, providing amenities such as a chapel, town hall, fitness center, and spa. A unique building cross section allows the interior 'street' in the village center to be a two-story skylit space. This addition is part of a larger project that will involve renovations to the existing health care unit and to the community center.

Major design objectives and responses

Accommodate two distinct populations of assisted living residents in a two-story building.
A unique building cross section creates two types of apartment plans and a central two-story atrium. The ground level accommodates two special-care dementia units. The second floor provides apartments and support spaces for residents who are frail but without major cognitive impairment.

Provide an environment that supports a high quality of life for cognitively impaired assisted living residents.
The village-like environment provides residents who have dementia with a familiar and interesting framework for their daily lives. Each resident has a home with a bedroom, living room, garden space, and front door opening onto an interior street. The street leads to a village center with a chapel, beauty shop, town hall, fitness center, and general store.

Provide an environment that supports a high quality of life for assisted living residents without significant cognitive impairment.
The second floor, for those without significant dementia, is an environment that simulates the character of the independent living areas in the community of which this facility is a part. Residents live in 640-square-foot apartments and have access to a living room/library and a dining room.

Improve quality of life for residents of the existing health care center.
The existing health care center, now part skilled nursing and part medical/institutional assisted living, will be converted to skilled

ARCHITECT	CALLOWAY JOHNSON MOORE & WEST, P.A.
SITE LOCATION	SUBURBAN
SITE AREA	1.34 ACRES/58,650 SQUARE FEET
CAPACITY	15 ASSISTED LIVING UNITS, 18 DEMENTIA-SPECIFIC UNITS
TOTAL PROJECT COST	$13.2 M

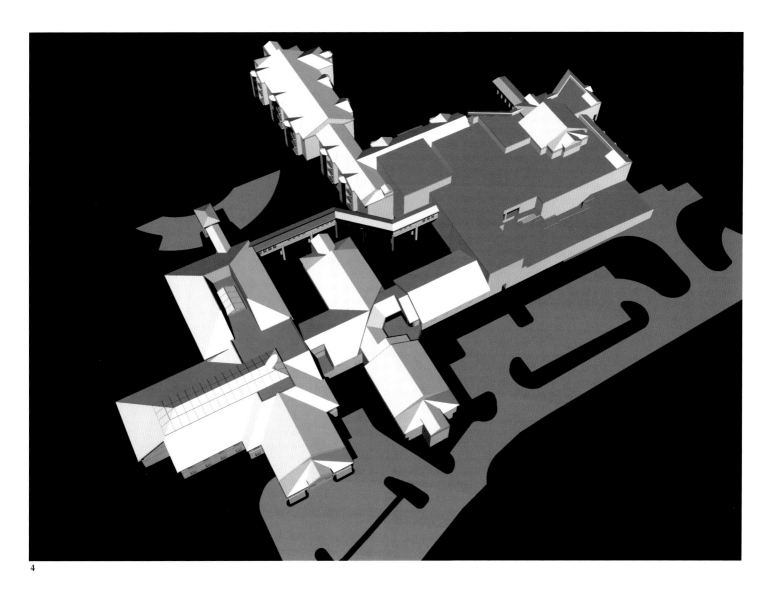

4

nursing care to meet the growing needs of the community. The new village center will provide common space and a focal point for the entire health care population.

Improve the circulation pattern between the existing community center and the health care center.
A new 'skyway' provides a connection between the third floor of the addition and the community center, enabling residents and staff to walk between the two without passing through the 'private' zones of resident rooms. The skyway also provides a direct route for residents to the new clinic, which is on the third floor of the addition. The existing clinic in the community center will be demolished to provide space for an expanded arts studio and other amenities.

Improve the quality of the food service for the health care center.
The new addition contains a 600-square-foot pantry kitchen on each floor. These new pantries will serve as dining rooms for the new assisted living building, as well as renovated dining rooms for the existing skilled nursing population.

5

1 Exterior elevation
2&3 Perspective, interior street
4 Site plan
5 Unit, rendering

FRAN AND RAY STARK VILLA

WOODLAND HILLS, CALIFORNIA

1

ARCHITECT'S STATEMENT

The Fran and Ray Stark Villa assisted living home provides leading-edge care and promotes aging in place. Residential clusters wrapped around garden courtyards and dining opportunities on all three levels allow for variety and flexibility for special care neighborhoods.

Distinct garden spaces, or outdoor rooms, encourage residents to interact. Activities range from working in the kitchen garden to dining in the alfresco courtyard. Abundant views along the interior walkways allow the therapeutic qualities of the natural elements to permeate.

Rooms are designed with a clean and simple aesthetic, so that they can be personalized. Open shelving encourages residents to display their belongings. Each unit has private and direct outdoor space.

The architectural flavor of the building was inspired by the industrial character of the old Hollywood studios and the typology of southern California architecture.

Major design objectives and responses
To exemplify aging in place, emphasizing dignity and independence for residents:
- Dining opportunities are provided on all three floors, so residents do not have to negotiate stairs or elevators.
- Multiple dining options allow variety and flexibility for aging in place.
- Building design, with residential 'arms,' creates natural clusters or neighborhoods ideal for dedicated care units that may evolve over time so residents do not have to move to get higher levels of care.
- Benches are located along walkways to stop and rest.

- Nurse call button is found in every room.
- Meaningful color contrasts throughout aid wayfinding.
- Grab bars and handrails are installed where needed.
- Color-coded hot and cold water faucets are included.
- Infrastructure supports an eventual need for more medical services.
- Outdoor spaces include an open lawn area, koi pond, garden walk with perennial and aromatic gardens, butterfly meditation retreat, and a wandering textural garden with waist-high turf and beach sand.

To provide a homelike atmosphere:
- nearby, accessible outdoor spaces and gardens
- balcony or patio for every unit

2

4

3

ARCHITECT   SMITHGROUP

SITE LOCATION   SUBURBAN

SITE AREA   2 ACRES/63,000 SQUARE FEET

CAPACITY   70 ASSISTED LIVING UNITS

TOTAL PROJECT COST $16 M

1 Plaza
2 Dining room
3 Activity pavilion and koi pond
4 Entry, interior
Photography: Tom Bonner (1,3); John Edward Linden (2,4)

- plants and animals cared for by residents
- family rooms at each residential cluster
- simple, unadorned interiors and open shelves, allowing residents to personalize
- building is designed like a home. Residents are encouraged to use the entire building as their home, with their unit as a bedroom. Dedicated activity spaces are scattered throughout to encourage mobility.

To support a sense of community and social interaction among residents:
- plentiful dedicated feature rooms, including an aviary, game room, spa, exercise room, business center, potting room, distinct gardens, alfresco dining courtyard, garden walk, and working kitchen garden
- corridors with benches along the way to promote casual interaction

- open family rooms at each residential neighborhood for residents to pass through and engage in casual interaction
- separate activity pavilion, koi pond, and rose garden with a labyrinth located directly outside the building to draw residents and staff from other parts of the campus to this destination.

To address the particular interests of the motion picture and television community:
- Internet access in every room; cable-TV and movies 'on command'
- radio production
- memorabilia gallery and nostalgia display along the main walkway, conveying the spirit of the industry
- business center with *The Wall Street Journal* and CNN available for continuous stock market updates

- activity pavilion to show first-run movies.

To link to other buildings on the campus:
- Site is envisioned with a pedestrian promenade linking buildings and outdoor spaces.
- Two entrance courtyards, rather than a single front door, give equal access from the parking area and from the pedestrian promenade.
- Roddy McDowell Rose Garden and labyrinth creates a destination link to the existing campus.
- Wasserman Koi Pond provides a destination spot for residents to gather and link to the greater campus.

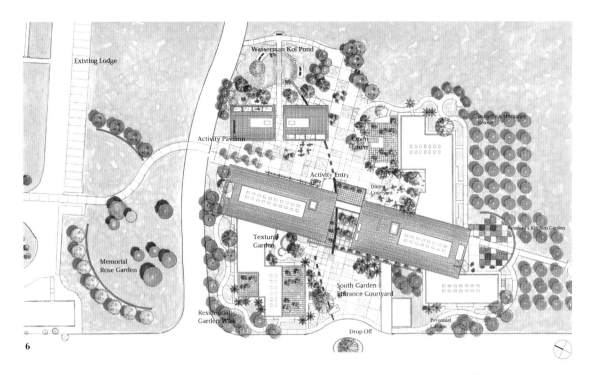

6

7

Opposite:
Entry, interior
6 *Roof and landscape plan*
7 *Corridor*
Photography: Tom Bonner

GRAND OAKS
WASHINGTON, D.C.

1

ARCHITECT'S STATEMENT

Grand Oaks, a hospital-based assisted living facility, completes a continuum of care for an aging population in its residential service area. Other components include the hospital's 237 acute care beds; extensive ambulatory care services; senior service, lifeline, and community outreach programs; and a recently completed skilled care facility.

Apartments are arranged in five- to seven-unit 'households,' each with its own small lounge area, around neighborhood activities at each floor and central community areas for dining, socializing, activities, and resident services. Offset hallways interspersed with solaria, porches, and reading areas provide directional cues and varying levels of spatial and social experience.

The cluster plan diminishes the mass of the building, defines garden areas, and creates sheltered patios and terraces of varying scale. Cluster planning also provides two exposures for most apartments, permitting cross-ventilation and extended and rhythmic patterns of natural light—important attributes of single-family residences.

Major design objectives and responses
Ensure resident dignity, privacy, and personal autonomy:
- opportunity for activity and socialization at varying scales, from personal to group
- variety of spatial experiences
- easy access to outside
- cluster planning, yielding homelike apartments with two exposures and operable widows for cross-ventilation

- upscale interior detailing and finishes
- dining choices: room, household lounge, clubroom, dining room
- one-seating dining.

Include maximum units on site in residential scale:
- cluster planning with maximum perimeter.

Enhance compatibility with residential neighborhood:
- breaking down building mass
- material, window, and color choices
- landscaping.

Provide shared services with hospital and skilled care facilities:
- tunnel connection.

ARCHITECT   OUDENS + KNOOP ARCHITECTS, PC

SITE LOCATION   URBAN

SITE AREA   2.6 ACRES/112,900 SQUARE FEET

CAPACITY   104 ASSISTED LIVING UNITS

TOTAL PROJECT COST $20.4 M

1 View from northeast
2 View from second floor, south terrace
3 Exterior detail
4 Exterior view, with sheltered patios and terraces
Photography: Alan Karchmer

ASSISTED LIVING

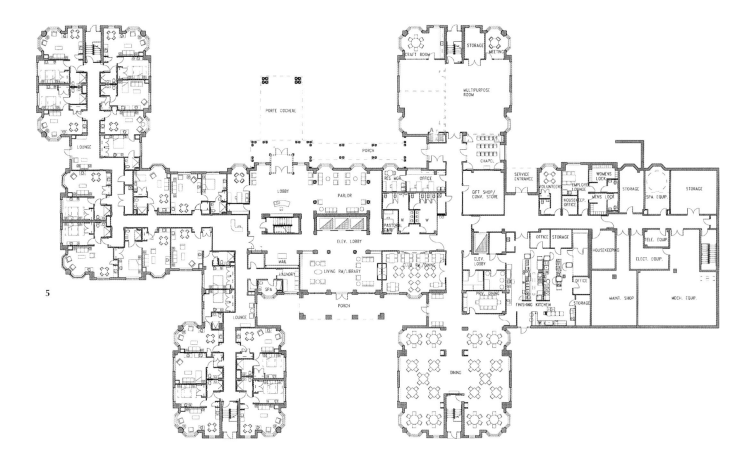

5

6

7

8

9

5   First floor plan
6   First floor elevator lobby and living room
7   Resident unit, typical living room
8   Resident services suite
9   Entrance lobby
Photography: Alan Karchmer

GRANITE LEDGES OF CONCORD

1

2

3

ARCHITECT'S STATEMENT

Designed to fit within the context of large neighboring 'shingle-style' homes, Granite Ledges offers 75 senior living apartments, 14 of which are dedicated to Alzheimer's residents. This senior community features a private 10-seat dining room, pub, activity room, lounge, gift shop, library, and octagonal sun porch. A warm, homelike ambience is enhanced with elegantly simple detailing that includes local artisans' works and reflects the Shaker simplicity one expects in rural New England. The working English garden allows residents to express their creativity, while the enclosed special-needs garden provides both enjoyment and safety for memory-impaired residents.

Major design objectives and responses

Create a sense of community.
The shingle-style design and elegantly simple detailing reflects the strong Shaker influence found among the surrounding historic communities. The screened-in front porch and central lobby provide a physical hub as well as a social hub, encouraging social activity. Moreover, these defined gathering places create an intimate, human scale within a 75-unit assisted living facility.

Facilitate privacy.
The dining room, designed to evoke a cozy sense of privacy, consists of small nooks within a larger room. Bay windows and fluctuating ceiling heights further enhance this notion of privacy without compromising space.

Maintain independence.
Residents are encouraged to pursue their passions. For example, one resident brought his own piano into the Alzheimer's living room, and he now graces residents and staff with his talents. Also, a two-sided glass cabinet located between the lobby and country kitchen is available for residents to exhibit their crafts and collections. All units are designed with a private bath and kitchenette to afford residents the utmost privacy and autonomy possible.

Provide therapeutic environments.
Warm terracotta colors, ample natural lighting, and plentiful use of natural wood finishes integrate the Shaker ideal of functional simplicity in all things and, in doing so, subtly transform institutional requirements into a pleasant residential environment.

ARCHITECT JSA INC.

SITE LOCATION SUBURBAN

SITE AREA 7.7 ACRES

CAPACITY 61 ASSISTED LIVING UNITS,
14 DEMENTIA-SPECIFIC UNITS

TOTAL PROJECT COST $7.35 M

4

Ensure site integration.
Set amid a wooded site in the heart of
New Hampshire, the design objective was
established by prospective residents who
expressed a desire for a 'well-established'
New England country club atmosphere.

1 Library
2 Front entrance
3 Living room
4 Dining room
5 Country kitchen
Photography: Dan Gair (1–3,5);
David Mendelsohn (4)

5

GUARDIAN ANGELS BY THE LAKE

ELK RIVER, MINNESOTA

1

ARCHITECT'S STATEMENT

Recalling the traditional lakeside lodge of a bygone era, this affordable 60-unit assisted living facility is part of an 11-acre master planned senior campus that respects the natural setting of the site. Phased expansion includes a 20-unit assisted living addition, town homes, and a medical office building.

A grand front porch warmly welcomes guests and is a favorite outdoor social area for the residents. The main lobby is central to the resident common area amenities, including fireplace lounge, parlor, post office, country store, café, barber/beauty shop, and fellowship lobby to the dining room. The second level features a library nook, gentlemen's clubroom, activities, and chapel.

The kitchen aerda was planned as part of the lakeside dining room. The residents enjoy the active nature of the kitchen in the preparation of their meals. Residents often arrive early for light conversation with kitchen staff.

Approximately 40 percent of resident units are clustered around neighborhood lounges. The two-story layout required slightly longer distances to dining and social areas, so seating areas with outdoor views are provided along the way.

Major design objectives and responses
Provide truly affordable assisted living facility with one- and two-bedroom dwelling units.
With a careful balance of overall building square footage, final total development costs were kept under $63,000 per unit.

Include common and activity areas that residents will use.
Common areas flow around the main entry lobby, where residents tend to congregate.

Ensure efficiency for health care staff.
The staff area is centrally located; a two-way voice emergency call system is provided in units and commons.

Provide interactive meal preparation as part of the family-style dining experience.
The kitchen area opens toward the dining area, giving the space a more casual feel of home.

Include ample wheelchair passage space in corridors.
Corridors are 7.6 feet clear.

ARCHITECT	TROSSEN WRIGHT ARCHITECTS, P.A.
SITE LOCATION	SUBURBAN
SITE AREA	11.11 ACRES/125,530 SQUARE FEET
CAPACITY	60 ASSISTED LIVING UNITS
TOTAL PROJECT COST	$3.77 M

2

0   10ft

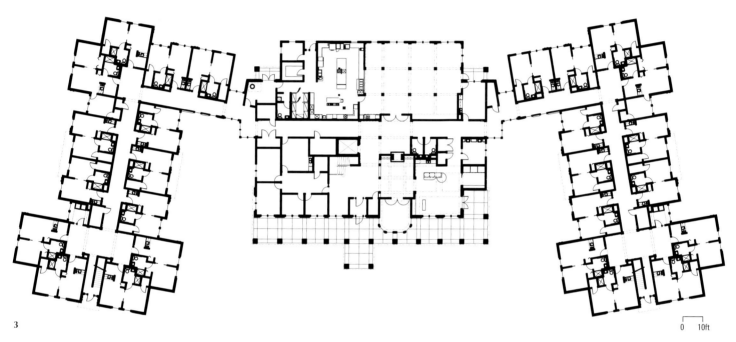

3

0   10ft

1 Aerial view, rendering
2 East elevation (main lodge)
3 First floor plan
4 Front porch at entrance
Photography: Jeff Zollman

4

ASSISTED LIVING

1   Living room
2   Bedroom
3   Bathroom
4   Kitchen
5   Walk-in closet
6   Neighborhood node

0   10ft

5

6

7

5 Typical unit plans
6 Entry lobby and grand stair
7 Parlor
8 North elevation (main lodge)
9 Lakeside dining room and kitchen beyond
Photography: Jeff Zollman

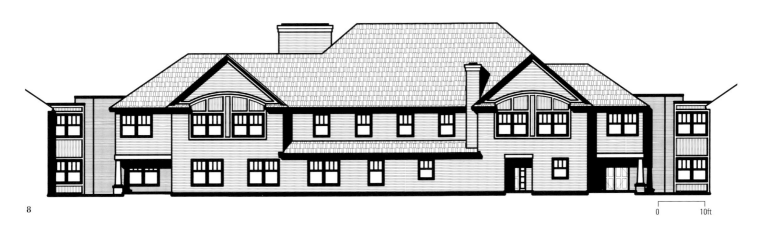

8

0   10ft

9

GURWIN JEWISH GERIATRIC CENTER
FAY J. LINDNER RESIDENCES
COMMACK, NEW YORK

1

2

ARCHITECT'S STATEMENT

The 160-unit building was designed to cater to community desires for a service-intensive assisted living program adjacent to an existing skilled care campus. Constrained by site considerations and utility setbacks, the undulating building form is finished in multiple colors of brick, stone, and cement.

Features include an abundance of interior and exterior common spaces dispersed throughout three floors. From the two-story lobby and social hall, one enters dynamic activity settings, visible from two levels.

Interior finishes feature maple-coffered ceilings, Jerusalem stone and granite fireplace surrounds, and maple casework and trim. Carpet patterns and colors were custom-tailored to enhance the architectural features of each space.

Large residential units, with corner-window views of the woodlands beyond, contain a tea kitchen and walk-in closets. A 19-resident special care area for those with Alzheimer's or related dementia provides program-specific common areas and secured outdoor gardens.

Major design objectives and responses

Maintain relationship to existing campus, identify image of a new residential model.
Brick color and contemporary building massing relate to the existing campus, but enriched exterior material colors and patterns, pitched roofs, planted terraces, and corner windows suggest a more residential character.

Ensure an abundance of daylight and views.
The building has large expanses of glass, shaded terraces, and corner windows to provide open views to the outdoor landscaped areas.

Include program spaces with individual identities.
There are many common spaces throughout the building, both one- and two-story, and varied furnishings; ceiling, lighting, and flooring conditions.

Provide a strong feeling of openness upon entering building.
The entrance is a two-story space with a strong visual connection directly through the building to surrounding activity spaces and the outdoor terrace.

Give units a residential feel.
Maple cabinetry; large, predominantly one-bedroom units; corner or bay windows; and generous closet space respond to an upscale market.

ARCHITECT	PERKINS EASTMAN ARCHITECTS PC
SITE LOCATION	SUBURBAN
SITE AREA	10 ACRES
CAPACITY	143 ASSISTED LIVING UNITS, 19 DEMENTIA-SPECIFIC SPECIAL CARE BEDS
TOTAL PROJECT COST	$26.5 M

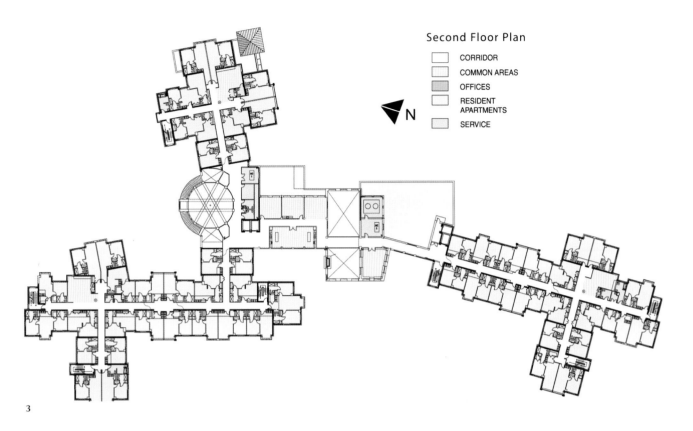

Second Floor Plan

- CORRIDOR
- COMMON AREAS
- OFFICES
- RESIDENT APARTMENTS
- SERVICE

N

3

4

5

1 Interior–living room with fireplace
2 Exterior–building front entrance
3 Second floor plan
4 Interior–main dining room
5 Private dining/conference room
Photography: Chuck Choi

Hearth and Home of Van Wert

Van Wert, Ohio

1

2

Architect's statement

Hearth and Home is a 30-unit assisted living facility designed with an eclectic cluster of cottage elements that feature varying styles of architecture. The mix of styles permits this small-town suburban facility to blend in with the surrounding residential character while diminishing the overall scale of the facility.

The design features 15-unit residential clusters radiating from an interior courtyard, which creates a streetscape with four distinct façades. The styling of each façade cues the residents to 'their house.'

The living units in each 'house' are arranged around a common family room or parlor with an adjacent dining room. The dining room is served by a family-style kitchen, which receives the prepared food from the main kitchen. A staff station is located in this kitchen to permit

supervision of activities and control of the residential group public spaces.

Major design objectives and responses

Create a residential character and scale in both mass and function.
The design combines a variety of styles and material in the mass and groups individuals of similar ability around smaller public spaces.

Deinstitutionalize staff areas.
The multifunctioning family kitchen in each wing is a serving kitchen, an activity center for baking cookies and the like, and a staff station. This space is open to the family and dining rooms and is detailed to look like a residential kitchen.

Minimize staffing requirements.
The staff station in the family kitchen has visual control over all the public spaces in each 15-unit cluster.

Permit the 15-unit clusters to function as either assisted living or dementia assisted living to permit flexibility in the market.
The two 15-unit clusters provide all the functions that would sustain the use of either program. A private courtyard and magnetic locks on each of the courtyard entry doors permit the facility to allow individuals of like abilities to live in a safe environment.

Permit the project to expand if the owner acquires the property to the east of the site.
The courtyard space has been designed to accommodate a third group of 15 units at a future date.

ARCHITECT	JMM ARCHITECTS, INC.
SITE LOCATION	SMALL TOWN
SITE AREA	3.03 ACRES/132,000 SQUARE FEET
CAPACITY	15 ASSISTED LIVING UNITS, 15 DEMENTIA-SPECIFIC UNITS
TOTAL PROJECT COST	$2.1 M

1 Living
2 Administration
3 Solarium/Walkway
4 Kitchen
5 Interior courtyard
6 Salon
7 Storage
8 Parlor
9 Family kitchen
10 Dining
11 Family room
12 Porch
13 Secured courtyard

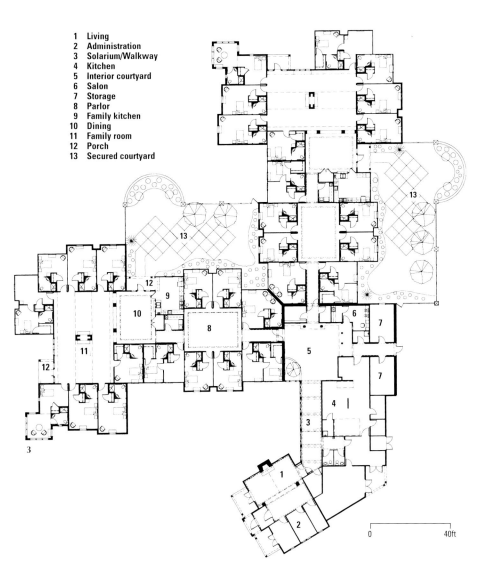

1 Main entry
2 Entry, dementia-specific house
3 Overall floor plan
4 Courtyard looking back to the main entry
Photography: Emery Photography

Jennings Residential and Community Services Center

Garfield Heights, Ohio

1

Architect's statement

Years after completing a master plan and new facility for Jennings Hall, Collins, Gordon, Bostwick Architects were commissioned to design Jennings Residential and Community Services Center. Key in designing the addition was maintaining the original design concept. The new center offers an adult day center, personal care apartments, dining room and activity centers, clinical center, and child care facility, adding a multigenerational component.

To accommodate the vast and diverse program requirements, the grading of the site was carefully considered. The ground floor level is open to grade on many sides to provide direct outside access required for the child care program, as well as from the dementia care resident rooms and outside program spaces. The entrance to the adult day center was required at grade

level to limit confusion for the participants and to provide easy access for family members bringing their loved ones.

The integration of exterior garden spaces was carefully considered throughout the design process, and several variations are included.

Major design objectives and responses

To provide a facility that is a natural extension of the existing nursing facility while developing a new identity.
By maintaining the existing entrance of the current facility as the primary entrance for the entire nursing and assisted living facility, the feeling of safety and association will be maintained.

To create a sense of the entire Jennings community being one entity.
The placement of the clinic space, a new snack shop as part of the existing gift shop,

and the current beauty parlor along the Main Street corridor will tie the various user groups together. These functions will be located conveniently for the adult day center, personal care residents, and current residents of the nursing facility. In addition, the existing chapel at the main entrance to the facility will serve the entire Jennings community as a spiritual center.

To maintain and increase multigenerational activities as part of the programming throughout the entire facility.
The existing child care center is located at the main lobby entrance. Although it will be moved to the ground level of the new building, the current location will be maintained for multigenerational activities. The new facility provides additional program spaces for similar activities, including the development of outside

ARCHITECT	COLLINS, GORDON, BOSTWICK ARCHITECTS
SITE LOCATION	SUBURBAN
SITE AREA	5.9 ACRES/278,271 SQUARE FEET
CAPACITY	55 ASSISTED LIVING UNITS, 18 DEMENTIA-SPECIFIC UNITS
TOTAL PROJECT COST	$10.075 M

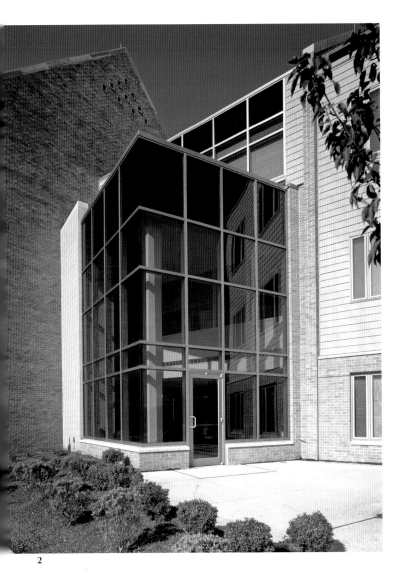

2

3

1 Exterior façade
2 Entrance
3 Exterior detail from garden
4 Site plan
Photography: William H. Webb, Infinity Studio

spaces to provide a playground and garden spaces for all the user groups.

To provide a homelike environment promoting self-sustaining activities for the dementia care residents.
The new dementia care facility is designed to resemble an individual residence. The kitchen will be stocked and supported by a food service pantry, but it will appear homelike to promote a user-friendly environment and maintain resident participation as a programming element. The laundry area will be similar. The entire unit will be secure, with a secure wandering garden to allow the residents freedom to circulate between the indoor and outdoor environments.

4

MADISON CENTER PROVIDENCE HOUSE

1

ARCHITECT'S STATEMENT

This project embodies the inherent value of aging well and, in the case of architecture, of adaptive reuse. The owner has taken a previously unoccupied building and combined it with a unique population to provide respite adult day care and 24-hour care for persons in stages 1, 2, or 3 of Alzheimer's disease.

This project consists of two buildings with long and varied histories. The original building was built around the late 1890s as a manufacturing plant for the Singer Sewing Machine Company. It is three stories tall and constructed with load-bearing exterior masonry walls and exposed heavy timber. It is located on the edge of the historic East Race Waterway, a hydraulic diversion from the St. Joseph River, from which it received its energy for the manufacturing process.

An addition to the building was built in the 1940s, and a renovation in the mid-1980s converted it for use as a restaurant and hotel, which closed in 1997. The previous owner then transferred ownership to its current not-for-profit owner, Madison Center. In 1998, after transfer of ownership, a portion of the first floor was renovated to a four-star restaurant, which continues operations today. In 2000, renovation began to convert it to its new use as an assisted living facility for persons in stages 1, 2, or 3 of Alzheimer's disease.

This project is part of a larger 25-acre urban health care campus providing mental health care on a regional basis from early childhood through older adulthood. It is a unique example of a mixed-use project in a historic urban setting.

Major design objectives and responses
Preserve the integrity of the original architecture.
The 100-year-old building was originally a manufacturing plant. The architects were able to work with local building officials in the rehab to address life safety issues in a manner that preserved the integrity of the original architecture.

1   Entrance, with patio garden beyond
2   Typical resident studio apartment
3   Second level plan
Photography: S.M. Lovinello

ARCIIITECT	MATHEWS-PURUCKER-ANELLA, INC.
SITE LOCATION	URBAN
SITE AREA	PART OF 25-ACRE CAMPUS
CAPACITY	55 SPECIAL CARE UNITS FOR PERSONS WITH DEMENTIA
TOTAL PROJECT COST	$1 M

2

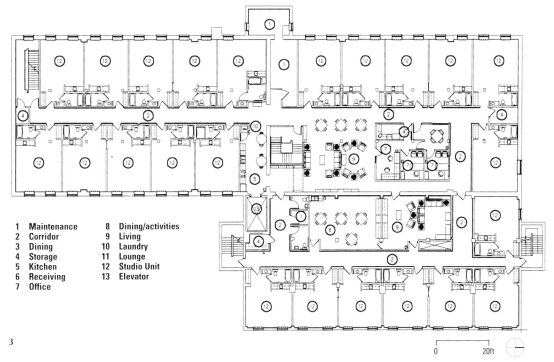

3

1	Maintenance	8	Dining/activities
2	Corridor	9	Living
3	Dining	10	Laundry
4	Storage	11	Lounge
5	Kitchen	12	Studio Unit
6	Receiving	13	Elevator
7	Office		

0   20ft

ASSISTED LIVING

4 *Second-floor, two-story living room with skylights*
Opposite:
    Suspended heavy timber stair
Photography: S.M. Lovinello

4

Masonic Homes of California

1

2

Architect's statement

Architects, planners, and trustees of the historic Masonic Home for Adults of Union City embarked on a plan guiding the rebirth of a century-old life-care complex into a cost-effective community of attractive, efficient, and profitable spaces. Composed of nine buildings ranging from 50 to 100 years old, the campus renovation spanned eight years and included four multistory buildings with a total of 200,000 square feet.

Basic components were larger apartments, new mechanical systems, and structural reinforcement. The historic administration building and two attached wings—constructed in 1868 to care for orphans and widows and then converted to residential care for Masons and their families—were seismically reinforced and completely reconfigured while perfectly

preserving their historic character. Living units in the Administration, Wollenberg, and Adams buildings were substantially enlarged from a scant 175 square feet to apartments of up to 475 square feet, complete with kitchenettes, ample natural light, and spacious living areas.

Major design objectives and responses

Increase the safety and well being of residents.
Completely new infrastructure of 100-year-old buildings provides state-of-the-art seismic strengthening and life safety.

Create a less institutional environment.
Expanding the corridors to become porches and gathering places diminishes institutional quality.

Expand residential units.
Combining two units to create one new, larger unit improves the quality of life for residents and provides flexibility in resident use of apartments.

Design residential units ergonomically for a senior population.
Bathrooms and kitchens focus on heights and access for limited mobility.

Distribute public spaces throughout the facility.
Public spaces optimize exterior exposure and views. Wayfinding and accessibility of public spaces and operational spaces help minimize travel distance between functions. Public spaces function as multipurpose spaces for various activities.

ARCHITECT	RATCLIFF
SITE LOCATION	SUBURBAN
SITE AREA	267 ACRES
CAPACITY	32 INDEPENDENT LIVING UNITS, 131 ASSISTED LIVING UNITS
TOTAL PROJECT COST	$60 M

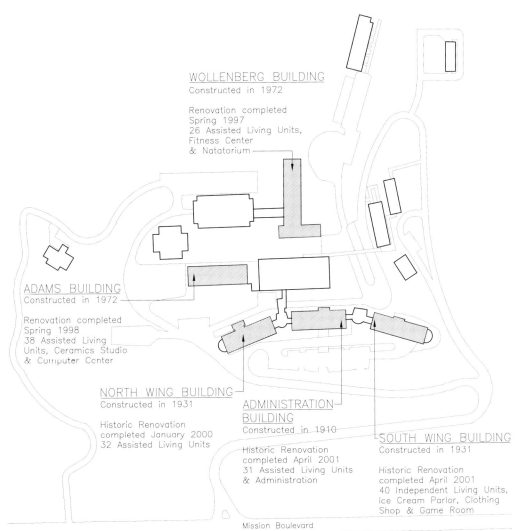

WOLLENBERG BUILDING
Constructed in 1972

Renovation completed
Spring 1997
26 Assisted Living Units,
Fitness Center
& Natatorium

ADAMS BUILDING
Constructed in 1972

Renovation completed
Spring 1998
38 Assisted Living
Units, Ceramics Studio
& Computer Center

NORTH WING BUILDING
Constructed in 1931

Historic Renovation
completed January 2000
32 Assisted Living Units

ADMINISTRATION
BUILDING
Constructed in 1910

Historic Renovation
completed April 2001
31 Assisted Living Units
& Administration

SOUTH WING BUILDING
Constructed in 1931

Historic Renovation
completed April 2001
40 Independent Living Units,
Ice Cream Parlor, Clothing
Shop & Game Room

Mission Boulevard

3

0   200ft

1 Administration building, exterior from west
2 Administration building connector, exterior
3 Site plan
4 Exterior, living units
5 Administration building lobby
6 Administration building parlor
Photography: Donna Kempner

4

5

6

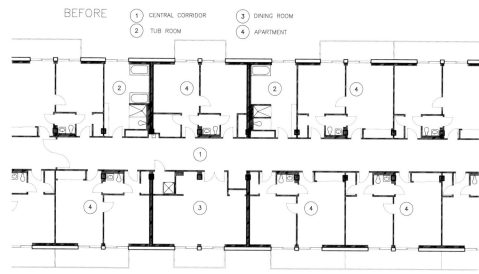
BEFORE
1 CENTRAL CORRIDOR 3 DINING ROOM
2 TUB ROOM 4 APARTMENT

7 Administration building library
8 'Before' and 'after' floor plans, North
building renovation
9&10 Administration building entry
Opposite:
Administration building ice cream parlor
Photography: Donna Kempner

7

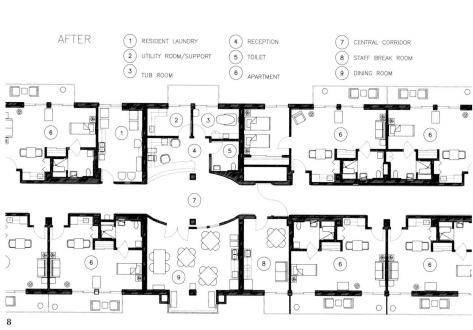

AFTER
1 RESIDENT LAUNDRY 4 RECEPTION 7 CENTRAL CORRIDOR
2 UTILITY ROOM/SUPPORT 5 TOILET 8 STAFF BREAK ROOM
3 TUB ROOM 6 APARTMENT 9 DINING ROOM

8

9

10

NORMANDY FARMS ESTATES

1

ARCHITECT'S STATEMENT

The floor plans for the three neighborhoods of the facility are similar, including a generous eat-in country kitchen with adjacent family room, dens, secured outdoor gardens, and an integrated care base at the center. Resident rooms flank both sides of the center area, making walking distances very reasonable.

The layout of the assisted living addition for the memory-impaired is similar to that of the skilled care component so that residents do not have to relearn circulation patterns. Details, materials, and images are consistent between the two levels of care, and resident room layouts are identical.

The design maximized flexibility to convert any of the three neighborhoods to skilled care or assisted living functions, depending on the future needs of the community.

Major design objectives and responses

Create cluster design.
The new 50-bed, special care facility for memory-impaired residents consists of three neighborhoods: two neighborhoods of 15 assisted living beds each and a third neighborhood of 20 skilled care beds.

Provide a homelike environment.
The homelike environment was created with residential care finishes, detailing, lighting, fabrics, and furnishings.

Maintain dignity.
Dignity was maintained through the use of private rooms, private baths, and small group settings.

Ensure control.
Control was achieved by the use of individual temperature controls, lighting, and territory.

Include choice.
Choice was supported via multiple programming and activity areas, both interior and exterior. Accessible outdoor spaces, courtyards, walking paths, and generous windows offer attractive indoor-outdoor connections.

Offer flexibility.
The design maximized flexibility to convert any of the three neighborhoods to skilled care or assisted living functions, depending on the future needs of the community.

1 Kitchen, dementia
2 Lounge, skilled care dementia
3 Spa, skilled care dementia
4 Corridor with memory boxes, skilled care dementia
Photography: Larry Lefever

ARCHITECT	REESE, LOWER, PATRICK & SCOTT, LTD.
SITE LOCATION	SUBURBAN
SITE AREA	101 ACRES
CAPACITY	50 SPECIAL CARE BEDS FOR PERSONS WITH DEMENTIA
TOTAL PROJECT COST	$6.9 M

2

3

4

OAK CREEK

STOCKTON, CALIFORNIA

1

ARCHITECT'S STATEMENT

This project includes an assisted living facility and independent cottages sited among beautiful 100-year-old oak trees. The main building includes 40 assisted living units and common dining, activity/craft room, administrative offices, nurses' area, and reception. One of the greatest assets to the project, and the greatest challenge, was the large number of mature trees scattered around the site. The buildings were carefully designed and sited to preserve as many of the trees as possible, creating an atmosphere of shade and dappled light that enhances the landscape. As a result, the buildings fit nicely into the site and look as though they have been there for a long time.

Major design objectives and responses
Incorporate the 100-year-old oak trees on the site into the design.
The cottages were sited among the trees.

Make the units larger.
One-bedroom units instead of two-bedroom units were provided.

Bring in a lot of natural light.
The use of skylights and large windows throughout the project provides the maximum amount of natural lighting.

1 Cottages
2 Entrance, assisted living facility
Photography: John Sutton

2

ARCHITECT	HARDISON KOMATSU IVELICH & TUCKER
SITE LOCATION	SUBURBAN
SITE AREA	5.5 ACRES/63,060 SQUARE FEET
CAPACITY	14 COTTAGES, 40 ASSISTED LIVING UNITS
TOTAL PROJECT COST	$6.88 M

3 Cottages
4 Exterior, assisted living
5 Lobby, assisted living facility
6 Exterior
7 Dining room
Photography: John Sutton

3

4

5

6

7

THE POINTE AT HAMILTON COMMUNITIES
NEW CARLISLE, INDIANA

1

ARCHITECT'S STATEMENT

The design provided for new assisted living and nursing care facilities on a 78-year-old continuing care retirement community campus. The overall mission was to provide facilities that would enhance the residents' quality of life and maximize their independent functioning.

The architect felt that a successful design should accommodate and encourage more self-care by the residents. The design is user-friendly, incorporating lever handles, tactile thermostats, package shelves at apartment entries, single-lever faucets, handrails and lean rails, grab bars, raised receptacles, lower windowsills, and hand-held shower sprays. In addition, the architect focused on a layout that reduced walking distances from living units to common-use areas, to enable residents to access these spaces independently and to minimize their need for walkers and wheelchairs.

The design unobtrusively compensates for the physical limitations of the residents so as not to emphasize those limitations. For example, in the assisted living area, it was decided to use lean rails—which resemble a wide chair rail—in lieu of standard handrails. This is a facility that responds well to age-related physical changes such as vision and hearing problems, decreased strength, and decreased mobility and loss of balance.

Major design objectives and responses
Focus on residential appearance.
The design incorporates residential massing, components, materials, and colors.

Maximize independent functioning.
User-friendly features, fixtures, and devices are included; travel distances are minimized.

Compensate for physical limitations.
The design addresses problems with vision, hearing, mobility, strength, and other age-related physical changes.

Focus on residential scale.
Small neighborhood clusters are used for nursing units.

Improve quality of life.
The design includes many areas for social interaction and use by families.

ARCHITECT	InterDesign
SITE LOCATION	Rural
SITE AREA	30 acres/1,305,842 square feet
CAPACITY	90 senior living units, 15 special care beds for persons with dementia, 10 skilled nursing care beds
TOTAL PROJECT COST	$12 M

2

3

4

1 Entrance
2 Lobby, assisted living
3 Main dining room, assisted living
4 Master plan
Photography: Aladin Images, Inc.

PROVIDENCE PLACE

MEMPHIS, TENNESSEE

1

ARCHITECT'S STATEMENT

This project had a limited amount of space on which to create an additional freestanding assisted living residence to meet the growing needs of occupants. The owners wanted to create a facility that would fill a niche market for transitional care. Although the model is social, the niche is to provide a place for people who do not fit the exact criteria for a nursing home or an assisted living center. Although there were medical considerations to take into account, the client did not want the medical areas revealed.

The unit is reserved for transitional care, which varies depending on the need of the resident. The design reflects open areas that allow for wheelchairs, walkers, and other types of assisted devices without referring to a medical facility. The suites provide adequate space for any type of resident or need. The atmosphere, with cathedral-style areas and open design, allows for independent spaces or group settings. One important design challenge was the criterion that there should be no place to categorize levels of care. Thus, all residents are cared for equally.

Major design objectives and responses

Create an atmosphere to which a resident of this age would respond.
As residents age, their sensory levels decrease. Adding cedar-lined closets keeps residents' clothing fresh, and the aroma reminds them where their items are stored. Marble windowsills in the suites are extra deep and flanked by built-in areas for personal items.

Look at behavioral issues.
More space was allowed for each resident, and large areas provided both group and individual space.

Address cultural issues specific to the South.
The front door opens into the kitchen—it is common practice in this region to enter a side door or back door when visiting someone, and often the kitchen is the heart of the home. The front door is seldom used.

2

ARCHITECT	McGEHEE, NICHOLSON, BURKE ARCHITECTS
SITE LOCATION	SUBURBAN
SITE AREA	1.22 ACRES/53,093 SQUARE FEET
CAPACITY	24 ASSISTED LIVING UNITS
TOTAL PROJECT COST	$3 M

1 Entrance porte-cochère
2 Suite entrance
3 Reading area
4 Model suite
5 Resident kitchen
6 Private dining room adjacent to main dining room
7 Resident laundry room
Photography: Woodliff Photography

3

4

5

6

7

RIDGEWOOD AT FRIENDSHIP VILLAGE OF COLUMBUS

COLUMBUS, OHIO

ARCHITECT'S STATEMENT

Friendship Village—operating primarily as an independent senior housing community, with a 90-bed skilled nursing facility on site—recognized the need to supplement its current program offering. A program was developed for assisted living-based care to bridge the gap between independent living and hospital care and provide choices to aging residents. As part of this project, a specialized unit for early-stage dementia care was planned to provide further choices and more resident-centered care.

The existing site provided multiple challenges regarding placement and interconnectivity of spaces. A Main Street causeway links the assisted living and

independent programs. Therapy, fitness facilities, aerobic spaces, an ice cream/soda shop, the Friendship Lounge, village store, community bank, art room, and media café are all accessed from this thoroughfare.

A 50-apartment assisted living community and a 14-bedroom dementia 'household' make up the majority of the 75,000-square-foot addition. All service/operational activities are kept 'behind the scenes' through below-grade tunnels and service elevators.

1 Courtyard/patio
2 Entrance, assisted living/dementia care
Photography: Brad Feinknopf

2

ARCHITECT	MADDOX NBD ARCHITECTURE
SITE LOCATION	SUBURBAN
SITE AREA	3.5 ACRES/152,479 SQUARE FEET
CAPACITY	49 ASSISTED LIVING UNITS, 10 DEMENTIA-SPECIFIC UNITS
TOTAL PROJECT COST	$11.9 M

ASSISTED LIVING

3 Dining room
4 South elevation
5 Living room, assisted living
6 Site plan, campus
7 Staff station
8 Sunlit foyer
9 Memory case, dementia care
Photography: Brad Feinknopf

3

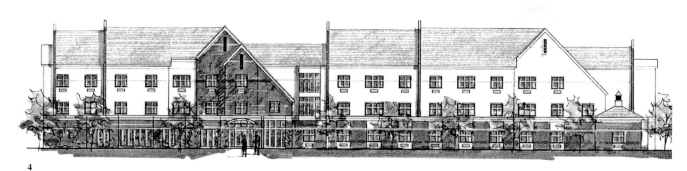

4

5

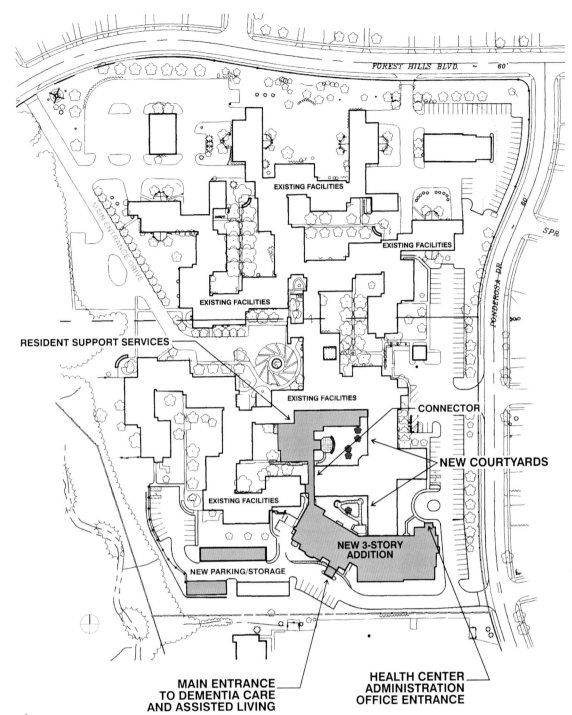

FOREST HILLS BLVD. ~ 60'

EXISTING FACILITIES

EXISTING FACILITIES

EXISTING FACILITIES

RESIDENT SUPPORT SERVICES

EXISTING FACILITIES

CONNECTOR

NEW COURTYARDS

EXISTING FACILITIES

NEW 3-STORY
ADDITION

NEW PARKING/STORAGE

HEALTH CENTER
ADMINISTRATION
OFFICE ENTRANCE

MAIN ENTRANCE
TO DEMENTIA CARE
AND ASSISTED LIVING

6

7

8

9

ASSISTED LIVING

SUNRISE ASSISTED LIVING

PACIFIC PALISADES, CALIFORNIA

1

ARCHITECT'S STATEMENT

The philosophy of care is represented by eight core principles of service that are integrated into the design and management of all Sunrise facilities: encouraging independence, preserving dignity, personalizing services, enabling freedom of choice, fostering individuality, protecting privacy, nurturing the spirit, and involving family and friends.

This building is targeted toward a frail population with an average age of 82 to 87 and a per-person average of two to four personal care needs for activities of daily living. The building is relatively small, with 40 units, but contains a dedicated floor of 15 secured units for residents with memory loss. The design of the building and interior uses residential themes, which make it look and feel like a house and not an institution.

Major design objectives and responses
Develop a Spanish Colonial Revival building that is consistent with the surrounding 1920s-vintage village center of Pacific Palisades.
Selected color, stucco texture, and stone/stucco detailing consistent with the dominant historic context.

Design a small, intimate building (similar to a bed and breakfast scale) that also includes the full range of services that characterizes the Sunrise national/international prototype.
Chose furniture consistent with the style of the building but also based on its fit with the sensory, anthropometric, and ergonomic requirements of this special population.

Developed a roof garden that overlooks the Pacific Ocean. Created a full floor of secured housing for a mentally frail dementia population. Provided life skills centers and activities related to the activities of food preparation, laundry, gardening, rummaging, and beauty.

The completed project exceeds expectations, having met—and in several aspects surpassed—all of its design objectives.

1 Exterior façade
2 Entry interior
3 Rooftop patio
4 Alzheimer's porch
5 First floor plan
Photography: Ronald Moore and Associates

ARCHITECT	HILL PARTNERSHIP INC.
SITE LOCATION	URBAN
SITE AREA	0.345 ACRES/15,009 SQUARE FEET
CAPACITY	25 ASSISTED LIVING UNITS, 15 DEMENTIA-SPECIFIC UNITS
TOTAL PROJECT COST	NOT AVAILABLE

2

3

4

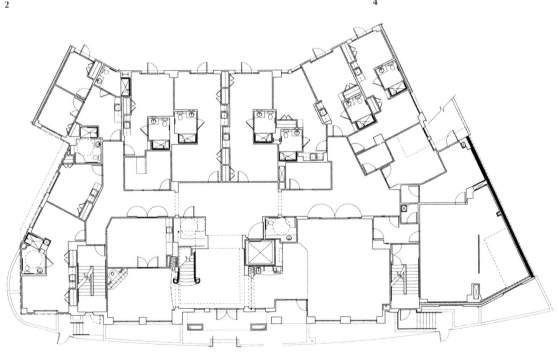

5

SUNRISE ASSISTED LIVING AT FAIR OAKS

FAIRFAX, VIRGINIA

1

ARCHITECT'S STATEMENT

The development of this assisted living residence resulted from a unique collaboration between an international assisted living provider and an acclaimed local health care organization. Their combined mission is to provide an assisted living environment that enhances the quality of life for area seniors and their families while simultaneously addressing specific community health care needs. Through this partnership, concepts such as living with dignity, wellness, and community outreach are realized through programs, operations, and facility design.

This partnership was developed to serve the specific needs of area seniors and the community in general. These needs encompass the areas of health care, wellness, and long-term care management. This facility has achieved the goal of providing area residents—not just seniors—

with an opportunity for rehabilitation and recovery in a therapeutic environment as an alternative to a medical-model nursing center after hospital discharge.

Major design objective and responses
Provide recovery options for hospital patients.
A short-stay wing was developed.

Offer community outreach.
The short-stay wing will be open to the local community.

Develop architecture sensitive to the community context.
The large manor home massing with traditional detailing is appropriate for the community.

Secure tax credit financing for nonprofits to reduce capital costs.
This is a joint venture of for-profit and nonprofit entities.

2

ARCHITECT	WILMOT/SANZ, INC.
SITE LOCATION	SUBURBAN
SITE AREA	12.58 ACRES/547,872 SQUARE FEET
CAPACITY	60 ASSISTED LIVING UNITS, 20 DEMENTIA-SPECIFIC ASSISTED LIVING UNITS
TOTAL PROJECT COST	$9.5 M

3

4

1 Entry porte-cochère
2 Rear courtyard
3 Dementia courtyard, exterior view
4 Dementia courtyard
5 Bay detail
Photography: Jerry Staley

5

6 Café
7 Dining room
8 Unit kitchen, with lower cabinets and refrigerator
  raised for ease of use
Photography: Jerry Staley

6

7

8

SUNRISE OF SAN MATEO

SAN MATEO, CALIFORNIA

1

ARCHITECT'S STATEMENT

This assisted living community, located on a tight urban site, offers residents a familiar, comfortable, and supportive setting. The aesthetic of the building embraces the vernacular California Mission style, with deep-set wood windows in thick stucco walls.

Major design objectives and responses
Create a residential environment.
High-quality wood windows and doors, integral colored stucco exteriors, detailed roof eaves, and a barrel-tile roof were used in the spirit of traditional building materials associated with the regional Mission style. Ample glazing and porches encourage outdoor excursions by emphasizing the relationship between the indoor rooms and outdoor gardens.

To create a familiar residential atmosphere and carry through the consideration to detail, the interior detailing received special attention, including a wood staircase, crown moldings, base and chair rail trim, Mission-style furnishings, and warm colors.

Make the transition from a commercial to a residential neighborhood.
The long axis of the building is set away approximately 15–20 feet from the street, reinforcing the street edge, which is appropriate in this urban context. An attractive landscaped buffer and trellis separates the dining/living areas from the busy arterial and allows the residents to view and participate in the busy street and pedestrian activities outside.

The main entry is located along a quiet side street, around the corner from the arterial, at the gateway to an established residential neighborhood. An elegant, landscaped front yard is adjacent to the clearly defined drop-off zone and garage entry.

1 Front
2 Third floor plan
3 Dining room
4 Grand room
Photography: Dennis Anderson

ARCHITECT	MITHUN, INC., SEATTLE
SITE LOCATION	URBAN
SITE AREA	0.528 ACRE
CAPACITY	46 ASSISTED LIVING UNITS, 17 DEMENTIA-SPECIFIC UNITS
TOTAL PROJECT COST	$9.77 M

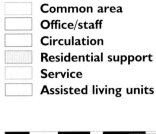

Common area
Office/staff
Circulation
Residential support
Service
Assisted living units

2

0   20ft

3

4

VERNON WOODS
RETIREMENT COMMUNITY
LA GRANGE, GEORGIA

1

ARCHITECT'S STATEMENT

Vernon Woods extends the fabric of its southern small town by organizing its independent and assisted living units into small-scale 'neighborhoods' linked by generous shared spaces. Lively outdoor courtyards, interstitial gardens, and a variety of dining areas and activity rooms connect the levels of care. Each group of resident units is arranged around a sunny lounge with its own tea kitchen and adjacent outdoor space. On the upper floors, lounges have trellised porches with seating; on the lower floors, each lounge entry functions as a front door that leads to convenient resident parking.

Design and material choices create a relaxed, residential atmosphere that is intentionally informal. Extensive paneling and millwork detailing, William Morris wall coverings, Mission light fixtures and furniture, and plantation shutters shading

double-hung multi-paned windows draw visitors through the building. Details including arts and crafts handrails subtly accommodate physical limitations of the aging residents.

Major design objectives and responses

To compensate for residents' disabilities sensitively.
Vernon Woods compensates for residents' disabilities in both plan organization (short travel distances, provision of window-walls and porches, etc.) and detail design. Light levels throughout are deliberately generous and evenly distributed to avoid glare. Mechanical systems are located away from conversation areas and baffled so as not to tax those with hearing problems; there is no overhead paging. Electrical switches glow in the dark. Handrails are constructed as part of the arts and crafts paneling detail

to be supportive and unobtrusive. Counter laminate colors contrast with floor and sink colors to emphasize edge locations and make them more obvious so that items will be dropped less frequently. Common spaces open wide into hallways, so residents have a sense of life throughout the entire building.

To encourage interaction throughout the community, stimulating residents' activity and independence.
Assisted living and independent living are closely linked by an active courtyard with outdoor dining porches and by lively interior spaces like the café/ice cream shop. Other activity spaces include the library, TV/cards room, crafts room, exercise room, chapel/lounge, bank, and two barber/beauty parlors, along with a variety of dining rooms located both

ARCHITECT	PERKINS & WILL
SITE LOCATION	SMALL TOWN
SITE AREA	24.4 ACRES/1,064,864 SQUARE FEET
CAPACITY	50 INDEPENDENT LIVING UNITS, 42 ASSISTED LIVING UNITS
TOTAL PROJECT COST	$18.1 M

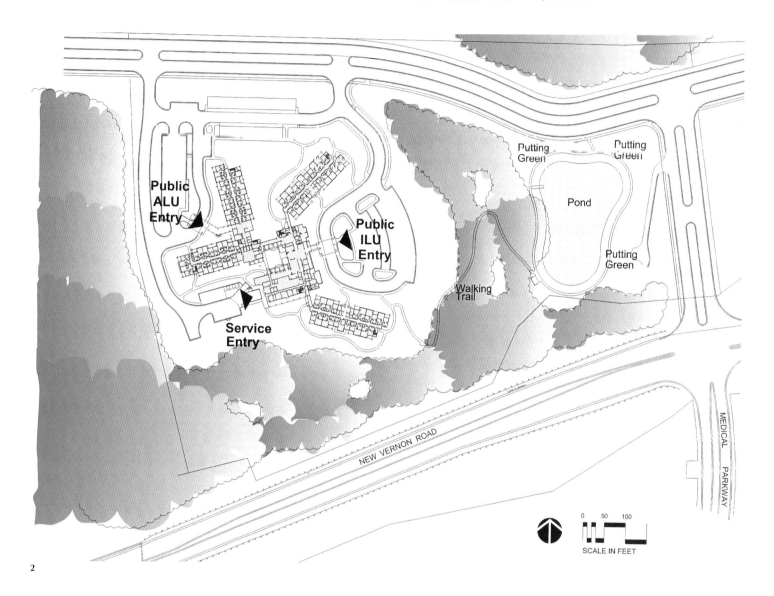

2

indoors and outdoors, sized for large and small groups.

Outdoor spaces include generous canopies and drop-offs to encourage visitors, as well as a pair of large fountains, a walking path down to the duck pond, and three putting greens. Trellised terraces and porches extend the living spaces into the landscape.

To provide units flexible enough to maintain each resident's sense of individuality and personality.
Resident units are paired with inset entry doors that widen hallways and offer opportunities for the seniors to personalize the plant and mail shelves. Wide wooden moldings, engraved doorknockers, and light sconces enhance the entry at each apartment. The project includes 11 types of independent living units and four types of assisted living units to suit differing resident preferences.

Unit sizes are generous enough to accommodate the variety of furniture and possessions seniors want to maintain. Structural cross-bracing was carefully located so that adjacent units can be combined to create even larger layouts. Every unit has a porch or a terrace and is served by a water-source heat pump that is individually controllable. Every living room has two or three window-walls and a ceiling fan.

3

1 Third-floor commons porch
2 Site plan
3 North wing independent living, neighborhood lounge entry, and porch
Photography: William Nelson

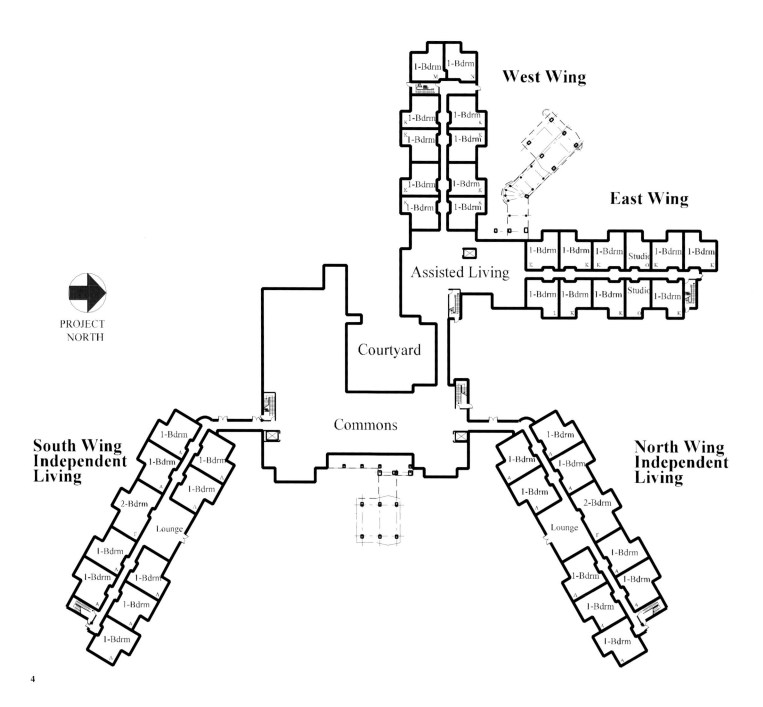

West Wing

1-Bdrm M | 1-Bdrm N

1-Bdrm K | 1-Bdrm K
1-Bdrm K | 1-Bdrm K

1-Bdrm | 1-Bdrm K
1-Bdrm K | 1-Bdrm K

East Wing

Assisted Living

1-Bdrm K | 1-Bdrm K | 1-Bdrm K | Studio O | 1-Bdrm K | 1-Bdrm K

1-Bdrm L | 1-Bdrm K | 1-Bdrm K | Studio O | 1-Bdrm K

Courtyard

Commons

PROJECT
NORTH

**South Wing
Independent
Living**

1-Bdrm A
1-Bdrm A | 1-Bdrm N
2-Bdrm | 1-Bdrm N
Lounge
1-Bdrm A
1-Bdrm A | 1-Bdrm A
1-Bdrm A

**North Wing
Independent
Living**

1-Bdrm
1-Bdrm A | 1-Bdrm A
1-Bdrm A | 2-Bdrm
Lounge
1-Bdrm A
1-Bdrm A | 1-Bdrm A
1-Bdrm A
1-Bdrm

4

5

6

4 First floor plan
5 North wing from entrance drive
6 Dining courtyard at independent/assisted living
   connecting corridor
7 Independent living/dining room
8 Commons library
9 Residential unit bath
10 Ice cream/café
11 Assisted living lounge
Photography: William Nelson

7

8

9

10

11

THE VILLAGE AT ROBINWOOD

1

ARCHITECT'S STATEMENT

A new 70-unit assisted living facility combined with a community center forms the heart of a small continuing care retirement community. The project is part of a campus being developed by the local health care system, along with a nonprofit provider of care for the elderly. The building was designed in the context of an existing large medical office building across the street but uses residential finishes, materials, and scale to render the assisted living building in a similar aesthetic.

Twelve of the 70 units in the residence are located in a dedicated wing for residents with dementia, and this wing also has a dedicated outdoor courtyard for resident wandering and activities. The remaining 58 units are designed around clustered living room areas that define various neighborhoods within the building. The residence contains a mix of one-bedroom and studio units.

Major design objectives and responses
Include shared amenities.
The dining and main activity areas are in a one-story wing that also serves as the main entrance for the facility. The community center has a separate entry. Independent cottage residents and assisted living residents share function rooms in the community center, such as an arts and crafts room, a salon, and a café.

Provide residentially scaled 'houses.'
The residence is arranged in 'neighborhoods' with 10 to 12 residents each. Corridors are articulated with offsets opening into clustered living room areas. Each unit features a small drop table to provide space for residents to rest items while entering their units or to display personal items.

To maintain a non-institutional environment, care assistants have alcoves in each neighborhood for a desk, a closet for clean linen and supplies, a housekeeping closet, and a laundry.

Create living units.
The living units are designed for a wide range of affordability to meet the needs of a diverse local market—they vary in size from 360 to 500 square feet. Every unit has a fully accessible bathroom with a barrier-free shower, equipped with a hand-held showerhead, non-institutional assist bars, and removable vanity fronts to permit ease of use by wheelchair occupants.

All units have kitchenettes with cabinets with rolling shelves, a refrigerator/freezer unit raised up to facilitate accessibility; lever-handled fittings, and a microwave. (For the residents' safety, no burners or

ARCHITECT	COCHRAN, STEPHENSON & DONKERVOET, INC.
SITE LOCATION	SUBURBAN
SITE AREA	1.85 ACRES/75,365 SQUARE FEET
CAPACITY	58 ASSISTED LIVING UNITS, 12 DEMENTIA-SPECIFIC UNITS
TOTAL PROJECT COST	$11 M

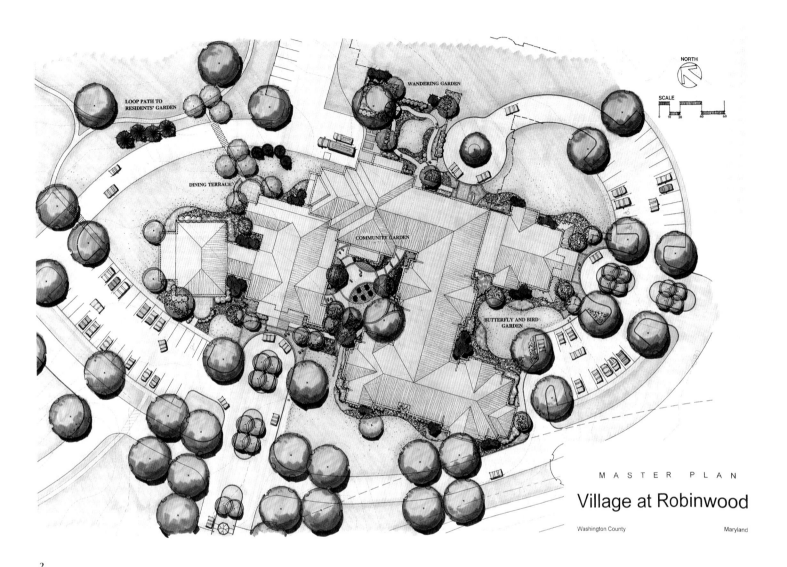

MASTER PLAN

Village at Robinwood

Washington County   Maryland

2

garbage disposals are provided.) Slip-resistant, hardwood-like floor coverings create a small foyer at the unit entrance.

The large windows, with lowered sills, provide wonderful views of the countryside or garden courtyard and increase the apparent size of the room. Units accommodate a bed, chair, dresser, table, and TV. The larger units are arranged to create distinct sleeping areas and sitting/eating areas. Residents provide their own furniture.

Heating and air-conditioning units are located in vertical enclosures that minimize the loss of square footage from the unit. The system is an energy-efficient central plant with individual controls that promote independence. Using a water system instead of air makes the comfort level quite adequate for the elderly.

1 Front porch, assisted living facility
2 Master plan
3 Dining room, assisted living facility
Photography: Alain Jaramillo

3

4

5

6

4   The commons provides a second entrance to the assisted living facility
5   Living room, dementia unit of the assisted living facility
6   Café, for residents of assisted living and independent living cottages
Photography: Alain Jaramillo

WESTMINSTER-CANTERBURY OF THE BLUE RIDGE,
CATERED LIVING BUILDING
CHARLOTTESVILLE, VIRGINIA

1

ARCHITECT'S STATEMENT

With views of Thomas Jefferson's Monticello, this new catered living building provides social-model assisted living for its 45 residents. The addition is part of a $67 million expansion of the Westminster-Canterbury of the Blue Ridge complex. The master plan outlines new independent living apartments and villas, a memory enhancement unit, expansions of the existing commons, and wellness facilities on the 50-acre site.

A primary design challenge was the site limitation. Connecting the building to the community without intruding on the surrounding cottages was accomplished by a creative, three-story infill design that steps up the site. Having the third floor connected to the community gives residents easy access to wellness and other activities.

The residents on the first floor need the highest level of support, and their units are smaller, creating another design challenge. Each resident has a private studio or bedroom apartment that features large windows and closets, private bath, and studio kitchen.

Historic Charlottesville greatly influenced the design, evoking the style of a southern home with formal living and dining rooms as well as places for individual and group activities. The color schemes showcase the interior architecture and reproductions of period furnishings.

The living rooms on the upper floors are connected to the dining/activity room by a passageway that features a bench seat and a large window where residents can wait for an activity or meal or just sit and read. The kitchen/family room is a casual space

that reflects the 'great room' concept. Around the corner is a sitting room with a magnifier for reading and an open library with a computer. Staff members are trained to help residents surf the internet.

Major design objectives and responses
Work with the steep topography of the site and the proximity to existing cottage residents.
Creative three-story, in-fill design that steps up the site and is connected to the main community. Porches were added to break up the mass of a three-story building so close to the cottages.

Meet Monticello view-shed regulations/ requirements.
Red brick was chosen for the exterior, as opposed to matching the look of the existing community, which is a combination of brick and white siding.

ARCHITECT	SFCS INC.
SITE LOCATION	SUBURBAN
SITE AREA	0.5 ACRE/21,800 SQUARE FEET
CAPACITY	45 ASSISTED LIVING UNITS
TOTAL PROJECT COST	$7.15 M

1   Main entrance
2   Rear of catered living building and
    bridge connecting it to the main building
3   Aerial view
4   Catered living, main entrance
Photography: Philip Beaurline

3

2

*Residents who need less assistance with
activities of daily living desire easy access
to the main community.*
These residents were located on the third
floor, which is connected to the main
community.

*Ensure that program-defined higher
functioning residents have larger units.*
Because of the site limitations and the
desire of the more active residents to have
access to the community center, the second
and third floors are occupied by residents
who need less assistance with activities of
daily living and have larger units. The first
floor residents have smaller units. This
created the challenge of designing a three-
story building. Stacking was not an option,
so porches were added on the first floor,
which provided additional opportunities
for residents to enjoy the outdoors.

4

5

6

7

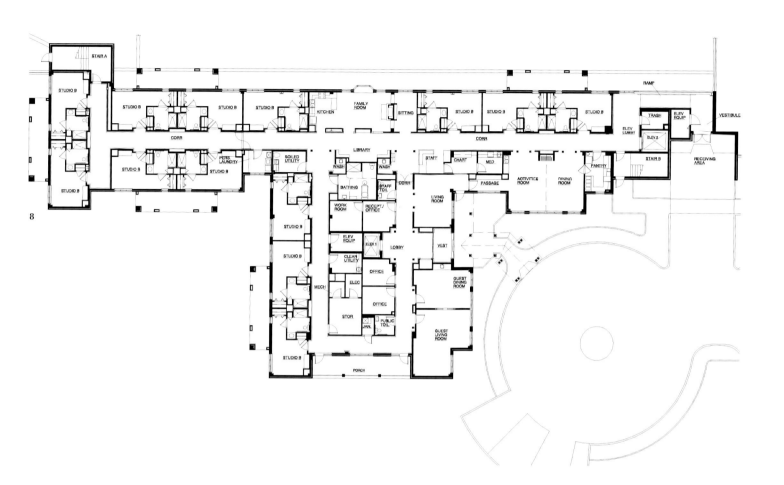

8

9

10

DESIGN for AGING REVIEW

NURSING

FOULKEWAYS AT GWYNEDD, SKILLED CARE FACILITY

1

ARCHITECT'S STATEMENT

Foulkeways, which was the first Quaker community and the first campus-style care facility in Pennsylvania, approached the new replacement skilled care facility with three objectives: (1) simple forms and materials, (2) a homelike setting, and (3) a strong connection to the outdoors.

These objectives inspired a design that used single-loaded corridors throughout, resulting in 'transparent' corridor walls that connect residents to nature in a bright and uplifting interior. All 40 private rooms include tiled, European-style showers and large walk-in closets. All social and dining spaces are central to the open plan for staff efficiency. These spaces are monitored through four care stations consisting of a simple wood desk and rear rolltop desk that houses a computer. An open residential country kitchen serves two flanking dining rooms.

Major design objectives and responses

Create a non-institutional aesthetic consistent with the Quaker philosophy of simplicity.
Simple materials of stucco and stone, varying roof heights of one and two stories, porches, distinctive chimney elements, overhangs, and wood brackets all translate into a simple but beautiful style reminiscent of a Quaker meeting house. The single-loaded resident corridors afford views into the building and translate well onto the exterior, creating a non-institutional and non-repetitious elevation not typically associated with skilled care facilities.

To diminish the traditional dark and institutional double-loaded corridors in resident wings.
Each resident corridor was designed to be single-loaded, with only five rooms per

wing. The explosion of natural light and connection to the outdoors immediately broke down the institutional medical-model stigma. The outdoors becomes part of the interior décor. Corridors are further animated with pocketed resident room doors and illuminated display niches at each resident room entry.

To decentralize the plan from a nursing care standpoint in order to diminish an institutional overtone.
Two wings of five rooms each radiate out from a simple wooden staff desk that also looks directly into the living and dining rooms. All charting and other medical-related functions occur in an adjacent back room, out of sight. This decentralization and residential detailing create a quiet, homelike setting.

ARCHITECT ■■ REESE, LOWER, PATRICK & SCOTT, LTD.

SITE LOCATION ■■ SUBURBAN

SITE AREA ■■ 3 ACRES/130,680 SQUARE FEET

CAPACITY ■■ 40 SKILLED NURSING CARE BEDS

TOTAL PROJECT COST ■■ $9.5 M

2

3

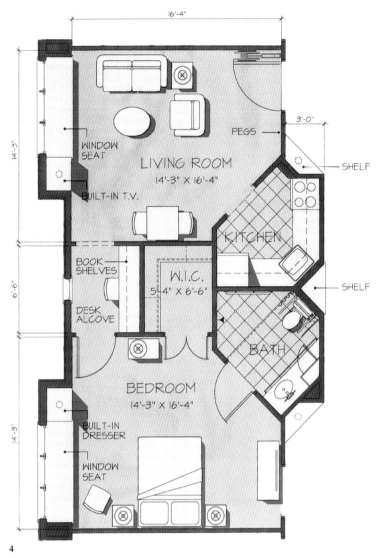

4

To provide a facility that makes resident dignity and privacy paramount to the success of the project.

In the new skilled-care facility, all 40 resident rooms are private. Each room is spacious and includes enough floor area for additional furniture belonging to residents. Each room also includes a large walk-in closet rather than the standard 2-foot by 3-foot wall closet, which allows residents to store more of their belongings close by and gives the staff an area to stock supplies needed by the individual resident. Medications are stored in a double-locked drawer in each closet. A shower in each private bathroom allows residents the dignity and comfort of bathing in their own rooms.

Provide a facility that is flexible enough to address any changes in the marketplace or industry.

The resident rooms are paired in the design to allow a simple conversion from two skilled-care rooms to a large, one-bedroom assisted living apartment. The conversion would entail removing one wall in a walk-in closet, creating a passageway, and renovating a private bath into an L-shaped kitchen.

1 Dining and kitchen
2 Central bathing area
3 Typical resident room
4 Plan, conversion to assisted living
Photography: Larry Lefever

BURLESON ST. JOSEPH'S MANOR

CALDWELL, TEXAS

1

ARCHITECT'S STATEMENT

The primary design objective, voiced both by administration and an elderly focus group, was to maximize the opportunity for resident choice while offering varying degrees of socialization. Response to this design criterion has been achieved primarily through a neighborhood plan concept with resident rooms situated in smaller groupings.

In order to stay within project cost parameters and maintain an all-private bedroom program, the floor plan was designed using the efficiency of double-loaded corridors. However, in order to avoid long, monotonous corridors, resident quarters are decentralized into three distinct 'neighborhoods.' Each of these neighborhoods contains four clusters of

eight resident rooms. Each neighborhood is situated for easy access to the dining hall, located at 'town center.'

Decentralized living rooms, screened-in porches, outdoor covered patios, and indoor activity areas all present comfortable amenities that reflect a warm residential scale. This design provides maximum opportunity for socialization, enabling residents to maintain their highest level of independence in a secure, nurturing, and pleasant environment. Mature oak trees surround the facility and are preserved in courtyard spaces. In addition, the 18-acre site is designed to accommodate future growth, including assisted living facilities.

2

ARCHITECT ▦ WATKINS HAMILTON ROSS ARCHITECTS

SITE LOCATION ▦ SMALL TOWN

SITE AREA ▦ 18 ACRES

CAPACITY ▦ 16 DEMENTIA-SPECIFIC BEDS,
80 SKILLED NURSING CARE BEDS

TOTAL PROJECT COST ▦ $4.6 M

5

3

6

4

1   Town center
2   Public waiting area
3   Exterior, front elevation
4   Dining room
5   Neighborhood living room
6   Resident room
Photography: Jud Haggard

FAIRMONT CROSSING

AMHERST, VIRGINIA

1

2

3

ARCHITECT'S STATEMENT

Nestled in the foothills of beautiful Amherst County, Fairmont Crossing was designed to capture the incredible views enjoyed by the local citizens it will serve. Amherst is home to rural people who enjoy their privacy but who are very active in their community, so the facility was also designed to meet those needs.

Every window enjoys a view of the countryside or a beautiful courtyard with gardens and wandering paths. The carpeted corridors contain alcoves to store and hide any of the nursing home equipment and wheelchairs normally associated with an institution. The unique configuration of the residents' semiprivate rooms gives a sense of privacy and personal space. The bathing facilities were designed to be spas, with

mirrors for grooming. Dayrooms with their low planter partitions are located across from the nursing stations so that residents can enjoy a café surrounding while being monitored.

The dining room/serving kitchens were developed to marry restorative health care with gracious, nutritional dining. Planters will divide the dining room to separate the independent diners from those needing assistance. Meals will be prepared in bulk in the lower main kitchen and served to residents by dining and health care staff from the serving kitchen on the floor. For residents who are bedfast, trays will be prepared in the serving kitchen and sent to the unit, thereby maintaining temperatures and faster service.

To provide a sense of community, large common areas offer sufficient space to meet the needs of large resident groups and open up to the general community for meetings, functions, and programs. A gas fireplace is the center of a homelike common area, while corridors are lined with windows to capture the views. The large multipurpose activity center that can be used for chapel, activities, resident council, and cooking is centrally located.

The facility was also designed to keep operations out of sight by having the kitchen, laundry, maintenance, delivery, and other functional areas located on a basement level and by keeping administrative and therapy areas out of the main resident areas.

ARCHITECT ▍▍▍ HUGHES ASSOCIATES ARCHITECTS

SITE LOCATION ▍▍▍ SMALL TOWN

SITE AREA ▍▍▍ 9 ACRES

CAPACITY ▍▍▍ 64 SKILLED NURSING CARE UNITS/120 BEDS

TOTAL PROJECT COST ▍▍▍ $6.7 M

4

5

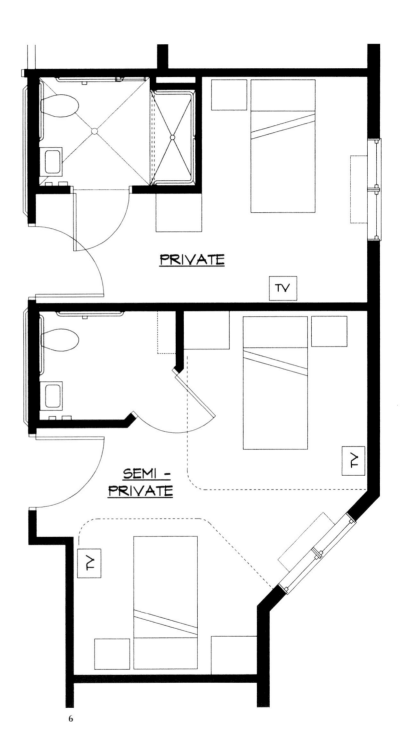

PRIVATE

TV

SEMI -
PRIVATE

TV

TV

6

Fairmont Crossing is positioned to continue a familiar way of life for Amherst citizens who depend on health care services—with accents on privacy, community, refinement, and appreciation of the surrounding country, without an institutional feeling.

Major design objectives and responses
Create a homelike facility.
Privacy and the use of residential materials add to the homelike atmosphere.

1 Front porch
2 Day room
3 Lounge
4 Great room
5 Dining room
6 Plan, typical resident rooms
Photography: Andrew Wildes

GURWIN JEWISH GERIATRIC CENTER
HARRY AND JEANNETTE WEINBERG RESIDENT PAVILION
AND COMMUNITY SERVICE CENTER

COMMACK, NEW YORK

1

ARCHITECT'S STATEMENT

The new Harry and Jeannette Weinberg Resident Pavilion and Community Service Center allows the Gurwin Jewish Geriatric Center to expand its existing programs. The new center contains 160 beds, as well as an outpatient diagnostic and treatment center, and increases the existing adult day health care program to 120 participants.

As with the original facility, courtyards and gardens separate elements of the building. The new center is designed around an open atrium used for outdoor recreation. Groups of nursing units are divided into 'neighborhoods' that help create a residential character, while colors and finishes were chosen to impart a sense of warmth and comfort.

Major design objectives and responses
Create a campus-like environment.
The new building ties in harmoniously to the original, with the use of courtyards and gardens between building elements as well as the same exterior brick.

Give the facility a residential character.
Nursing units are divided into a series of neighborhoods, imparting a residential scale. Colors and finishes were chosen to convey a sense of warmth and comfort.

Provide a sense of privacy and dignity for the residents.
Resident rooms are either single or bi-axial doubles. The bi-axial double room provides each resident with his or her own window and HVAC unit and the dignity of a private room.

Build flexibility into the design.
The home can vary the types of care provided by concentrating homogeneous populations in distinct 'neighborhoods.' The populations being served can change as needs change.

Allow for unobtrusive supervision.
The building's configuration creates a 'wandering loop' for residents with dementia. The location of the staff station at the confluence of the neighborhoods, where the lounges, dining room, and exterior balcony are situated, allows the staff unobtrusive supervision of all resident areas.

ARCHITECT ▦ LANDOW AND LANDOW ARCHITECTS

SITE LOCATION ▦ SUBURBAN

SITE AREA ▦ 4 ACRES

CAPACITY ▦ 160 SKILLED NURSING CARE UNITS

TOTAL PROJECT COST ▦ $35 M

2

3

1 Weinberg Pavilion, entry
2 Staff station and lounge
3 Aerial view
4 First floor plan
Photography: Paul Warchol Photography Inc.

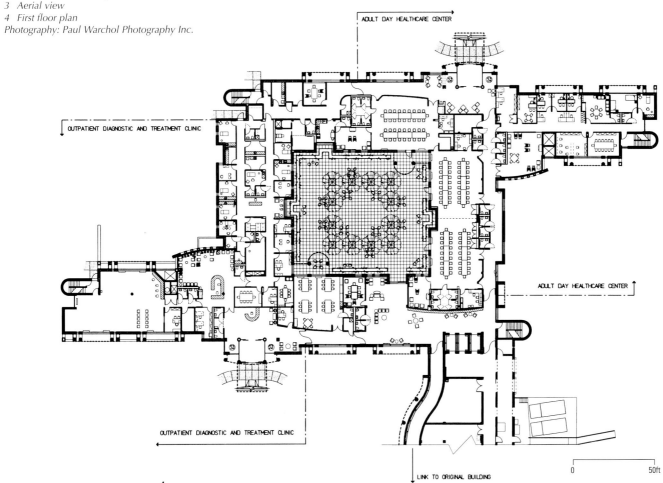

ADULT DAY HEALTHCARE CENTER

OUTPATIENT DIAGNOSTIC AND TREATMENT CLINIC

ADULT DAY HEALTHCARE CENTER

OUTPATIENT DIAGNOSTIC AND TREATMENT CLINIC

LINK TO ORIGINAL BUILDING

0   50ft

4

JEWISH HOME OF CENTRAL NEW YORK

SYRACUSE, NEW YORK

1

ARCHITECT'S STATEMENT

An extensive plan was developed to improve and expand the Jewish Home's facilities and services. The firm designed The Oaks, an independent living center on the upper campus, in 1995. For the lower campus, the firm designed:

- A new health center to replace the existing nursing home: resident areas are divided into small clusters of rooms; two clusters form a 'neighborhood,' with a shared 'great room.' Nursing desks at the center of each neighborhood increase staff efficiency. Each floor has its own dining room, divided into three distinct areas for 14 residents each, as well as an activity room and library

- The Inn: transformed an existing nursing home into assisted living and memory-enhancement residences

- New rehabilitation center
- New main entrance: Main Street, along with the activity and circulation artery, seamlessly connects the existing building to new construction.

Major design objectives and responses
Establish a continuum of care campus— options for level of care.
The campus includes a new skilled nursing facility, dementia care, assisted living, frail assisted apartments, independent living.

Incorporate the cluster concept.
Several distinct living areas are grouped around shared great rooms, creating 'neighborhoods.'

Increase staff/resident interaction and care.
Nursing desks are clustered near the residents' bedrooms.

Minimize travel distances.
Living clusters are arranged so that dining/activity areas are connected.

Minimize dining room scale and improve dining experience.
Three dining area clusters per floor help reduce confusion and improve food quality.

1 Entrance
2 Lobby/welcome center
3 Corridor
4 Chapel

ARCHITECT ▪▪ KING & KING, ARCHITECTS LLP,
MANLIUS, NY

SITE LOCATION ▪▪ SUBURBAN

SITE AREA ▪▪ 14.9 ACRES/649,425 SQUARE FEET

CAPACITY ▪▪ 18 ASSISTED LIVING UNITS,
25 DEMENTIA-SPECIFIC UNITS,
87 SKILLED NURSING CARE UNITS/132 BEDS

TOTAL PROJECT COST ▪▪ $16 M

2

3

4

JONES-HARRISON RESIDENCE

MINNEAPOLIS, MINNESOTA

1

ARCHITECT'S STATEMENT

The scope of the Jones-Harrison Residence project was to remodel virtually every room in the five-story nursing and assisted living facility to meet contemporary expectations for senior housing and health care. The challenges were significant: while the facility was occupied, all finishes would be updated and existing square footage would be significantly reconfigured. Two complex design challenges were embedded in this project: reconfiguring an entire floor to meet the unique needs of residents with Alzheimer's and dementia, and creating a wellness center, complete with pool, in the existing basement of the facility.

Major design objectives and responses

Create a floor plan for residents with dementia within the constraints of an existing building.
Five 'neighborhoods' were developed on a single floor, with a 'great room' located at the end of each wing and one in the center of the plan.

Create a wellness center with a club-like atmosphere in the existing basement.
The basement was reconfigured to create separate therapy, pool, and exercise spaces with internal circulation space allowing users to move from one space to another without having to go through the central lobby.

Create a uniform interior design with the feel of an elegant hotel.
High-quality finishes with common detailing were used throughout all floors of the facility. The main entry lobby introduces the use of these finishes at the reception desk, continuing throughout the public spaces.

Replace the institutional character of the building with a more residential feeling.
Additional spaces for resident use were created. Warmer, softer finishes enhance the residential nature of the spaces.

1 Lake cabin great room and nurses' station
2 Lower floor plan
3 Country corridor
4 Lake cabin corridor
Photography: Joel Butkowski

ARCHITECT ▦ GLTArchitects

SITE LOCATION ▦ Urban

SITE AREA ▦ 5.3 ACRES/230,868 SQUARE FEET

CAPACITY ▦ 57 ASSISTED LIVING UNITS,
78 DEMENTIA-SPECIFIC UNITS,
85 SKILLED NURSING CARE BEDS

TOTAL PROJECT COST ▦ $5.39 M

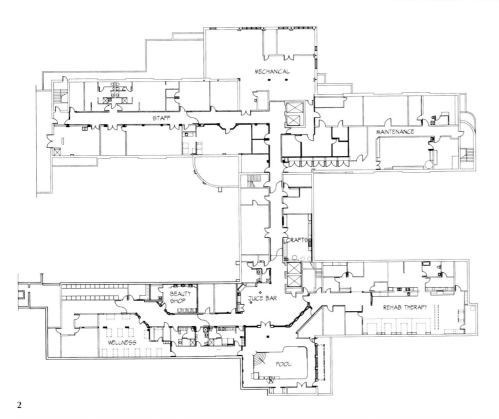

2

3

4

1

Architect's statement

The 'neighborhood' concept as a model of care that integrates a smaller grouping of resident rooms with dedicated common and support spaces provided the direction for this project from its inception. The exploration of this concept clearly defined the project goals of (1) creating distinct neighborhoods within an existing, cross-shaped, medical-model, skilled care building and (2) enlivening and expanding communal spaces in the linear assisted living building. The design process integrated this concept with the physical constraints dictated by the existing building and its site.

Fundamental issues such as establishing separate neighborhood identities through material and color changes, exposure to natural light, openness, sensitivity to acoustics and lighting, and the inherent characteristics of residential detailing were

addressed to strengthen the organizing structure of a neighborhood, thereby enhancing the residents' daily quality of life.

Major design objectives and responses
Break down the medical model of existing skilled care resident rooms into neighborhood groups with separate common areas.
Some resident rooms were deleted and new construction square footage was added to create separate neighborhoods and common spaces.

Enliven and expand assisted living communal spaces.
Existing common areas were totally renovated, and some new construction was added.

Enhance residents' quality of life with characteristics of residential detailing.
The design included material and color changes, wood detailing, improved lighting, an open-plan arrangement, and increased exposure to natural light.

Reinforce 'neighborhood' by providing separate dining accommodation.
Each neighborhood now has an individual, residentially detailed serving kitchen and dining area.

Develop an assisted living café.
The design addresses an open-plan café, library, and living room layout adjacent to a country store and mailroom.

1 New addition at neighborhood (skilled care)
2 Café, library, and family room (assisted living)
3 Care base adjacent to open dining and family
   room (skilled care)
4 Care base and dining area (skilled care)
Photography: Larry Lefever

ARCHITECT ▚ REESE, LOWER, PATRICK & SCOTT, LTD.

SITE LOCATION ▚ SUBURBAN

SITE AREA ▚ 78 ACRES

CAPACITY ▚ 100 SENIOR LIVING UNITS,
            134 SKILLED NURSING CARE BEDS

TOTAL PROJECT COST ▚ $4.25 M

2

3

4

Missouri Veterans' Home

1

2

Architect's statement

A residential scale, access to the outdoors, and efficient operation were the primary objectives in planning this project. The one-story design uses natural materials—wood and stone—and brick inside and out, bringing continuity and warmth to the facility.

Residential scale was achieved by organizing resident rooms around small living rooms, each with a hearth element that gives focus to the space. Views and easy access to the outdoors are evident throughout the plan. Interiors are bathed in natural light, and views to the outside aid orientation and wayfinding.

Resident social and activity spaces, grouped together at the center of the plan, create a Main Street. In addition to traditional nursing care, the facility provides two specially designed dementia care units.

Efficiency is enhanced by a decentralized approach that distributes support/service spaces throughout the units. The project was designed as a prototype facility that can be replicated on other sites.

Major design objectives and responses

Ensure easy access for all residents.
The design has a single-story layout.

Create a residential feel.
Use of wood, stone, and brick, along with an abundance of daylighting and exterior views, creates a residential feel.

Instill a sense of place and community.
The sense of community is enhanced by the centralized placement of two small and one large 'cluster lounges' per wing.

Provide decentralized support functions.
Laundry, showers, nutrition, and medication are positioned to optimize staff efficiency. These functions are located in each residential wing, rather than one of each to serve the entire complex.

1   Dining room
2   Dementia dining room
3   Site plan
4   Main lobby approach with natural daylight
5   Small cluster lounge
6   Garden view
7   Hydrotherapy suite
Photography: Michael Spillers

ARCHITECT ▦ RAFAEL ARCHITECTS, INC.

SITE LOCATION ▦ SMALL TOWN

SITE AREA ▦ 22 ACRES/955,500 SQUARE FEET

CAPACITY ▦ 200 SKILLED NURSING CARE BEDS

TOTAL PROJECT COST ▦ $17.6 M

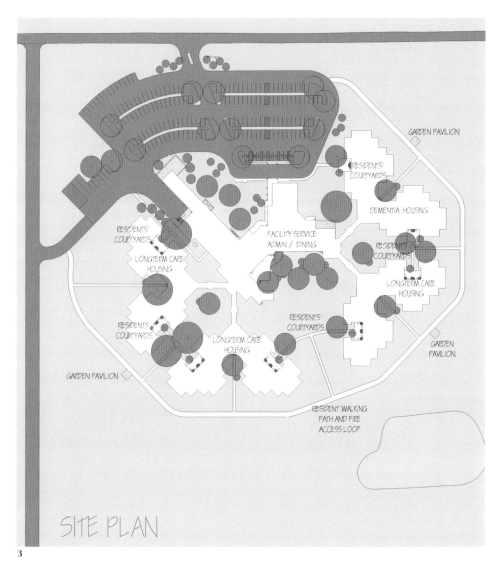

GARDEN PAVILION

RESIDENTS' COURTYARDS

DEMENTIA HOUSING

RESIDENTS' COURTYARDS

LONGTERM CARE HOUSING

GARDEN PAVILION

RESIDENTS' COURTYARDS

LONGTERM CARE HOUSING

FACILITY SERVICE ADMIN / DINING

RESIDENTS' COURTYARDS

LONGTERM CARE HOUSING

RESIDENTS' COURTYARDS

GARDEN PAVILION

RESIDENT WALKING PATH AND FIRE ACCESS LOOP

SITE PLAN

3

4

5

6

7

NURSING

MOTHER ANGELINE McCRORY MANOR

COLUMBUS, OHIO

1

ARCHITECT'S STATEMENT

This skilled nursing facility is situated along a major corridor leading into downtown Columbus. Its existing campus encompasses an assisted living and independent living facility surrounded by a mature landscape with a nearby river. The building orientation takes full advantage of the vistas connecting residents to the rural and urban qualities of the community.

The northern façade faces local streetscape elements while the southern exposure opens to views of Walnut Creek. As people enter the facility, they are greeted by the sensory stimulation of the 'city center,' which resembles a small town's Main Street, with a coffeehouse, library, and chapel as anchored communication hubs to the outdoor piazza. These landmarks provide a sense of place, with natural light reinforcing time.

The facility has a total of 147 beds, of which 21 are dedicated to dementia care. Each resident room is part of a 'household' (cluster of 21 rooms) that forms a 'neighborhood pavilion' with resident room entry features such as porch lights and 'memory boxes.' There are also small seating areas for private conversations, a resident laundry, and a hydrotherapy spa. Each neighborhood pavilion shares a typical home's gathering spaces such as the kitchen, activity area, dining room, and living rooms with fireplaces and bookshelves. Both the dementia and non-dementia pavilions have access to their own roof-garden terrace.

Major design objectives and responses
Maintain one staff member for every seven residents.
Neighborhood pavilions of 21 beds each make for shortened travel distances and increase staff efficiency (maximum distance 75 feet).

Provide resident rooms with views.
Half the rooms view Walnut Creek; the remainder view the piazza and courtyards.

Respond to urban context and surrounding region.
A local vernacular design using materials of the area, such as stone and brick, and a 'city center' evoke memories for residents who lived and worked in Columbus.

ARCHITECT	THW DESIGN
SITE LOCATION	SUBURBAN
SITE AREA	15 ACRES/653,400 SQUARE FEET
CAPACITY	126 SKILLED NURSING CARE UNITS, 21 DEMENTIA-SPECIFIC UNITS
TOTAL PROJECT COST	$18.7 M

2

1   Entrance
2   Piazza
3&5   City center
4   Neighborhood pavilion

3

4

Use a neighborhood social model.
Smaller 'neighborhood/homelike wings'
provide residents with opportunities for
socialization and seating/resting points
on their journey to the 'city center.'

Design for sensory and mobility loss.
Extensive use of non-gloss surfaces,
indirect lighting, and acoustical treatments
throughout the building help maximize
resident abilities.

5

NURSING

NEW HAMPSHIRE VETERANS HOME

TILTON, NEW HAMPSHIRE

1

ARCHITECT'S STATEMENT

The project integrates 100 new skilled nursing and dementia beds into an existing 150-bed campus, with provision for 50 additional beds in the future. Major challenges included addressing inefficiencies in function, flexibility, wayfinding, engineering, and quality of environment.

To start with, a new circulation spine was established to simplify wayfinding and circulation and to establish an appropriate master framework for the campus. A new, vertically expandable two-story addition compactly and efficiently integrates with the design, with minimal site impact, and improves operational convenience. In addition, a generic 'racetrack' decentralized pod design for nursing units creates a homelike, flexible, and efficient environment, anticipating change as a reality in health care.

Generous daylight, views, indoor and outdoor activity areas, indirect lighting, therapeutic gardens, and a Shaker aesthetic combine to create a supportive, healing environment that helps all residents, not just those with dementia, to connect with everyday life in a non-institutional manner.

Major design objectives and responses

Enhance the therapeutic value of contact with nature and natural light for residents with dementia.
Interior atrium courtyards with plants were included, and exterior therapeutic gardens were developed.

Improve the therapeutic value of contact with everyday household activities and the supervision of residents.
A country kitchen is the focal element in the common/activity/dining area and serves as a decentralized nursing station.

Consider the tendency for dementia patients to wander and problems associated with corridors ending in a closed door.
A 'racetrack' walking loop was included around communal areas. This creates a common area concept appropriate for the entire community.

Ensure flexibility in planning health care facilities and the need to look beyond the immediate future in an ever-changing field.
A semi-generic pod design is appropriate for various population types. This affected room design, pod size, and architectural design concepts.

Avoid residents being disturbed by service activity.
There is double access to all housekeeping, utility, and linen rooms.

ARCHITECT ▮▮ MorrisSwitzer Environments for Health

SITE LOCATION ▮▮ Small town

SITE AREA ▮▮ 28.944 acres/1,260,807 square feet

CAPACITY ▮▮ 50 special care beds for persons with dementia, 50 skilled nursing care beds

TOTAL PROJECT COST ▮▮ $10.5 M

1   View from the courtyard
2   Ground floor plan
3   Longitudinal section
4   Perspective and elevation

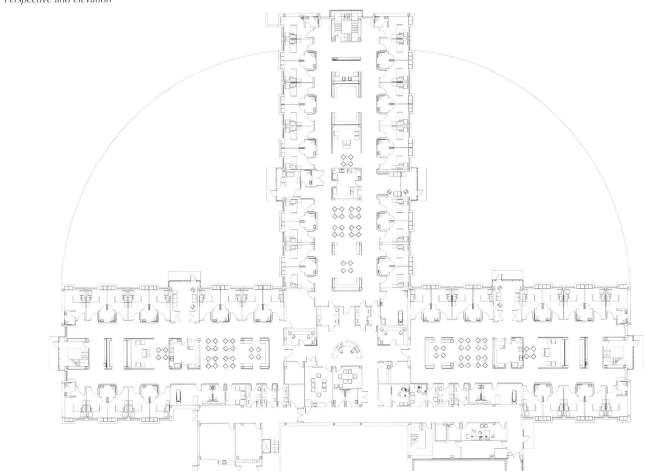

2

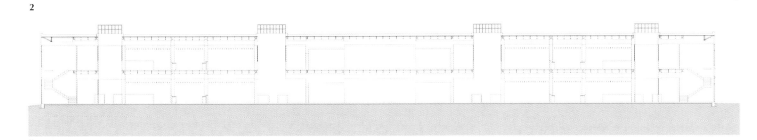

3

4

NURSING

Pathways Center for Alzheimer's Care

Springfield, Ohio

1

Architect's statement

This single-story, residential-style brick and stone facility contains 60 units within its 46,900 square feet. Licensed for skilled nursing care, the building is scaled down into four 'households' of 15 bedrooms each. The shared resident spaces in each household feature a family room, living room with fireplace, dining room, large farmhouse kitchen, and private courtyard. Each 'household' is approximately 10,000 square feet and has been designed to have its own identity, to be 'self-supporting,' and to encourage family-like interaction and person-centered care among staff and residents.

The commons comprise a central kitchen, administration offices, hair salon, and family meeting/conference rooms. Meal preparation is finished in the butler kitchens before the meal is served 'family style.'

A great deal of attention was given to the interior trim and the use of 'warm' materials to provide the residents with a familiar feeling of home. The blending of circulation and socialization spaces further defines the residential scale and atmosphere desired. Furniture, artwork, accessories, and physical environment were all designed to work together to stimulate memory, recall familiar surroundings, and encourage a positive and interactive lifestyle.

1 Dining room, dementia household
2 Floor plan, dementia household
3 Resident bedroom, with memory case
4 Family/guest room
Photography: Feinknopf Photography

ARCHITECT ▓▓ MADDOX NBD ARCHITECTURE
SITE LOCATION ▓▓ SMALL TOWN
SITE AREA ▓▓ 6.17 ACRES
CAPACITY ▓▓ 60 DEMENTIA-SPECIFIC UNITS
TOTAL PROJECT COST ▓▓ $6.87 M

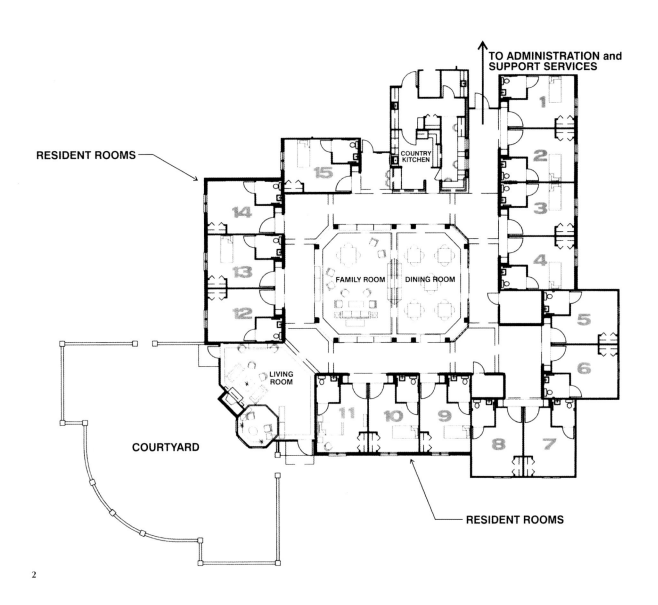

RESIDENT ROOMS

TO ADMINISTRATION and
SUPPORT SERVICES

COUNTRY
KITCHEN

FAMILY ROOM   DINING ROOM

LIVING
ROOM

COURTYARD

RESIDENT ROOMS

2

3   4

THE RENAISSANCE
WASHINGTON, D.C.

1

ARCHITECT'S STATEMENT

This 94-bed skilled nursing addition, with all private rooms, at the west end of Sibley Memorial Hospital, completes an on-campus care continuum that includes ambulatory, acute, and skilled care; assisted living; and senior service, lifeline, and community outreach programs.

The two buildings connect at the second-, third- and fourth-floor nursing levels, permitting staff and supply movement and convenient patient access to therapeutic services. Patient rooms are clustered for nursing support in eight-bed groups. Two clusters form a 16-bed unit with a certified nurse assistant; country kitchen; and dining, social, and rehab space. Two 16-bed units per floor share access and service facilities.

The sloping site permits at-grade access at the second level to sheltered gardens with wandering paths for Alzheimer's patients. Social space is expanded at this level and planned to minimize unit corridors.

The first-floor concourse provides community access to the rehabilitation center, education and conference facilities, the hospital's senior program, and the skilled care facility lobby and administrative offices.

Major design objectives and responses
Provide multiple levels of care.
This project adds skilled and Alzheimer's care and ambulatory rehab to acute, ambulatory, and assisted living.

Ensure patient privacy and dignity:
- private rooms with window bays
- small-group nursing clusters
- country kitchen replaces nurses' station
- a variety of social and activity spaces, including porches
- for Alzheimer's patients: generous social space, minimal corridors, direct access to outside, choices of social venues.

Establish staffing and service economies:
- clustered nursing groups
- direct link to hospital.

1 Southwest entrance
2 Second floor plan
3&4 Exterior view
5 Detail, southeast view
Photography: Alan Karchmer

ARCHITECT	Oudens + Knoop Architects, PC
SITE LOCATION	Urban
SITE AREA	1.5 acres/66,300 square feet
CAPACITY	94 skilled nursing care beds
TOTAL PROJECT COST	$19.6 M

2

3

4

5

NURSING

6

6 First floor concourse
7 Entry corridor
8 Therapeutic pool
Photography: Michael Dersin (6); Alan Karchmer (7,8)

7

8

Westminster Towers
Rock Hill, South Carolina

1

Architect's statement

Westminster Towers is a high-rise continuing care retirement community (CCRC) located on the campus of a church and school. While enjoying a close, ongoing association with the church and school, Westminster Towers used the need for a 66-bed nursing addition as an opportunity to begin a phased master planning process for the site. The new entry sequence was reinvented to focus on the CCRC campus, giving it more independence from the church and school.

The addition opens toward a residential area and mitigates the change in scale and material between the adjacent suburban houses and the existing residential tower.

Consistent with a resident-focused, operations-driven approach, the design creates comfortable, residentially scaled and textured bedrooms and living areas, while providing operationally efficient service areas for the staff.

Major design objectives and responses
Create semiprivate rooms that respect privacy.
L-shaped rooms have a shared vestibule and toilet; ceiling soffits differentiate space.

Provide homelike bedrooms.
Bedrooms have six-panel doors, a writing desk with display shelves, a residential over-bed light, and a non-institutional head wall/light.

Create pleasing, non-institutional corridors.
Short, offset corridors with quality carpet, sconces, and ceiling soffits contribute to the residential effect.

Avoid dead-end corridors.
Corridors terminate in comfortable seating alcoves.

Provide comfortable dining on the residents' schedule.
Decentralized dining is available with upscale features (lighting, fireplace, finishes, French doors) and bulk food service to pantries, allowing residents to eat when they are ready.

Limit bulk food carts in corridors.
There is direct access from the kitchen to the elevator and a short run to serving pantries.

Decentralize service, but don't isolate nurses.
Nurses' aide stations are on separate pods but are closely linked through the dining area.

ARCHITECT ▦ FreemanWhite Senior Living

SITE LOCATION ▦ Suburban

SITE AREA ▦ 7.978 acres/50,340 square feet

CAPACITY ▦ 66 skilled nursing care beds

TOTAL PROJECT COST ▦ $6.5 M

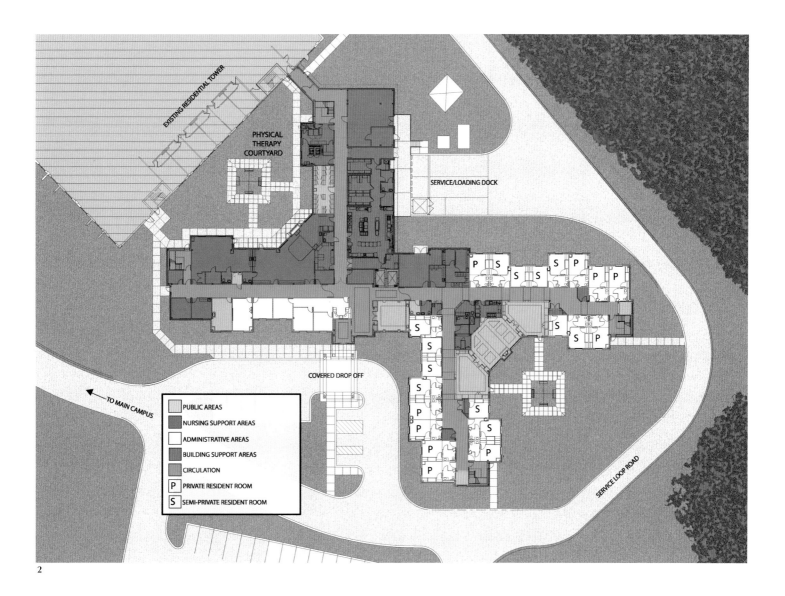

2

Create living spaces 'where the action is'
but out of the corridors.
Living rooms are easily accessible to
bedrooms and open to the corridor;
adjacent nurses' aide stations are screened,
and the nurses' station overlooks activity at
the front entry.

1 Front entry and porte-cochère
2 Site plan
3 Exterior of nursing addition
Photography: Tim Buchman

3

4

6

5

4 Private seating area
5 Nursing station and corridor
6 Patient room
7 Dining room
8 Public seating area
Photography: Tim Buchman

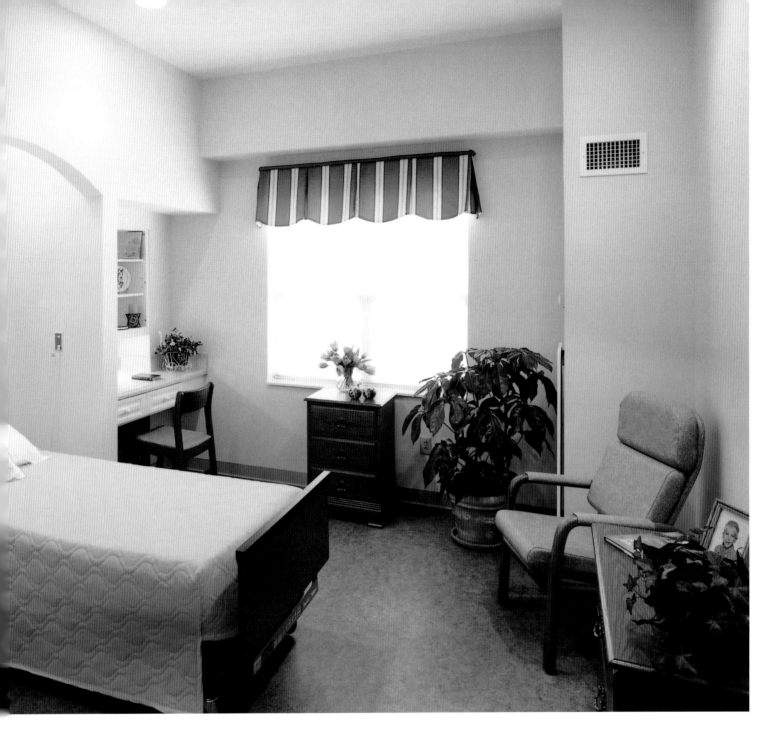

7

8

WILLIAM BREMAN JEWISH HOME
ATLANTA, GEORGIA

1

2

ARCHITECT'S STATEMENT

This 96-bed skilled nursing facility complements the range of care previously offered on the home's 10-acre campus, consisting of a 200-unit independent living facility and a 60-unit supportive housing facility.

Though the limitations of the site dictated a vertical solution, the resultant configuration of two 'neighborhoods' on each floor actually contributes to the quality of care. Providing a smaller number of residents per caregiver results in more personalized attention, higher staff retention, and less likelihood that residents will experience collective agitation.

The use of residential-like materials adds to a comfortable and homelike atmosphere rather than an institutional one. Various group activity spaces throughout the facility encourage community involvement and provide a balance between the public and private needs of the residents.

Major design objectives and responses

Increase use of outdoor spaces.
The facility is designed to tie in with existing buildings on the site, creating a courtyard between spaces; the use of glass in the garden rooms helps bring the outside in, inviting the residents to participate outdoors.

Balance between public and private needs.
The buildings create a separation and transition from the public arrival points, through community spaces, decentralized activity areas and neighborhood day rooms, to private bedrooms.

Work with limited site area; minimize impact on the adjacent neighborhood.
The limitations of the site dictated a vertical solution, with two neighborhoods on each floor. The zoning approval process reflects the collaboration of the facility, city officials, and neighbors in achieving their

respective goals. Precise siting to minimize the visual impact of the new facility, preserve mature trees, and create an extensive buffer addressed community concerns while enhancing the natural campus setting.

Expand programs that encourage community involvement.
Spaces such as an auditorium, outdoor courtyards, and public activity areas serve campus residents as well as seniors and disabled persons who live in the community. Programs offered in public spaces include adult day care, computer training, sheltered workshop, and myriad educational offerings.

Provide the most attentive patient care possible.
Living units are divided into 12-unit neighborhoods. Each includes

ARCHITECT ▓▓ STEVENS & WILKINSON OF GEORGIA, INC.

SITE LOCATION ▓▓ URBAN

SITE AREA ▓▓ 5.84 ACRES/254,535 SQUARE FEET

CAPACITY ▓▓ 60 ASSISTED LIVING UNITS,
72 SKILLED NURSING UNITS

TOTAL PROJECT COST ▓▓ $18.1 M

3

1 Exterior at night
2 Exterior view and courtyard
3 Exterior detail
Photography: Gary Knight & Associates

decentralized and intimate dining in an area that features a kitchen with a kitchen counter that also serves as a nurses' station (kitchen cabinets house the medical records). This configuration contributes to the quality of care in several ways:

• With 12 residents in each cluster, fewer residents compete for the caregivers' time. The owner attributes the unusually high staff retention rate to the concept of the neighborhood cluster. The staff experience less competition among the residents for their attention and a more defined and well-planned work environment.

• In smaller groups, residents are less likely to experience collective agitation.

• Residents dine in groups of 12, rather than in groups of up to 60 that are typical of large dining rooms, allowing

for more personalized and responsive attention from the staff.

• Residents can enjoy the benefits of a wander garden, even in this mid-rise facility.

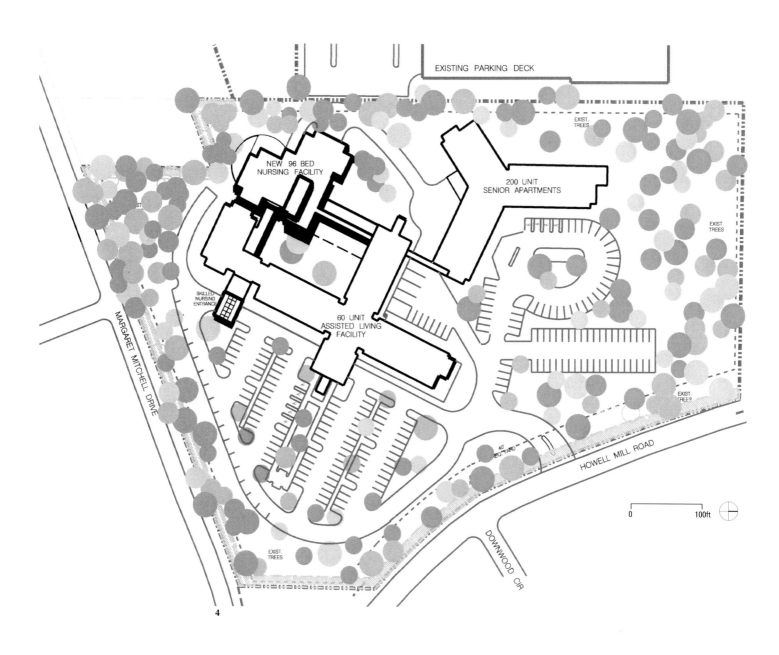

EXISTING PARKING DECK

NEW 96 BED
NURSING FACILITY

200 UNIT
SENIOR APARTMENTS

EXIST.
TREES

EXIST.
TREES

SKILLED
NURSING
ENTRANCE

60 UNIT
ASSISTED LIVING
FACILITY

EXIST.
TREES

MARGARET MITCHELL DRIVE

40'
BUFFARD

HOWELL MILL ROAD

DOWNWOOD CIR

EXIST.
TREES

0   100ft

4

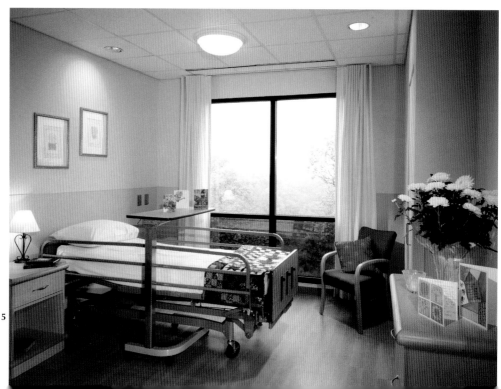

5

6

7

4 Campus site plan
5 Typical living unit
6 Day room with kitchen
7 Activity room
Photography: Gary Knight & Associates

Woon en Zorg H. Hart

1

Architect's statement

The original premises housed a general hospital of about 180 beds, run by a congregation of sisters. When the government decided to restructure the health care sector to reduce the number and increase the size of the hospitals, the institution decided to diversify its activities.

The campus now comprises 90 apartments (service flats), a children's day and possible night care (children's hotel) center, and a senior living and care community of 170 elderly.

The main constraint was of a physical nature: how to replace an old conglomerate of buildings with a completely new complex in the center of a town with almost no free space, while all the occupants continue to live on the spot.

The main goal was to create an open and diversified environment, with all modern

comfort and care facilities, in a stylish way, with the intention of making the inhabitants feel as if they were staying in a hotel.

Major design objectives and responses
Create a hotel-like, yet also home-like, feeling.
Special attention was given to the choice of materials and the design of the fixed and mobile furniture, light fittings, etc.

Create an 'open' environment in the social areas.
Several functions are mixed within the same area, enabling overflowing activities without formal boundaries, by using (if any) transparent screens—for example, in the entrance, reception, self-service, bar, dining, multipurpose, and day care areas.

Encourage residents' participation in normal daily activities, such as food preparation, and stimulate them by enabling interwoven functions.
The living and dining rooms form a continuum. The fixed kitchen furniture has integrated working, cooking, and dining surfaces, and the kitchen areas are situated next to the living rooms.

Create a diversified environment, seen in both the exterior and interior.
Each section of the building (three per floor) is treated differently in layout, use of materials, and color of finishes to create separate identities.

1 Entrance
2 Resident room
3 Therapy kitchen
4 Back of building
Photography: Studioboa

ARCHITECT ▓ VAN KERCKHOVE B.V.B.A.

SITE LOCATION ▓ URBAN

SITE AREA ▓ 10,618 SQUARE METERS

CAPACITY ▓ 50 SPECIAL CARE UNITS (DEMENTIA),
105 SKILLED NURSING CARE BEDS,
23 CHILDREN'S HOTEL BEDS

TOTAL PROJECT COST ▓ $14.2 M

2

3

4

RES

RESIDENCE

DENCE

THE SUMMIT AT FIRST HILL

1

2

ARCHITECT'S STATEMENT

Kline Galland Center, an organization established to address the needs of the Jewish elderly, decided to expand their services to seniors in an active downtown setting. While not adjacent to their existing urban skilled nursing campus, the organization acts as a virtual continuum of care. For their new high-rise, they wanted to:

- attract sophisticated, well-traveled, educated, upper-income seniors
- integrate seniors into an urban neighborhood where services such as stores, theaters, public transportation, and medical offices are located
- respect and celebrate the symbolic and ritualistic needs of the full spectrum of the Jewish population
- express the community's love of learning

- fit into the existing urban residential neighborhood
- encourage community and intergenerational activities
- create a long-term, enduring building.

Major design objectives and responses

Fit into the residential neighborhood.
To fit into the existing residential neighborhood, the three-story brick base is modulated to reflect the scale of a series of row houses. Some of the functions are expressed subtly on the exterior of the building. On the east corner is a synagogue, articulated as a hexagonal two-story element and topped with a metal-pitched roof.

The café is set back from a covered outdoor terrace that overlooks the activity of the street and the neighborhood park.

The base, spanning the entire block and supporting a thinner tower, incorporates all of the common areas and the higher care floors. The tower is set back from the base of the building to minimize its apparent mass from pedestrians.

Express the community's love of learning.
The library is designed as the heart and soul of the community. It is the first room seen directly past the lobby from the main entry. The centrally located, skylit location encourages residents and their families to gather, read, and play games.

Provide comprehensive orientation.
A series of elevator lobbies facing east, looks out over the roof garden and views of mountains beyond, and helps orient residents to their floor and to the seasons.

ARCHITECT	MITHUN
SITE LOCATION	URBAN
SITE AREA	0.66 ACRES/28,800 SQUARE FEET
CAPACITY	102 APARTMENTS, 10 ASSISTED LIVING UNITS, 13 DEMENTIA-SPECIFIC UNITS
TOTAL PROJECT COST	$25.26 M

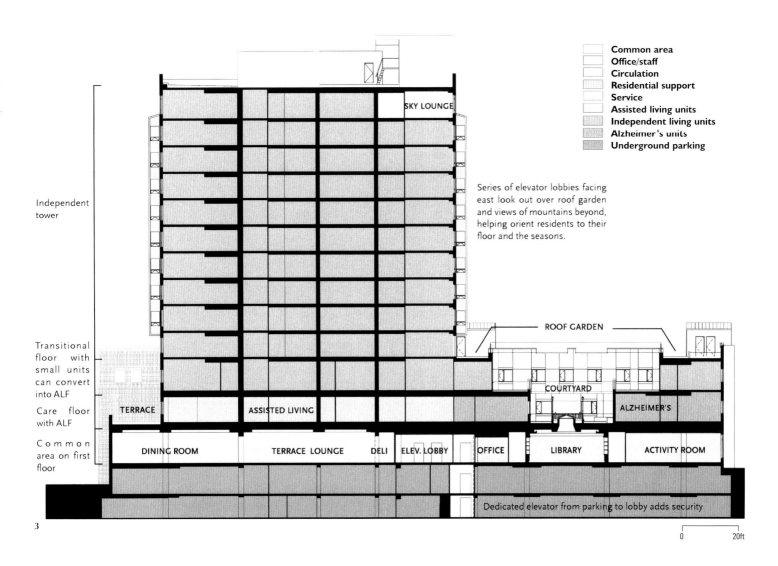

Legend:
- Common area
- Office/staff
- Circulation
- Residential support
- Service
- Assisted living units
- Independent living units
- Alzheimer's units
- Underground parking

SKY LOUNGE

Series of elevator lobbies facing east look out over roof garden and views of mountains beyond, helping orient residents to their floor and the seasons.

Independent tower

ROOF GARDEN

Transitional floor with small units can convert into ALF

COURTYARD

Care floor with ALF

TERRACE   ASSISTED LIVING   ALZHEIMER'S

Common area on first floor

DINING ROOM   TERRACE LOUNGE   DELI   ELEV. LOBBY   OFFICE   LIBRARY   ACTIVITY ROOM

Dedicated elevator from parking to lobby adds security

3

0   20ft

1 Fourth-floor terrace
2 Exterior
3 Section
4 Library
Photography: Lara Swimmer

4

THE ATRIUM AT CEDARS

PORTLAND, MAINE

1

ARCHITECT'S STATEMENT

The facility was designed with three residential wings extending from a three-story skylit atrium to create residential-scaled building masses. The atrium, formed by offsetting the north wing of the T-shaped plan, was oriented toward views of majestic pine trees to the north. It was strategically located at the core of the building to aid residents' orientation. Internal public circulation spaces and gallery areas are infused with daylight from the atrium and receive borrowed light through glazed interior partitions.

The building shape combined with the adjacent nursing center forms a landscaped courtyard. The facility will connect in the future to an assisted living facility, currently being designed, and the administration wing of the existing nursing center, providing direct enclosed access between facilities for staff and residents. Great care was taken to preserve the natural wooded site with its wetlands.

Major design objectives and responses

Minimize building mass of new structure.
A modified T-shaped building was created.

Provide connections to the existing nursing center and future assisted living facility.
A new service connector was installed at the rear for central receiving and food service collaboration and master plan at front for the new assisted living facility.

Provide natural light to enhance living experience and aid in orientation.
A skylit three-story atrium courtyard and interior glazed corridor partitions on the ground floor at commons areas were incorporated in the design.

Experience and aid in orientation.
Corridor partitions were installed on the ground floor at commons areas.

Maximize spaciousness of individual apartment units.
Balconies in all units, kitchens that accommodate a small table for snacking, and additional windows in kitchens and living rooms of corner apartments contribute to this goal.

Maximize number of corner apartments.
Eight corner apartments per typical floor were created.

1 Main entrance (north elevation)
2 Courtyard (south elevation)
3 Three-story atrium
4 Site plan
Photography: Bonjour Studio

ARCHITECT	TSOMIDES ASSOCIATES ARCHITECTS PLANNERS, TAAP
SITE LOCATION	SUBURBAN
SITE AREA	4.15 ACRES/180,774 SQUARE FEET
CAPACITY	61 APARTMENTS
TOTAL PROJECT COST	$12 M

2

3

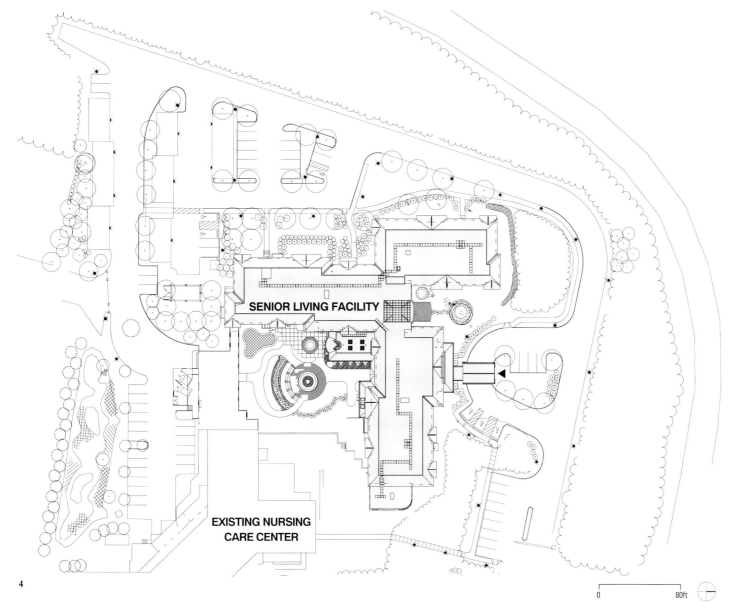

SENIOR LIVING FACILITY

EXISTING NURSING
CARE CENTER

4

0   80ft

FISCHER HOMES, SENIOR HOUSING VILLAGE

NEW ORLEANS, LOUISIANA

1

ARCHITECT'S STATEMENT

The Senior Housing Village at Fischer Homes is the first phase of the rebuilding of this major public housing development. Designed using the principles of new urbanism, 100 independent housing units and a community center are spread over a 9.5-acre site with traditional streets, sidewalks, private and public yards and gardens, and a 'great lawn' surrounded by shaded walkways and gazebos. This complex will replace the existing 11-story elderly housing complex, which will be demolished when construction is completed.

The individual one- and two-story apartment buildings have front porches, kitchen windows, and backyards surrounded by picket fences. The style of the buildings is similar to those in traditional New Orleans neighborhoods, with bungalow, shotgun, and classic Greek

Revival styling, and gives the residents the ambience of nearby historic Algiers Point and other classic historic districts of New Orleans.

The community center is designed to serve not only the residents but also the neighborhood, with visitor parking, dining and multi-use activities, and health-screening facilities available. The center is designed in a Greek Revival style, like most turn-of-the-century community and public buildings in New Orleans.

Major design objectives and responses
Create a sense of place and territoriality.
Apartments are organized in small groups and buildings along traditionally landscaped streets and paths. Shaded paths guide residents to activities and meals in the community center, the heart of the community. Individual living units have

front and back doors, private and public gardens, porches, and kitchen windows and are larger than similar low-income units.

Establish a neighborhood community.
The community is focused around the community center and 'great lawn,' with gardens and lawn areas near all of the units. Clusters of apartments share green space, gazebos, trellises, mailbox gathering spaces, and other pedestrian-friendly elements.

Respect New Orleans' traditions and ambience.
The individual buildings are styled with New Orleans' context in mind. Color schemes will reflect the pastels of older historic neighborhoods, and wrought-iron railings are used on the two-story buildings with traditional design and detailing.

ARCHITECT	BLITCH KNEVEL ARCHITECTS, NEW ORLEANS
SITE LOCATION	URBAN
SITE AREA	9.5 ACRES/415,000 SQUARE FEET
CAPACITY	100 APARTMENTS
TOTAL PROJECT COST	$11.52 M

2

3

1 Aerial view
2 Side elevation, building A and community center
3 Front elevation, community center
4 Interior, community center

Reduce the institutional scale and feeling of typical public housing.
Small buildings of three to 10 units break up the community into streetscapes similar to a traditional neighborhood. Residents can walk along sidewalks to visit neighbors and friends, sit on their front porch in a rocker, tend to their private garden behind a picket fence, or walk to the community center. Input from residents of the current high-rise facility was sought throughout the design phase.

Embrace and involve the local senior community.
The community center is located near the entrance to the complex and is convenient to public transportation. Activities scheduled in the center will be directed to seniors in surrounding neighborhoods as well as the onsite residents. Ample visitor parking is provided at the community center.

4

New Madonna Residence

San Francisco, California

1

Architect's statement

Located in the Tenderloin area of San Francisco, this senior center and residential facility will provide comfortable, supportive housing and services for 50 low-income senior women, enabling them to remain independent. The project brings an array of services to one location to serve both the residents and the community. Specifically, the center will house programs for poor and homeless seniors, including an adult day health center, a drop-in center, and offices for various social services such as medical doctors and psychiatrists. Each of these elements of the project has a front door facing a secure interior courtyard within sight of the gated main entrance.

The communal dining facilities are on the second level and open onto an interior balcony overlooking the landscaped courtyard. The design allows the residents

to stay in self-contained private living quarters above and away from the more public spaces located on the first floor.

The building was specifically oriented so that the interior courtyard would face south. Solar shading was built into the design. The units are not air-conditioned but have operating windows for natural ventilation.

Major design objectives and responses

Integrate a variety of program elements around a central courtyard and entry.
All elements are designed around a central ground-level court with 'eyes-on' approach and access to the street.

Provide a safe haven for indigent women and elderly members of the community.
The residential component is located on the upper floors.

Locate activities at street level to serve the surrounding community.
The entrance is off the secure central courtyard.

Provide security for residents on upper floors.
Upper floors can function independently from lower floors.

ARCHITECT	Hardison Komatsu Ivelich & Tucker
SITE LOCATION	Urban
SITE AREA	0.43 acres/18,931 square feet
CAPACITY	51 assisted living units
TOTAL PROJECT COST	$6.7 M

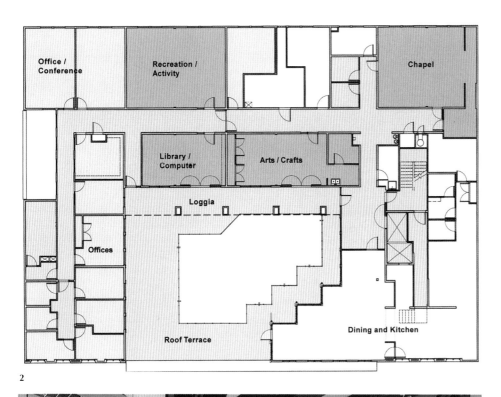

2

3

4

5

1 Exterior
2 Second floor plan
3 Activity room
4 Dining room
5 Courtyard
Photography: John Sutton

NORTHPOINTE

LENEXA, KANSAS

1

ARCHITECT'S STATEMENT

The site available was a narrow, steeply graded area bordering an undeveloped lakefront. The challenge was to design a building with the maximum number of one-, two-, and three-bedroom units having a view of the lake and nearby wooded area. Access to parking and to a fishing dock had to be provided without steps or steep slopes. A six-story complex hugging the curve of the lake took full advantage of the view and yielded 96 units on the 9-acre site. The design provides a balcony for each unit and lakeside terraces off the main lobby level and the two lower-level dining areas.

Providing opportunity for residents to socialize in a comfortable atmosphere was a prime concern. Each residential level has a community room and activity spaces designed for club meetings or workout areas. Safety features include a keyless

building entry system, electronic security, hazard alarm systems, and emergency pull stations. Future plans for further lakeside development include walking paths, picnic pavilions, and recreational areas.

As a complement to the overall retirement community, Northpointe provides an additional social destination for surrounding residents. All residents can take advantage of daily planned meals, private parties, and scheduled social events within walking distance (the original high-rise apartment building is on the opposite side of the 90-acre development, serving residents in close proximity to that building as well).

Due to a more active lifestyle, more residents are retaining second cars, recreational vehicles, and watercraft. Long- and short-term storage of such vehicles necessitates discrete parking areas and

some off-site locations. Restricted sites and local zoning regulations can pose problems.

Major design objectives and responses
Provide visual access and orientation to the existing lake.
The number of units and public areas facing the lake was maximized. All corridors and elevator lobbies have natural light sources—eliminating dark, disorienting, enclosed spaces.

Design accommodating slopes to the lake from the facility.
A walk-out lower level was provided for residents, with subtle use of ramped exterior pathways as necessary.

Create opportunities for social interaction.
Community rooms and dining areas were oriented to the lake. Laundry rooms are large and amply lighted.

ARCHITECT █ BURNS & McDONNELL

SITE LOCATION █ SUBURBAN

SITE AREA █ 9 ACRES/392,000 SQUARE FEET

CAPACITY █ 96 APARTMENTS

TOTAL PROJECT COST █ $18.2 M

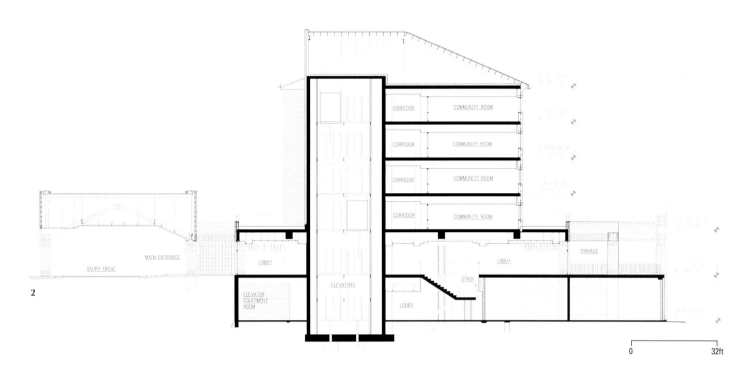

2

0 ——————— 32ft

3

Ensure flexibility for future development.
Unfinished space on the lower level facing
the lake offers prime space for
development into a variety of functions.

*Accommodate transition from single-family
to multifamily lifestyle.*
The environment is safe and secure. Units
have large rooms and ample storage that
reflect greater space needs of contemporary
seniors.

4

1 Main entry
2 Building section
3 Apartment unit dining
4 Aerial view to the north
Photography: courtesy Burns & McDonnell
Engineers-Architects

5

6

7

8

5 Main dining room
6 First level lobby
7 Lower level lobby
8 Apartment entry and kitchen
9 Typical bedroom
10 Lower level floor plan

Photography: courtesy Burns & McDonnell Engineers-Architects

9

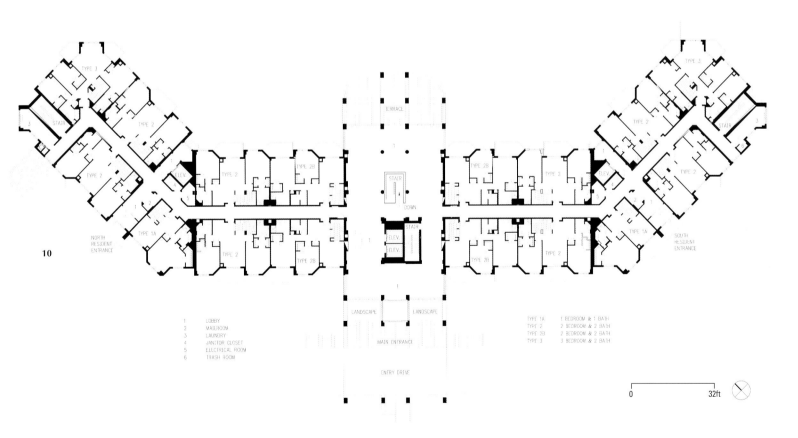

10

1	LOBBY
2	MAILROOM
3	LAUNDRY
4	JANITOR CLOSET
5	ELECTRICAL ROOM
6	TRASH ROOM

TYPE 1A	1 BEDROOM & 1 BATH
TYPE 2	2 BEDROOM & 2 BATH
TYPE 2B	2 BEDROOM & 2 BATH
TYPE 3	3 BEDROOM & 2 BATH

0   32ft

RESIDENCE

FAC

OTHER FACILITIES

JAMES F. ROSBOROUGH JR.
CULTURAL ARTS AND WELLNESS CENTER

GAITHERSBURG, MARYLAND

1

ARCHITECT'S STATEMENT

The building was designed to serve the growing wellness and cultural needs of a large 74-year-old continuing care retirement community (CCRC) located on a 130-acre rolling pastoral campus in the suburbs of Washington, D.C.

The owner desired a building that would demonstrate the commitment of the CCRC to wellness and cultural arts and become the heart of the campus for both residents and the greater community. A prominent, easily accessible location was selected at the intersection of two primary roads in the core of the campus, and the goal is realized both literally and symbolically.

The program is a complex mix that required integrating four major and numerous minor functions into one building on a small, constrained site. Major functions include a theater, indoor pool, multipurpose/ community room, and fitness center.

Other functions are as varied as a branch bank and a television studio. The design responds to each function's needs in area, height, mechanical demands, and interior finishes. During design, careful attention was paid to the logic and sequence of spaces and activities; special needs of older adults; adjacencies; and the use patterns of residents, visitors, and staff.

Major design objectives and responses

Demonstrate the CCRC's commitment to wellness and culture for residents and the community and become the heart of the campus for residents and the community.
The facility will be used by people other than CCRC residents so an easily accessible, prominent location was needed.

- The building is accessible on four sides by pedestrians.

- Locating the main entrance at the corner gives the center a strong public presence and high visibility.

- Parking lot/road design allows easy access for shuttle vans and visitors.

Integrate four major, and numerous ancillary functions into one building on a relatively small and constrained site within an existing CCRC campus.
Attention was paid during design to the logic and sequence of spaces and activities, interrelationships between functions, and resident flow through the building.

Express the center's internal functions on the building exterior yet minimize its height and mass to better blend in with its residential neighbors.

- The pool is located on the site's main loop road. Its height and large arched window clearly indicate that something special is occurring.

- The main entrance's curved canopy and two-story skylight lobby lead to the front door.

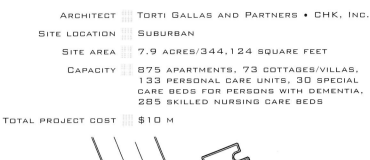

ARCHITECT   TORTI GALLAS AND PARTNERS • CHK, INC.

SITE LOCATION   SUBURBAN

SITE AREA   7.9 ACRES/344,124 SQUARE FEET

CAPACITY   875 APARTMENTS, 73 COTTAGES/VILLAS,
133 PERSONAL CARE UNITS, 30 SPECIAL
CARE BEDS FOR PERSONS WITH DEMENTIA,
285 SKILLED NURSING CARE BEDS

TOTAL PROJECT COST $10 M

1 Main entrance
2 Site plan
Photography: Rick M. Jolson, AIA

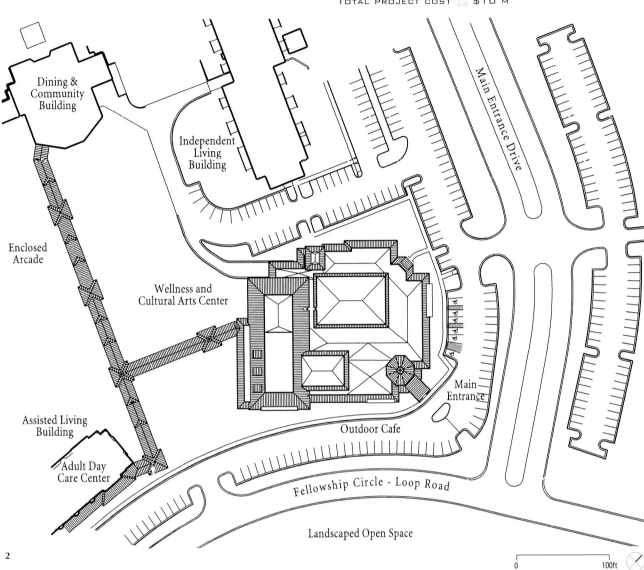

2

- The north side of the center, containing support areas, is built into the grade to minimize mass and height.

Tight integration of the building into the fabric of the existing campus with a design that is as non-institutional as possible.
- The center's site plan and orientation work within the guidelines of the CCRC's master plan.

- Internal spaces and functions are organized to break up the building's mass and visually diminish its height.

- Exterior materials and colors are similar to or match its neighbors.

Meet program requirements for a complex mix of uses, as well as special requirements for HVAC and interior finishes.
There was careful evaluation of adjacencies and logic of user flow through the building.

The major space (theater) is at the center with smaller spaces arranged in a ring outside the exercise corridor.

Provide a secure, barrier-free, and comfortable pedestrian link between the center and adjacent buildings while maintaining existing sight lines through open space.
An enclosed, conditioned arcade located to minimize walking distance from the assisted living facility links the center with the assisted living/adult day care facility (west) and an apartment/dining/community complex (north).

Include a first-class theater with 287 seats to accommodate plays, concerts, lectures, and performances and serve the needs of both CCRC residents and the public.
Located near the main entrance, the theater has a sloped floor and offset seating for

better sight lines, acoustical treatment on walls, assisted hearing devices, a tiered ceiling for acoustics and to conceal lighting, ramp and steps to stage, and space for wheelchairs.

Include an indoor pool to facilitate water-based exercise classes and recreational use. A Jacuzzi is also to be provided.
- The pool is 60 feet by 40 feet. To accommodate water exercise classes and free swimming, the depth varies from 3 feet to 5 feet across the pool's narrow dimension.

- To assist mobility into the pool, a hydraulic lift is provided, along with two deep-treaded sets of steps.

- Custom long-span exposed steel trusses allow for an open, well-lighted space.

- A lifeguard and an aquatics coordinator are on staff.

CARLETON-WILLARD VILLAGE WELLNESS CENTER

BEDFORD, MASSACHUSETTS

1

ARCHITECT'S STATEMENT

The master plan for this facility called for a centrally located, readily accessible, comprehensive wellness center for this existing continuing care retirement community (CCRC). The center includes a revitalized and expanded outpatient health clinic, a newly landscaped central courtyard, a new recreational lap pool/therapy pool, a physical therapy fitness center, a new meditation room with custom-designed stained-glass windows reflecting the flora of the landscaped courtyard, and a garden room. Newly designed and revitalized main circulation corridors wrap around the courtyard and access all areas of the wellness center.

The new natatorium, adjacent to the main administration farmhouse, is carefully detailed and intimately scaled, enclosed in walls sheathed with gray-stained wood shingles to convey a welcoming residential

quality. A large skylight located over the pool provides a cheerful, stimulating environment bathed in natural light.

Major design objectives and responses
Revitalize and expand the outpatient health clinic.
The existing clinic was completely gutted, redesigned, and expanded, recapturing portico space around the courtyard.

Provide new wellness center with recreational lap and therapy pool.
The new natatorium and physical therapy department were located next to the clinic and are accessible from outside.

Create a wellness center with a hospitality-type ambience.
The constrained site for the natatorium led to a large skylight over the pool and windows with integral horizontal blinds for privacy.

Provide natural light to enhance living experience and aid in orientation.
The pool is skylit and the glazed walls of corridors wrap around the landscaped courtyard.

Strategically locate a new meditation room accessible to all residents.
The room is located off the courtyard and is accessible to all residents from the main circulation corridor.

1 Natatorium exterior, northeast elevation
2 Exterior, wellness center
3 Exterior, detail
4 First floor plan
Photography: Hutchins Photography

ARCHITECT ‖ TSOMIDES ASSOCIATES ARCHITECTS
PLANNERS, TAAP

SITE LOCATION ‖ SUBURBAN

SITE AREA ‖ 0.53 ACRE/23,000 SQUARE FEET

CAPACITY ‖ 224 PEOPLE IN COMMON SOCIAL AREAS,
80 DAILY VISITS TO FITNESS/REHAB/
WELLNESS, 90 USERS FOR POOL AND
RELATED AREAS

TOTAL PROJECT COST ‖ $4.5 M

2

3

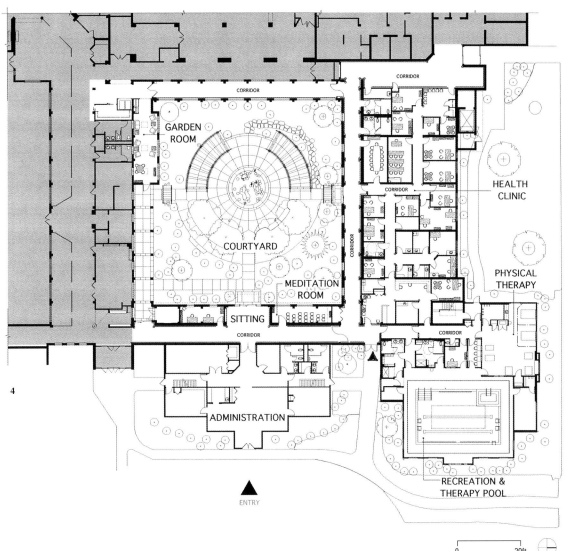

4

GARDEN ROOM

COURTYARD

MEDITATION ROOM

SITTING

CORRIDOR

CORRIDOR

HEALTH CLINIC

PHYSICAL THERAPY

CORRIDOR

ADMINISTRATION

RECREATION & THERAPY POOL

ENTRY

0   20ft

OTHER FACILITIES

5 Recreational/therapy pool natatorium, interior
6 Transverse section, wellness center
7 Corridor
Photography: Hutchins Photography

5

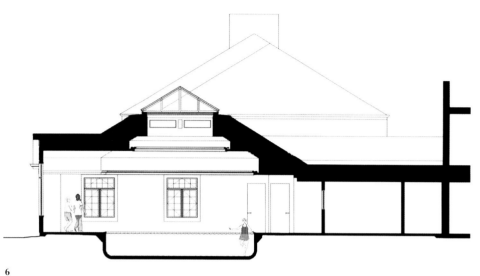

6

7

CAROL WOODS, CLUSTER HOME AND CHILD DAY CARE CENTER
CHAPEL HILL, NORTH CAROLINA

A Bedroom suite
B Living room
C Parlor
D Dining room
E Garden dining
F Kitchen
G Activities
H TV room
I Welcoming alcove
J Front porch
K Porte-cochère
L Pantry/staff room
M Staff office
N Bathing suite
O Utility room
P Laundry
Q Mechanical room

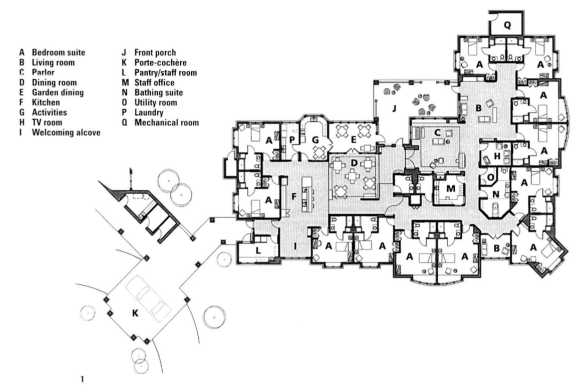

1

2

ARCHITECT'S STATEMENT

The two goals of this project were to design a state-of-the-future, intergenerational center that would meet the high standards of this innovative retirement community and to create a unique, resident-focused setting. The intergenerational center provides a supportive care setting where daily domestic routines are maintained. Residents can prepare food and enjoy the outdoors; the typical household arrangement of a home provides a familiar setting. The kitchen, dining, and living rooms are the centers of activity. Adjacent to the home is a child development center and playground, visible from the cluster home porches. The daily life of both programs encourages frequent interaction.

Major design objectives and responses
Create a familiar residential setting where residents can be physically active and find purpose in their daily life.

The two 12-suite cluster homes create an intimate architectural scale. The staff can tailor programming and daily activities around the needs and desires of small groups. A variety of small rooms provide places for residents who prefer individual rather than group activities.

The life of the home revolves around normal household activities and social life.
The design of the cluster home is similar to that of a single-family house. Public rooms face a front porch, and bedrooms are reached by short hallways. The kitchen is the center of most daily activities. The open plan of the living room, dining room, and kitchen makes it easy for residents to find these spaces and encourages them to join in activities.

Gardening is a major program element.
A large front porch, facing a pleasant courtyard, was an important feature of the design. All public spaces in the cluster home face the porch and courtyard, and residents can participate in gardening activities in the courtyard. The porch area is the residents' front door to the home, and visitors and staff enter from the discreetly located back door.

The home, garden, and child development center provide places for children and residents to spend time together every day.
The cluster home was carefully sited to provide a view of the children's play area. The play area and the cluster home flow together to encourage daily interaction.

Staff constantly engages residents in the life of the home.
Although there is an enclosed staff area for paperwork, private conferences, and a quiet retreat, staff members spend most of their time with the residents.

ARCHITECT	Dorsky Hodgson and Partners, Cleveland
SITE LOCATION	Suburban
SITE AREA	3.6 acres/43,560 square feet
CAPACITY	Two 12-suite cluster homes, 24 assisted living units, and one children's day care center
TOTAL PROJECT COST	$4.6 M

Courtyard

Playground

12 Suite Cluster Home

Child Development Center

Gazebo

Porte Cochere

12 Suite Cluster Home

Courtyard

3

Intergenerational Child Development Center
This center located in close proximity to the cluster home offers residents an opportunity to actively interact with children on a daily basis.

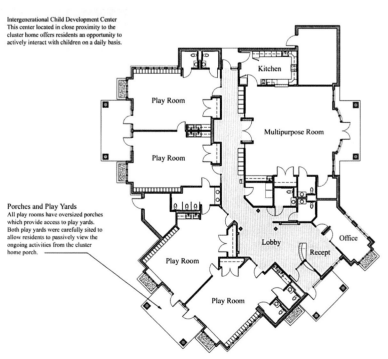

Kitchen

Play Room

Multipurpose Room

Play Room

Porches and Play Yards
All play rooms have oversized porches which provide access to play yards. Both play yards were carefully sited to allow residents to passively view the ongoing activities from the cluster home porch.

Play Room

Lobby

Office

Recept

Play Room

Play Room

4

5

1   Cluster home, floor plan
2&5   Elevations
3   Site plan
4   Child development center, floor plan

NORTH SHORE SENIOR CENTER, ARTHUR C. NIELSEN JR. CAMPUS

NORTHFIELD, ILLINOIS

1

ARCHITECT'S STATEMENT

Serving more than 29,000 members, the Arthur C. Nielsen Jr. Campus, North Shore Senior Center, in Northfield, Illinois, moved into a renovated, 40,000-square-foot former warehouse in September 2000. The vastness of this column-free space meant the architects could create smaller environments within a stunning open space.

Defined by street lamps and floor patterns, Main Street leads visitors to flexible areas ranging from high-volume gathering spaces to an intimate café and library. Main Street opens onto a light-filled winter garden, which provides sunshine and warmth year-round and hosts many of the center's activities.

The center provides critical social services; education, spiritual, and health/wellness programs; and opportunities for seniors to socialize with peers. The café, adjacent to the main entrance, offers a casual setting where older adults can receive assistance from social service agencies. The center promotes independence by providing a safe and accessible environment for area seniors.

Major design objectives and responses

Create a safe and accessible environment for seniors that brings aspects of the outdoors inside.
This was accomplished through the use of Main Street as the unifying design concept, using exterior materials throughout portions of the building and flooding the space with natural light.

Create an inviting environment in which to provide seniors with necessary services.
The center offers professional counselors to assist seniors. Services range from grief counseling to social service help to more casual support.

Create a place to learn and have fun.
The center houses an auditorium, fitness/wellness center, art studios, library, and music room, as well as ample gathering and social space. Diverse programs range from tai chi to language classes and day trips.

Create a variety of experiences.
Main Street links the center's varying volumes, which range from large-scale gathering places to private nooks.

ARCHITECT	OWP&P ARCHITECTS
SITE LOCATION	SUBURBAN
SITE AREA	123,700 SQUARE FEET
CAPACITY	40,000-SQUARE-FOOT WELLNESS CENTER
TOTAL PROJECT COST	$10 M

Social Areas / Main Street
Continuing Education
Fine Arts
Volunteer
Wellness/Fitness
Offices
Support

1 Main entry and gift shop
2 Floor plan
3 The café
4 The wintergarden
Photography: Steve Hall

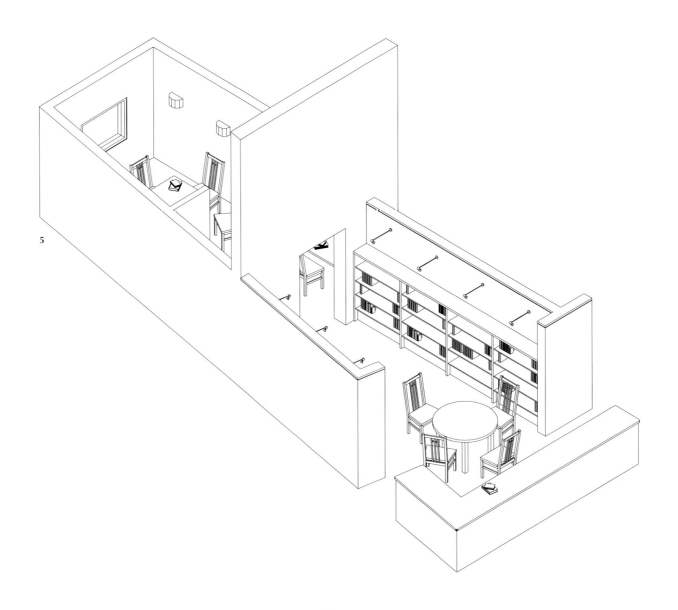

5

6

7

8

9

5 Library and classroom
6 Main Street
7 Main Street looking toward the wintergarden
8 Library
9 The café
Photography: Steve Hall

WELLNESS CENTER/TWIN TOWERS

COLLEGE HILL, OHIO

1

ARCHITECT'S STATEMENT

This Methodist facility for the elderly, renowned for its outstanding care, has served the community for over 100 years. The owner strove to implement a new vision, beyond providing services for the ailments and frailties of the facility's residents, by embracing a new trend in the health care community.

A new wellness center was planned with specialized facilities aimed at improving both the quality and quantity of life. This ambitious project totals just over 11,000 square feet and includes a 25-meter pool, a 1,400-square-foot weight room, a 1,200-square-foot aerobics and multipurpose room, an integrative therapy room, and locker rooms that rival those of private health clubs in the area.

As part of an existing facility, the new wellness center needed to be integrated into the existing building. Because of the size of the existing and new buildings, a firewall was needed to separate the structures. This presented a significant challenge since the wellness center was a one-story addition to a three-story building. Fire shutters could not be used because of the danger of injury when deployed.

Major design objectives
Provide a 25-meter pool that can be used for competitive swimming.

Provide easy access for the residents and outside members.

Provide state-of-the-art equipment and programs.

Provide space for integrative therapies.

1   Entrance
2   Lobby
3   Whirlpool
4   25-meter pool
5   Wellness Center
Photography: J. Miles Wolf Photography

ARCHITECT	PDT Architects
SITE LOCATION	Suburban
SITE AREA	113 ACRES
CAPACITY	11,000 SQUARE FEET FOR HEALTH CENTER
TOTAL PROJECT COST	$1.94 M

2

3

4

5

PROJECT DATA

ALDERSGATE

Status of project: Completed July 2002
Facility Administrator: Reverend Raymond O. Hall
Owner: The Methodist Home, Inc.
Architect: FreemanWhite Senior Living
Interior designer: FreemanWhite, Inc.
Structural engineer: King Guinn Associates
Mechanical engineer: FreemanWhite, Inc.
Electrical engineer: FreemanWhite, Inc.
Civil engineer: Site Solutions
Contractor: Bovis Lend Lease

PROJECT AREAS

	Units, Beds or Clients	New GSF	Renovated GSF	Total Gross Area GSF
Apartments (units, new)	60	86,190		86,190
Cottages/villas (units) (Phase I)	15	23,600		23,600
Special care for persons with dementia	45	34,000		34,000
Common social areas (people)		37,750	26,750	37,750
Fitness/rehab/wellness (daily visits) (included in commons)		12,000		12,000

RESIDENTIAL FACILITIES

Project Element		Cottages			Apartments	
	No.	Typical Size GSF	Size Range GSF	No.	Typical Size GSF	Size Range GSF
One-bedroom units				8	840	6,720
Two-bedroom units	6	1,465	8,750	46	1,250	57,500
Two-bedroom + den units	9	1,650	14,850	9	1,350	12,150
Total, all units	15		23,600	63		99,970
Residents' social areas (lounges, dining, and recreation spaces)						15,200
Medical/health/fitness and activities areas						12,000
Administrative, public, and ancillary support service areas						5,400
Service, maintenance, and mechanical areas						5,000
Total gross area						161,170

ASSISTED LIVING FACILITIES
Dementia-Specific Assisted Living Models

Project Element	New Construction		Renovations
	No. Units	Typical Size GSF	Typical Size GSF
Studio units	45	285	
Total, all units	45	12,825	
Residents' social areas (lounges, dining, and recreation spaces): 1,450/household			4,350
Therapies and activities spaces: Town Square			4,600
Administrative, public, and ancillary support services, clinic for CCRC			35,600
Service, maintenance, and mechanical areas			1,200
Total gross area			34,000

CONSTRUCTION COSTS
The following information is based on actual bids received September 2000.

Total Project Costs (est.)	$23.8 M

THE ATRIUM AT CEDARS

Status of project: Completed December 1999
Facility administrator: Kathryn Callnan, CEO
Owner: Jewish Home for Aged
Architect: Tsomides Associates Architects Planners, TAAP
Interior designer: Currier & Associates
Structural engineer: Foley & Buhl Engineering, Inc.
Mechanical engineer: Am-Tech Engineers, Inc.
Electrical engineer: Am-Tech Engineers, Inc.
Civil engineer: Land Use Consultants
Contractor: C.M. Cimino, Inc.

PROJECT AREAS

Project Element	Included in this Project		
	Units, Beds or Clients	New GSF	Total Gross Area GSF
Apartments (units)	61	70,000	70,000
Common social areas		10,000	10,000
Kitchen		2,000	2,000
Fitness/rehab/wellness		400	400
Pool(s) and related areas		2,000	2,000

RESIDENTIAL FACILITIES

Project Element	No.	Typical Size GSF
One-bedroom units	26	720
Two-bedroom units	30	1,000
Two-bedroom + den units	5	1,170
Total, all units	61	70,000
Residents' social areas (lounges, dining, and recreation spaces)		10,000
Medical/health/fitness and activities areas		5,000
Administrative, public, and ancillary support services		5,000
Service, maintenance, and mechanical areas		15,000
Total gross area		105,000

CONSTRUCTION COSTS
The following information is based on actual costs.
Final construction cost as of December 1999.

Building Costs

New construction	$9.8 M
Medical equipment costs	$600,000
Total building costs	$10.4 M

Site Costs

New	$800,000
Renovation	$200,000
Total site costs	$1M
Total Project Costs	$12 M

BRISTOL GLEN

Status of project: Completed March 2001
Facility Administrator: Scott Norton
Owner: United Methodist Homes of New Jersey
Architect: Donnelly Wagner Nelson Rebilas Architects, LLC
Interior designer: Merlino Design Partnership, Inc.
Structural engineer: Thomas R. Kulp, P.E.
Mechanical engineer: Kelter & Gilligo, P.C.
Electrical engineer: Kelter & Gilligo, P.C.
Civil engineer: Suburban Consulting Engineers, Inc.
Contractor: The Henderson Corporation

PROJECT AREAS

Project Element	Included in this Project	
	Units, Beds or Client	New GSF
Apartments (units)	88	77,347
Senior living/assisted living/ personal care (units)	40	23,156
Skilled nursing care (beds)	60	15,819
Common social areas (people)		14,350
Kitchen (daily meals served)		3,598
Retail space (shops, restaurants, etc.)		1,098
Fitness/rehab/wellness (daily visits)		2,886

RESIDENTIAL FACILITIES

Project Element	Apartments		
	No.	Typical Size GSF	Size Range GSF
One-bedroom units	64	660	647–844
Two-bedroom units	24	1,134	1,120–1,489
Total, all units	88	77,347	
Residents' social areas (lounges, dining, and recreation spaces)		4,170	
Administrative, public, and ancillary support areas		1,435	
Service, maintenance, and mechanical areas		2,851	
Total gross area		99,267	

ASSISTED LIVING FACILITIES
General Social/Residential Assisted Living Models

Project Element	New Construction		
	No. Units	Typical Size GSF	Typical Size GSF
One-bedroom units	36	580	
Two-bedroom units	4	764	
Total, all units	40	23,156	
Residents' social areas (lounges, dining, and recreation spaces)			4,936
Medical, health care, therapies and activities spaces			4,394
Administrative, public, and ancillary support services			9,948
Service, maintenance, and mechanical areas			1,592
Total gross area			57,071

NURSING FACILITIES
Skilled Nursing Facilities

Project Element	New Construction		Renovations
	No. Beds	Typical Room Size GSF	Typical Room Size GSF
Residents in one-bed/single rooms	12	326	
Residents in two-bed/double rooms	48	502	
Total no. of rooms/residents: Rooms: 36 Beds:	60	15,819	
Social areas (lounges, dining, and recreation spaces)			3,021
Medical, health care, therapies, and activities spaces			785
Administrative, public, and ancillary support services			6,258
Service, maintenance, and mechanical areas			6,052
Total gross area			41,609

CONSTRUCTION COSTS
The following information is based on actual costs.
Financing sources: non-taxable bond offering

Building Costs

New construction	$24.35 M
Total building costs	$24.64 M

Site costs

Total site costs	$2.05 M

Total Project Costs | $26.7 M |

BUCKINGHAM'S CHOICE

Status of project: Completed March 2000
Facility administrator: Charles Clark, Executive Director
Owner: Episcopal Ministries to the Aging, Inc.
Architect: Perkins Eastman Architects
Interior designer: Perkins Eastman Architects
Structural engineer: Columbia Engineers
Mechanical engineer: Spears Votta Associates, Inc.
Electrical engineer: Spears Votta Associates, Inc.
Civil engineer: Harris Smariga Associates, Inc.
Contractor: Morgan-Keller, Inc.

PROJECT AREAS

Project Element	Included in this Project				
	Units, Beds or Clients	New GSF	Renovated GSF	Total Gross Area GSF	Total on Site or Served by Project
Apartments (units)	80	92,200		92,200	92,200
Cottages/villas (units)	130	196,300		196,300	196,300
Senior living/assisted living/ personal care (units)	45	34		35,210	35,210
Skilled nursing care (beds)	42	23,910		23,910	23,910
Common social areas (people)	360	19,985		19,985	19,985
Kitchen (daily meals served)	492	6,195		6,195	6,195
Retail space (shops, restaurants, etc.)	3	1,680		1,680	1,680
Fitness/rehab/wellness (daily visits)		1,680		1,680	1,680
Pool(s) and related areas (users)	38	3,920		3,920	3,920
Other		11,655		11,655	11,655

RESIDENTIAL FACILITIES

Project Element	Cottages			Apartments		
	No.	Typical Size GSF	Size Range GSF	No.	Typical Size GSF	Size Range GSF
Studio units	0			0		
One-bedroom units	76	1,050	875–1,070	70	850	750–950
Two-bedroom units	26	1,170	1,100–1,200	10	1,200	1,150–1,250
Two-bedroom + den units	8	1,800	1,800	0		
Three-bedroom and larger units	20	3,350	3,350	0		
Total, all units	130		196,300			92,200
Residents' social areas (lounges, dining, and recreations spaces)						17,535
Medical/health/fitness and activities areas						9,240
Administrative, public, and ancillary support service areas						3,465
Service, maintenance, and mechanical areas						17,850
Total gross area						336,590

ASSISTED LIVING FACILITIES
General Social/Residential Assisted Living Models

Project Element	New Construction		Renovations	
	No. Units	Typical Size GSF	No. Units	Typical Size GSF
Studio units	0			
One-bedroom units	45	435		
Two-bedroom units	0			
Total, all units	45	29,365		
Residents' social areas (lounges, dining, and recreation spaces)				2,715
Medical, health care, therapy, and activity spaces				1,690
Administrative, public, and ancillary support services				1,000
Service, maintenance, and mechanical areas				440
Total gross area				35,210

continued

NURSING FACILITIES
Skilled Nursing Facilities

Project Element	New Construction		Renovations	
	No. Beds	Typical Room Size GSF	No. Beds	Typical Room Size GSF
Residents in one-bed/single rooms	42	230		
Total no. of rooms/residents:				
Rooms: 42 Beds:	42	15,460		
Social areas				
(lounges, dining, and recreation spaces)				3,280
Medical, health care, therapy, and activity spaces				2,950
Administrative, public, and ancillary support services				1,080
Service, maintenance, and mechanical areas				1,140
Total gross area				23,910

CONSTRUCTION COSTS
The following information is based on actual costs.
Final construction cost as of March 2000.
Financing sources: non-taxable bond offering

Building Costs
Total building costs	$32.7 M

Site Costs
Total site costs	$3.4 M

Total Project Costs
	$36.1 M

BURLESON ST. JOSEPH'S MANOR

Status of project: Completed May 1999
Facility administrator: Sister Alice Warrick
Owner: St. Joseph Health System
Architect: Watkins Hamilton Ross Architects
Interior designer: Watkins Hamilton Ross Architects
Structural engineer: Cagley, Conti & Jumper
Mechanical engineer: Garner Engineering & Consulting
Electrical engineer: Garner Engineering & Consulting
Civil engineer: Walter P. Moore & Associates
Contractor: Vaughn Consulting Co.

PROJECT AREAS

	Units, Beds or Clients	New GSF
Special care for persons with dementia	16	271
Skilled nursing care (beds)	80	284
Common social areas (people)	5	4,829
Kitchen (daily meals served)	240	2,688
Chapel		466

NURSING FACILITIES
Nursing Homes and Intermediate Care Facilities

Project Element	New Construction		Renovations	
	No. Beds	Typical Room Size GSF	No. Beds	Typical Room Size GSF
Residents in one-bed/single rooms	96	281		
Social Areas				
(lounges, dining, and recreation spaces)				5,360
Medical, health care, therapies, and activities spaces				1,473
Administrative, public, and ancillary support services				12,736
Service, maintenance, and mechanical areas				3,354
Total gross area				50,000

CONSTRUCTION COSTS

Building Costs
New construction	$3.7 M
Medical equipment	$495,000
Total building costs	$4.2 M

Site Costs
Total site costs	$420,700

Total Project Costs
	$4.6 M

CARLETON-WILLARD VILLAGE WELLNESS CENTER

Status of project: Completed March 2000
Facility administrator: Barbara A. Doyle, CEO
Owner: Carleton-Willard Village, Inc.
Architect: Tsomides Associates Architects Planners, TAAP
Interior designer: Woodman Design Group
Structural engineer: Foley & Buhl Engineering, Inc.
Mechanical engineer: Zade Company, Inc.
Electrical engineer: Zade Company, Inc.
Civil engineer: Commonwealth Engineering, Inc.
Contractor: Linbeck/Kennedy & Rossi, Inc.
Stained-glass artist: Lyn Hovey Studio

PROJECT AREA

Project Element	Included in this Project			
	New GSF	Renovated GSF	Total Gross Area GSF	Total on Site or Served by Project
Apartments (units)				67
Cottages/villas (units)				88
Senior living/assisted living/personal care (units)				69
Special care for persons with dementia				30
Skilled nursing care (beds)				70
Common social areas (people)	1,840	1,830	3,670	224
Fitness/rehab/wellness (daily visits)	1,380	5,380	6,760	80
Pool(s) and related areas (users)	3,090		3,090	90

OTHER FACILTIES

Project Element	New Construction		Renovations	
	No.	Size GSF	No.	Size GSF
Recreational/therapy pool		3,090		
Physical therapy department		1,380		
Outpatient health clinic				5,380
Meditation room		240		
Garden room, computer room, corridors		1,600		1,830
		6,310		7,210
Service, maintenance, and mechanical areas				410
Total gross area				13,930

CONSTRUCTION COSTS

The following information is based on actual costs.
Financing sources: taxable bond offering, tax-exempt bonds

Building Costs

New construction	$1.90 M
Renovations	$1.10 M
Medical equipment costs	$300,000
Total building costs	$3.3 M

Site Costs

New	$300,000
Renovation	$900,000
Total site costs	$1.2 M

Total Project Costs	$4.5 M

CAROL WOODS, CLUSTER HOME AND CHILD DAY CARE CENTER

Status of project: Completed May 2002
Facility administrator: Patricia Sprigg, Executive Director
Owner: Carol Woods Retirement Community
Architect: Dorsky Hodgson and Partners
Associate architect: DTW Architects and Planners, Ltd
Interior designer: Dorsky Hodgson and Partners
Landscape architect: Beckwith Chapman
Structural engineer: Neville Engineers
Mechanical engineer: Knott Benson Spring Engineers
Electrical engineer: Knott Benson Spring Engineers
Civil engineer: Coulter Jewell Thames Associates
Acoustical consultant: Dewey T. Lawson, PhD
Contractor: Clancey & Theys Construction Company

PROJECT AREAS

	Units, Beds or Clients	New GSF	Total Gross Area GSF
Special care for persons with dementia—assisted living	24	19,300	19,300
Children's day care (clients)	64	6,900	6,900

DEMENTIA FACILITIES
Dementia-Specific Assisted Living Models

	New Construction	
	No. Units	Typical Size GSF
Studio units	24	370
Total, all units	24	9,900
Residents' social areas (lounges, dining, and recreation spaces)		5,124
Medical, health care, therapies, and activities spaces		2,838
Administrative, public, and ancillary support services		860
Service, maintenance, and mechanical areas		578
Total gross area		19,300

OTHER FACILITIES
Child Day Care

	New Construction	
	No. Units	Typical Size GSF
Playrooms	4	1,108
Social areas (lounges, dining, and recreation spaces)		1,200
Administrative, public, and ancillary support services		688
Service, maintenance, and mechanical areas		582
Total gross area		6,900

CONSTRUCTION COSTS

The following information is based on estimates.

Building Costs

New construction	$2.6 M
Total building costs	$1 M

Site Costs

New	$1 M

Total Project Costs	$4.6 M

THE CEDARS OF CHAPEL HILL

Status of project: Under construction, estimated completion date August 2004
Facility administrator: Robert Woodruff
Owner: Meadowmont Retirement Community, LLC
Architect: Calloway Johnson Moore & West, P.A.
Interior designer: One Design Center
Structural engineer: Calloway Johnson Moore & West, PA
Mechanical engineer: David Sims & Associates
Electrical engineer: Haas & Kennedy
Civil engineer: The John R. McAdams Company
Contractor: Bovis Lend Lease

PROJECT AREAS

	Units, Beds or Clients	Total Gross Area
Apartments (units)	251 units	507,711
Cottages/villas (units)	49 units	108,929
Special care for persons with dementia	36 beds	24,118
Skilled nursing care (beds)	52 beds	30,606
Common social areas (people)		43,566
Kitchen (daily meals served)		4,879
Retail space (shops/restaurants, etc.)		1,273
Fitness/rehab/wellness (daily visits)		1,499
Pool(s) and related areas (users)		3,246

RESIDENTIAL FACILITIES

Project Element	Cottages			Apartments		
	No.	Typical Size GSF	Size Range GSF	No.	Typical Size GSF	Size Range GSF
One-bedroom units				12	1,094	981–1,094
Two-bedroom units				89	1,585	1,158–1,961
Two-bedroom + den units	49	2,159	1,522–2,783	150	1,813	1,395–2,442
Total, all units	49	108,929		251	507,711	
Residents' social areas (lounges, dining, and recreation spaces)					19,844	
Service, maintenance, and mechanical areas					27,740	
Total gross area					616,640	

ASSISTED LIVING FACILITIES
Dementia-Specific Assisted Living Models

Project Element	New Construction	
	No. Units	Typical Size GSF
One-bedroom units	12	269
Two-bedroom units	12	281
Total, all units	24	6,600
Residents' social areas (lounges, dining, and recreation spaces)		4,875
Medical, health care, therapies, and activities spaces		2,820
Administrative, public, and ancillary support services		1,795
Service, maintenance, and mechanical areas		784
Total gross area		24,118

NURSING FACILITIES
Skilled Nursing Facilities

Project Element	New Construction	
	No. Beds	Typical Room Size GSF
Residents in one-bed/single rooms	20	269
Residents in two-bed/double rooms	32	354
Residents share multi-bed rooms/wards		
Total no. of rooms/residents		
Rooms: 36 Beds:	52	16,708
Social areas (lounges, dining, and recreation spaces)		5,931
Medical, health care, therapies, and activities spaces		644
Administrative, public, and ancillary support services		1,112
Service, maintenance, and mechanical areas		690
Total gross area		32,977

OTHER FACILITIES
Project Element

Clubhouse	Size GSF
Main hall 1 & 2, living room, balcony library, and library/conference	3,238
Card room, billiards, art studio, community room, and main lobby	4,773
Third-floor lobby, computer room, classroom	1,183
Bar, informal dining, formal dining, and private dining	4,910
Spa, manicure/pedicure, treatment 1 and 2, bank, and beauty/barber	1,024
Pool and exercise	3,734

CONSTRUCTION COSTS
The following information is based on contractor's estimate dated December 2000.

Building Costs

New construction	$82.85 M
Total building costs	$82.85 M

Site Costs

New costs	$8.02 M

Total Project Costs	$91.8 M

CHASE POINT

Status of project: Completed November 1999
Facility Administrator: Miles Health Care
Owner: Miles Health Care
Architect: JSA Inc.
Interior designer: JSA Inc.
Structural engineer: JSA Inc.
Mechanical engineer: Panitsas Associates, Inc.
Electrical engineer: Dilorio, Inc.
Civil engineer: Underwood Engineers Inc.
Contractor: Langford & Low Inc.

PROJECT AREAS

Project element	Units, Beds or Clients	New GSF	Total Gross Area GSF
Senior living/assisted living/ personal care (units)	24	10,392	10,392
Special care for persons with dementia	18	5,040	5,040
Common social areas (people)		8,122	8,122
Kitchen (daily meals served)	141		
Elder day care (clients)	18	2,000	2,000

ASSISTED LIVING FACILITIES

General Social/Residential Assisted Living Models

Project Element	New Construction		Renovations
	No. Units	Typical Size GSF	Typical Size GSF
Studio units	7	350–380	
Alzheimer's studio units	18	225	
One bedroom units	17	480–500	
Total, all units	42	15,432	
Residents' social areas (lounges, dining, and recreation spaces)			8,122
Service, maintenance, and mechanical areas			4,868
Total gross area			38,000

CONSTRUCTION COSTS

The following information is based on actual costs.

Building Costs
Total building costs	$2.5 M

Site Costs
Total site costs	$500,000

Total Project Costs — $3.5 M

COVENANT MANOR COURTYARD, ADDITION

Status of project: Completed July 2001
Facility Administrator: Gary Gardeen
Owner: Covenant Retirement Communities, Inc.
Architect: Horty Elving & Associates, Inc.
Interior designer: Horty Elving & Associates, Inc.
Structural engineer: Structural Design Associates
Mechanical engineer: Horty Elving & Associates, Inc.
Electrical engineer: Horty Elving & Associates, Inc.
Civil engineer: Paramount Engineering
Contractor: Kraus Anderson Construction Company, St. Paul Division

PROJECT AREAS

	Units, Beds or Clients	New GSF	Renovated GSF
Apartments (units)	125	222,166	10,000

RESIDENTIAL FACILITIES

Project Element	Apartments		
	No.	Typical Size GSF	Size Range GSF
Studio units	2	495	450–540
One-bedroom units	18	720	620–960
Two-bedroom units	13	1,080	1,030–1,250
Two-bedroom + den units	4	1,280	1,270–1,450
Total, all units	125		123,612
Residents' social areas (lounges, dining, and recreation spaces)			47,359
Medical/health/fitness and activities areas			5,943
Administrative, public, and ancillary support service areas			4,702
Service, maintenance, and mechanical areas			3,056
Total gross area			222,166

CONSTRUCTION COSTS

The following information is based on contractor's estimate dated March 2000.

Building Costs
New construction	$17.32 M
Renovations	$1 M
Total building costs	$18.32 M

Site costs
New	$285,000

Total Project Costs — $21 M

CYPRESS COVE AT HEALTHPARK FLORIDA

Status of project: Completed September 2000
Facility administrator: Douglas A. Dodson
Owner: HealthPark Florida, Inc.
Architect: Reese, Lower, Patrick & Scott, Ltd
Interior designer: Stanzione Associates
Structural engineer: A.W. Lookup Corporation
Mechanical engineer: ABS Consultants, Inc.
Electrical engineer: Reese Engineering, Inc.
Civil engineer: Johnson Engineering, Inc.
Contractor: The Weitz Company, Inc.

PROJECT AREAS

Project Element	No.	Cottages Typical Size GSF	Size Range GSF	No.	Apartments Typical Size GSF	Size Range GSF
Studio units				6	679.5	679.5
One-bedroom units				126	782.1	716.2–920
Two-bedroom units	12	1,525		64	1,152.7	1,152.7–1,338.6
Two-bedroom + den units	18	1,561	1,561–1,770	32	1,360.7	1,360.7–1,530.4
Total, all units	30	55,444		228	229,174	
Residents' social areas (lounges, dining, and recreation spaces)		12,461				
Medical/health/fitness and activities areas						
Administrative, public, and ancillary support service areas		998				
Service, maintenance, and mechanical areas		15,455				
Total gross area		380,319				

ASSISTED LIVING FACILITIES
General Social/Residential Assisted Living Models

Project Element	New Construction No. Units	New Construction Typical Size GSF	Renovations No. Units	Renovations Typical Size GSF
One-bedroom units	42	495		
Total, all units	42	21,780		
Residents' social areas (lounges, dining, and recreation spaces)				4,668
Medical, health care, therapy, and activity spaces				1,933
Administrative, public, and ancillary support services				16,505
Service, maintenance, and mechanical areas				1,200
Total gross area				46,086

NURSING FACILITIES
Skilled Nursing Facilities

Project Element	New Construction No. Beds	New Construction Typical Room Size GSF	Renovations No. Beds	Renovations Typical Room Size GSF
Residents in one-bed/single rooms	64	277		
Total no. of rooms/residents: Rooms: 64 Beds:	64	17,728		
Social areas (lounges, dining, and recreation spaces)				4,740
Medical, health care, therapy, and activity spaces				4,215
Administrative, public, and ancillary support services				980
Service, maintenance, and mechanical areas				2,304
Total gross area				48,283

OTHER FACILITIES

Project Element	New Construction No.	New Construction Size GSF	Renovations No.	Renovations Size GSF
Pool/spa	1	3,706		
Wellness Center	1	1,386		
Total	2	5,092		
Social areas (lounges, dining, and recreation spaces)				21,582
Administrative, public, and ancillary support services				2,117
Service, maintenance, and mechanical areas				12,149
Total gross area				56,610

CONSTRUCTION COSTS

The following information is based on actual costs.
Final construction cost as of September 2000
Financing sources: non-taxable bond offering

Building Costs

Total building costs	$53.19 M

Site Costs

Total site costs	$1.23 M

Total Project Costs | $54.42 M |

FAIRMONT CROSSING

Status of project: Completed
Facility administrator: Centra Health
Owner: Centra Health
Architect: Hughes Associates Architects
Interior designer: Donna Miles & Associates
Structural engineer: Day & Kinder Consulting Engineers, PLLC
Mechanical engineer: HCYu and Associates
Electrical engineer: HCYu and Associates
Civil engineer: Hurt & Proffitt
Contractor: Coleman-Adams Construction, Inc.

PROJECT AREAS

	Units, Beds or Clients	New GSF
Skilled nursing care (beds)	120	37,008
Common social areas (people)	280	5,595
Kitchen (daily meals served)	400 +/-	1,440

Nursing Homes and Intermediate Care Facilities:

Project Element	New Construction		Renovations	
	No. Beds	Typical Room Size GSF	No. Beds	Typical Room Size GSF
Residents in one-bed/single rooms	8	230		
Residents in two-bed/double rooms	112	314		
Total no. of rooms/residents:				
Rooms: 64 Beds:	120	37,008		37,008
Social areas (lounges, dining, and recreation spaces)				5,595
Medical, health care, therapies, and activities spaces				6,190
Administrative, public, and ancillary support services				3,065
Service, maintenance, and mechanical areas (including vertical circulation)				8,097
Total gross area				59,955

CONSTRUCTION COSTS
The following information is based on actual bids received July 2001.

Building Costs
New construction $5.12 M

Site Costs
New $475,582

Total Project Costs $6.67 M

FISCHER HOMES, SENIOR HOUSING VILLAGE

Owner: Housing Authority of New Orleans
Architect: Blitch Knevel Architects, Inc.
Interior designer: Blitch Knevel Architects
Landscape architect: Blitch Knevel Architects
Structural engineer: Morphy Makofsky, Inc.
Mechanical engineer: M-K Engineering, Inc.
Electrical engineer: Jolly Consults, Inc.
Civil engineer: Morphy Makofsky, Inc.
Contractor: Harvey Honore Construction Co, Inc.

PROJECT AREAS

	Units, Beds or Clients	Total Gross Area GSF
Apartments (units)	100	79,110
Common social areas (people)	120	
Community center		9,013

RESIDENTIAL FACILITIES

	Number	Typical Size GSF
One-bedroom units	91	572
Two-bedroom units	9	741
Total, all units	100	58,721
Residents' social areas (lounges, dining, and recreation spaces)		9,013
Administrative, public, and ancillary support service areas		2,300
Service, maintenance, and mechanical areas		1,850
Total gross area		88,123

CONSTRUCTION COSTS
The following information is based on bids.

Building Costs
New construction $9.74 M
Total building costs $9.74 M

Site Costs
Total site costs $1.78 M

Total Project Costs $11.52 M

THE FOREST AT DUKE, ADDITION

Status of project: Under construction
Facility administrator: Leslie Jarema
Owner: The Forest at Duke, Inc.
Architect: Calloway Johnson Moore & West, P.A.
Structural engineer: Calloway Johnson Moore & West, P.A.
Mechanical engineer: David Sims & Associates
Electrical engineer: Calloway Johnson Moore & West, P.A.
Civil engineer: The John R. McAdams Company
Contractor: Weaver Cooke Construction

PROJECT AREAS

	Units, Beds or Clients	New GSF	Renovated GSF	Total Gross Area GSF
Senior living/assisted living/ personal care (units)	15	22,657		22,657
Special care for persons with dementia	18	16,752		16,752
Skilled nursing care (beds)				
Common social areas (91 people served by this project; total CCRC independent living population is 309)	91	3,232	1,560	4,792
Kitchen	273	1,200		1,200
Retail space (shops, restaurants, etc.)	91	274		
Clinic/administrative (average visits per day)		9,297		

ASSISTED LIVING FACILITIES
General Social/Residential Assisted Living Models

	New Construction		Renovations	
	No. Units	Typical Size GSF	No. Units	Typical Size GSF
One-bedroom units	15	641		
Total, all units	15	9,615		
Residents' social areas (lounges, dining, and recreation spaces)		975		
Medical, health care, therapy, and activity spaces		1,874		
Administrative, public, and ancillary support services		184		
Service, maintenance, and mechanical areas		1,809		
Total gross area		22,657		

CONSTRUCTION COSTS
The following is based on contractor's estimates.

Building Costs
New construction	$9.66 M
Medical equipment costs	$25,000
Total building costs	$9.68 M

Site Costs
New	$655,000
Total site costs	$655,000
Total Project Costs	**$13.2 M**

FOULKEWAYS AT GWYNEDD, SKILLED CARE FACILITY

Status of project: Completed August 2001
Facility administrator: Douglas A. Tweddale
Owner: Foulkeways at Gwynedd
Architect: Reese, Lower, Patrick & Scott, Ltd.
Interior designer: Reese, Lower, Patrick & Scott, Ltd.
Structural engineer: Zug & Associates, Ltd.
Mechanical engineer: Consolidated Engineers
Electrical engineer: Reese Engineering, Inc.
Civil engineer: Bursich Associates
Contractor: C. Raymond Davis & Sons, Inc.

PROJECT AREAS

Project Element	Units, Beds or Clients	New GSF	Total Gross Area GSF	Total on Site or Served by Project
Apartments (units)				236
Cottages/villas (units)				11
Senior living/assisted living/personal care (units)				32
Skilled nursing care (beds)	40	52,223	52,223	
Kitchen (daily meals served)				1,100/day
Children's day care (clients)				32
Fitness/rehab/wellness (daily visits)				35 persons/day
Pool(s) and related areas (users)				20 persons/day

NURSING FACILITIES
Skilled Nursing Facilities

Project Element	New Construction		Renovations
	No. Beds	Typical Room Size GSF	Typical Room Size GSF
Residents in one-bed/single rooms	40	350	
Total no. of rooms/residents: Rooms: 40 Beds:	40	14,000	
Social areas (lounges, dining, and recreation spaces)			4,900
Medical, health care, therapy, and activity spaces			4,000
Administrative, public, and ancillary support services			3,200
Service, maintenance, and mechanical areas			7,040
Total gross area			52,223

CONSTRUCTION COSTS
The following information is based on actual costs.
Final construction cost as of August 2001
Financing sources: non-taxable bond offering through Montgomery County Higher Education Authority

Building Costs
Total building costs	$8.38 M

Site Costs
New	$792,000
Renovation	$342,000
Total site costs	$1.13 M
Total Project Costs	**$9.51 M**

Fran and Ray Stark Villa

Status of project: Completed October 2001
Facility administrator: David Tillman, MD/CEO;
 Ed Malinowski, Facilities Director
Owner: The Motion Picture and Television Fund
Architect: SmithGroup
Interior designer: SmithGroup
Structural engineer: Taylor & Gaines
Mechanical engineer: Store Matakovich & Wolfberg (MEP)
Electrical engineer: Store Matakovich & Wolfberg (MEP)
Civil engineer: RBA Partners
Contractor: Millie & Severson

PROJECT AREAS

Project Element	Units, Beds or Clients	New GSF	Renovated GSF	Total Gross Area GSF	Total on Site or Served by Project
Cottages/villas (units)					62 units
Senior living/assisted living/ personal care (units)	70 units				62 + 70 new
Skilled nursing care (beds)					256
Common social areas (people)	92				
Pool(s) and related areas (users)	koi pond				

ASSISTED LIVING FACILITIES
General Social/Residential Assisted Living Models

Project Element	New Construction No. Units	New Construction Typical Size GSF	Renovations No. Units	Renovations Typical Size GSF
Studio units	48	450		
One-bedroom units	18	650		
Two-bedroom units	4	850		
Total, all units	70	38,000		
Residents' social areas (lounges, dining, and recreation spaces)				9,000
Medical, health care, therapy, and activity spaces				4,000
Administrative, public, and ancillary support services				4,000
Service, maintenance, and mechanical areas				8,000
Total gross area				63,000

Total Project Costs	$16 M

Grand Oaks

Status of project: Completed September 2000
Facility administrator: Life Care Services Corporation
Owner: Sibley Memorial Hospital
Architect: Oudens + Knoop Architects, PC
Interior designer: Design Innerphase
Structural engineer: SK&A Consulting Engineers
Mechanical engineer: Hankins & Anderson
Electrical engineer: Hankins & Anderson
Civil engineer: Hankins & Anderson
Contractor: Forrester Construction Company

PROJECT AREAS

Project Element	Units, Beds or clients	New GSF	Renovated GSF	Total Gross Area GSF	Total on Site or Served by Project
Senior living/assisted living/personal care (units)	104	122,645		122,645	104
Skilled nursing care (beds)					94
Other					237

ASSISTED LIVING FACILITIES
General Social/Residential Assisted Living Models

Project Element	No. Units	Typical Size GSF
Studio units	16	450
One-bedroom units	83	600
Two-bedroom units	5	950
Total, all units	104	61,750
Residents' social areas (lounges, dining, and recreation spaces)		15,700
Medical, health care, therapy, and activity spaces		5,700
Administrative, public, and ancillary support services		25,995
Service, maintenance, and mechanical areas		13,500
Total gross area		122,645

CONSTRUCTION COSTS
The following information is based on actual costs.
Final construction cost as of September 2000
Financing sources: non-taxable bond offering

Building Costs
New construction	$17.19 M
Medical equipment costs	$431,000
Total building costs	$17.62 M

Site Costs
Total site costs	$1.21 M
Furniture/Fees/Miscellaneous costs	$1.6 M

Total Project Costs	$20.43 M

GRANITE LEDGES OF CONCORD

Status of project: Completed June 1999
Facility Administrator: Genesis Eldercare
Owner: Capital Region Healthcare Corporation
Architect: JSA Inc.
Interior designer: JSA Inc.
Structural engineer: Ocmulgee Associates
Mechanical engineer: Engineered Systems, Inc.
Electrical engineer: Engineered Systems, Inc.
Civil engineer: Provan & Lorber
Contractor: MacMillan Company

PROJECT AREAS

Project Element	Included in this Project			
	Units, Beds or Clients	New GSF	Total Gross Area	Total on Site or Served by Project
Senior living/assisted living/ personal care (units)	61 units	22,441	22,441	22,441
Special care for persons with dementia	14 units	5,320	5,320	5,320
Common social areas (people)	84			84
Kitchen (daily meals served)	3/day/pp			3/day/pp
Retail space (shops, restaurants, etc.)	1 shop			1 shop
Fitness/rehab/wellness (daily visits)	1 room, voluntary			1 room, voluntary

ASSISTED LIVING FACILITIES
General Social/Residential Assisted Living Models

Project Element	New Construction		Renovations	
	No. Units	Typical Size GSF	No. Units	Typical Size GSF
Studio units	51	305–600		
Dementia studio units	14	320–600		
One-bedroom units	6	538		
Two-bedroom units	4	802		
Total, all units	75	30,980		
Residents' social areas (lounges, dining, and recreation spaces)				10,717
Medical, health care, therapies, and activities spaces				385
Administrative, public, and ancillary support services				1,175
Service, maintenance, and mechanical areas				14,363
Total gross area				57,620

CONSTRUCTION COSTS
The following is based on: actual costs (completed).
Financing sources: conventional (privately financed)

Building Costs

Total building costs	$4.9 M

Site Costs

Total site costs	$500,000

Total Project Costs — $7.35 M

GUARDIAN ANGELS BY THE LAKE

Status of project: Completed September 1999
Facility administrator: Sherry Emerson-Mutterer, Vice President of Operations
Owner: Guardian Angels of Elk River, Inc.
Architect: Trossen Wright Architects, P.A.
Interior designer: Guardian Angels of Elk River, Inc.
Landscape architect: Guardian Angels of Elk River, Inc.
Structural engineer: Larson Engineering of Minnesota
Mechanical engineer: Steen Engineering
Electrical engineer: Steen Engineering
Civil engineer: John Oliver & Associates
Contractor: Frana & Sons

PROJECT AREAS

	Units, Beds or Clients	Total Gross Area GSF
Apartments (units)	60	52,125

ASSISTED LIVING FACILITIES
General Social/Residential Assisted Living Models

	New Construction		Renovations	
	No. Units	Typical Size GSF	No. Units	Typical Size GSF
Studio units	2	520		
One-bedroom units	54	460		
Two-bedroom units	4	650		
Total, all units	60			26,640
Residents' social areas (lounges, dining, and recreation spaces)				8,475
Medical, health care, therapy, and activity spaces				1,375
Administrative, public, and ancillary support services				985
Service, maintenance, and mechanical areas				3,600
Total gross area				52,125

CONSTRUCTION COSTS
The following is based on actual costs.

Building Costs

New construction	$2.98 M
Medical equipment costs	$223,424
Total building costs	$3.2 M

Site Costs

New	$275,454
Total site costs	$275,454

Total Project Costs — $3.77 M

GURWIN JEWISH GERIATRIC CENTER
FAY J. LINDER RESIDENCES

Status of project: Completed June 2001
Facility administrator: Herbert Friedman
Owner: Gurwin Jewish Geriatric Center—Fay J. Linder Residences
Architect: Perkins Eastman Architects PC
Interior designer: Perkins Eastman Architects PC
Structural engineer: Goldstein Associates
Mechanical engineer: Jack Stone Engineers PC
Electrical engineer: Jack Stone Engineers
Civil engineer: James LaSala & Associates LLP
Contractor: Gotham Construction Co., LLC

PROJECT AREAS

Project Element	Included in this Project		
	Units, Beds or Clients	New GSF	Renovated GSF	Total Gross Area GSF
Senior living/assisted living/personal care (units)	143			84,418
Special care for persons with dementia	17 units 19 beds			8,403
Common social areas (people)				32,680
Kitchen (daily meals served)				5,200
Retail space (shops, restaurants, etc.)				380
Fitness/rehab/wellness (daily visits)				1,300

ASSISTED LIVING FACILITIES
General Social/Residential Assisted Living Models

Project Element	New Construction		Renovations	
	No. Units	Typical Size GSF	No. Units	Typical Size GSF
Studio units	1	440		
One-bedroom units	130	565		
Two-bedroom units	13	888		
Total, all units	144	85,434		
Residents' social areas (lounges, dining, and recreation spaces)				32,680
Medical, health care, therapy, and activity spaces				1,300
Administrative, public, and ancillary support services				1,544
Service, maintenance, and mechanical areas				4,000
Total gross area				149,262

Dementia-Specific Assisted Living Models

Project Element	New Construction		Renovations	
	No. Units	Typical Size GSF	No. Units	Typical Size GSF
Studio units	15	250		
One-bedroom units	2	388		
Total, all units	17	4,526		
Residents' social areas (lounges, dining, and recreation spaces)				2,225
Medical, health care, therapy, and activity spaces				128
Administrative, public, and ancillary support services				100
Total gross area				8,403

Total Project Costs $26.5 M

GURWIN JEWISH GERIATRIC CENTER—
HARRY AND JEANNETTE WEINBERG RESIDENT PAVILION AND COMMUNITY SERVICE CENTER

Status of project: Completed September 2000
Facility administrator: Herb Friedman, Executive Vice President
Owner: Gurwin Jewish Geriatric Center
Architect: Landow and Landow Architects
Interior designer: Landow and Landow Architects
Landscape architect: Goldberg and Rodler
Structural engineer: Severud Associates
Mechanical engineer: Altieri Sebor Weber LLC
Electrical engineer: Altieri Sebor Weber LLC
Contractor: Gotham Construction Corp.

PROJECT AREAS

	Units, Beds or Clients	New GSF	Renovated GSF	Total Gross Area GSF
Skilled nursing care (beds)	160	27,440		27,440
Common social areas (people)	280	3,730	3,700	7,430
Kitchen (daily meals served)	600		9,300	9,300
Elder day care (clients)	120	11,000		11,000
Other		7,000		7,000

NURSING FACILITIES
Skilled Nursing Facilities

	New Construction	
	No. Beds	Typical Room Size GSF
Residents in one-bed/single rooms	16	230
Residents in two-bed/double rooms	144	330
Total	160	27,440
Social areas (lounges, dining, and recreation spaces)		7,430
Medical, health care, therapies, and activities spaces		7,000
Administrative, public, and ancillary support services		10,000
Service, maintenance, and mechanical areas		38,000
Total gross area		154,500

OTHER FACILITIES

	New Construction	
	No.	Size GSF
Adult day health care center	1	11,000
Diagnostic and treatment clinic	1	7,000
Total gross area		18,000

CONSTRUCTION COSTS
The following is based on actual costs.

Building Costs

New construction	$22.6 M
Renovations	$3.4 M
Medical equipment costs	$1.5 M
Total building costs	$27.5 M

Site Costs

New	$800,000
Total site costs	$800,000

Total Project Costs $35 M

HEARTH AND HOME OF VAN WERT

Status of project: Completed August 2000
Facility administrator: AdCare Health System
Owner: Hearth and Home of Van Wert, LLC
Architect: JMM Architects, Inc.
Interior designer: Artistic Interiors
Structural engineer: Jack D. Walters & Associates
Mechanical engineer: Hill Engineering
Electrical engineer: Hill Engineering
Civil engineer: Hartman Engineering
Contractor: McKnight Development Corporation

PROJECT AREAS

Project Element	Included in this Project			
	Units, Beds or Clients	New GSF	Total Gross Area GSF	Total on Site or Served by Project
Senior living/assisted living/personal care (units)	30	21,577	21,577	30

ASSISTED LIVING FACILITIES
General Social/Residential Assisted Living Models

Project Element	New Construction		Renovations
	No. Units	Typical Size GSF	Typical Size GSF
Studio units	13	303	
One-bedroom units	2	430	
Total, all units	15	4,796	
Residents' social areas (lounges, dining, and recreation spaces)			4,214
Administrative, public, and ancillary support services			408
Service, maintenance, and mechanical areas			1,117
Total gross area			11,867

Dementia-Specific Assisted Living Models

	No. Units	Typical Size GSF	Typical Size GSF
Studio units	13	303	
One-bedroom units	2	430	
Total, all units	15	4,796	
Residents' social areas (lounges, dining, and recreation spaces)	2,273		
Administrative, public, and ancillary support services			408
Service, maintenance, and mechanical areas			1,117
Total gross area			9,690

CONSTRUCTION COSTS
The following information is based on actual costs.
Final construction cost as of August 2000
Financing sources: conventional (private) limited liability corporation

Building Costs
Furniture costs	$111,228
New construction	$1.76 M

Site Costs
New	$240,202

Total Project Costs
New	$2.11 M

HILLSIDE COMMUNITIES

Status of project: Completed May 2001
Facility administrator: Jacklyn P. Friedman
Owner: Hillside Communities
Architect: Mithun
Interior designer: Arthur Shuster, Inc.
Landscape architect: Greenworks P.C.
Structural engineer: Kramer Gehlen and Associates, Inc.
Mechanical engineer: HV Engineering Inc.
Electrical engineer: Interface
Civil engineer: Group Mackenzie
Contractor: Swinerton Builders

PROJECT AREAS

	Units, Beds or Clients	Total Gross Area GSF
Apartments (units)	69	78,050
Cottages/villas (units)	54	92,600
Senior living/assisted living/personal care (units)	40	25,780
Special care for persons with dementia	20	14,325
Skilled nursing care (beds)	20	17,900
Common social areas (people)	140	6,850
Kitchen (daily meals served)	3	3,000

ASSISTED LIVING FACILITIES
General Social/Residential Assisted Living Models

	New Construction		Renovations	
	No. Units	Typical Size GSF	No. Units	Typical Size GSF
Studio units	36	325		
One-bedroom units	4	490		
Two-bedroom units				
Total, all units	40	13,875		
Residents' social areas (lounges, dining, and recreation spaces)				3,075
Medical, health care, therapies, and activities spaces				623
Administrative, public, and ancillary support services				800
Service, maintenance, and mechanical areas				835
Total gross area				25,780

Dementia-Specific Assisted Living Models

	New Construction		Renovations	
	No. Units	Typical Size GSF	No. Units	Typical Size GSF
Studio units	20	325		
Total, all units	20	6,750		
Residents' social areas (lounges, dining, and recreation spaces)				3,085
Medical, health care, therapies, and activities spaces				570
Administrative, public, and ancillary support services				390
Service, maintenance, and mechanical areas				630
Total gross area				14,325

NURSING FACILITIES
Skilled Nursing Facilities

	New Construction		Renovations	
	No. Beds	Typical Room Size GSF	No. Beds	Typical Room Size GSF
Residents in one-bed/single rooms	20	325		
Residents in two-bed/double rooms				
Social areas (lounges, dining, and recreation spaces)				1,935
Medical, health care, therapies, and activities spaces				1,490
Administrative, public, and ancillary support services				1,140
Service, maintenance, and mechanical areas				1,965
Total gross area				17,900

CONSTRUCTION COSTS
The following information is based on actual costs.

Building Costs
New construction	$23.2 M
Total building costs	$23.2 M

James F. Rosborough Jr.
Cultural Arts and Wellness Center

Status of project: Completed 2001
Facility administrator: Robert Hechtman
Owner: Asbury Methodist Village
Architect: Torti Gallas and Partners • CHK, Inc.
Interior designer: Partners in Planning
Structural engineer: Smislova, Kehnemui and Associates, PA
Mechanical engineer: Don Johnson
Electrical engineer: Don Johnson
Civil engineer: Bengston, Debell and Elkin, Ltd.
Contractor: Donohoe Construction Company

PROJECT AREAS

Project Element	Total on Site or Served by Project
Apartments (units)	875
Cottages/villas (units)	73
Senior living/assisted living/ personal care (units)	133
Special care for persons with dementia	30
Skilled nursing care (beds)	285
Common social areas (people)	1,700
Kitchen (daily meals served)	3,000
Elder day care (clients)	35
Fitness/rehab/wellness (daily visits)	New
Pool(s) and related areas (users)	1,385

Project Element Cultural Arts and Wellness Center	New Construction No.	Size GSF
Indoor pool/Jacuzzi/lockers/office	1	8,407
Theater/backstage/control	1	5,037
Fitness center	1	1,505
Exercise loop/corridors 3, 4, 5, and 6	1	3,412
Multipurpose room/pantry	1	4,450
Media and technology center	1	686
TV studio	1	1,154
Resident's organization office/storage	1	419
Branch bank	1	1,114
Wellness resource center/office/message	1	676
Shop/cafe	1	1,361
Post office	1	135
Exhibit room and display cases	3	886

CONSTRUCTION COSTS
The following information is based on actual costs.

Building Costs

New construction	$7.44 M
Total building costs	$7.44 M

Site Costs

Total site costs	$600,000

Total Project Costs	$10 M

Jennings Residential and Community Services Center

Status of project: Completed September 2002
Facility administrator: Martha Kutik
Owner: Martha Kutik
Architect: Collins, Gordon, Bostwick Architects
Landscape architect: McKnight and Associates
Structural engineer: Lienweber and Associates
Mechanical engineer: K.D. Hausmann Co.
Electrical engineer: KME Consulting , LCC
Civil engineer: Donald Bohning and Associates
Contractor: The Krill Company

PROJECT AREAS

	Units, Beds or Clients	Total Gross Area GSF
Senior living/assisted living/ personal care (units)	55	26,400
Special care for persons with dementia	18	4,320
Common social areas (people)		5,100
Common social areas servicing the dementia care facility		3,000
Common areas—multigenerational		1,100
Kitchen (daily meals served)	4	1,400
Elder day care (clients)	40	2,880
Children's day care (clients)	63	5,000
Other (clinic)		2,200

ASSISTED LIVING FACILITIES
General Social/Residential Assisted Living Models

	New Construction No. Units	Typical Size GSF	Renovations No. Units	Typical Size GSF
Studio units	1	250		
One-bedroom units	54	480		
Total, all units	55	26,170		26,170
Residents' social areas (lounges, dining, and recreation spaces) (on 1, 2, and 3 only)				7,288
Medical, health care, therapies, and activities spaces				2,200
Administrative, public and ancillary support services (on 1, 2, and 3 only)				1,480
Service, maintenance, and mechanical areas (on 1, 2, and 3 only)				3,080
Total gross area				40,218

Dementia-Specific Assisted Living Models

	New Construction No. Units	Typical Size GSF	Renovations No. Units	Typical Size GSF
Studio units	18	240		
Total, all units		4,320		4,320
Residents' social areas (lounges, dining, and recreation spaces)				3,000
Medical, health care, therapies, and activities spaces				540
Administrative, public, and ancillary support services				330
Service, maintenance, and mechanical areas				550
Total gross area				8,740

CONSTRUCTION COSTS
The following is based on the contractor's estimate in August 2001.

Building Costs

Medical equipment costs	$270,000
Total building costs	$9.53 M

Site Costs

Total site costs	$275,000

Total Project Costs	$10.07 M

JEWISH HOME OF CENTRAL NEW YORK

Facility administrator: Harvey Finkelstein
Owner: Jewish Home of Central New York
Architect: King & King, Architects LLP
Landscape architect: Appel Osborne Landscape Architecture
Structural engineer: Burns Consulting Engineer
Mechanical engineer: Robson & Woese, Inc.
Electrical engineer: Robson & Woese, Inc.
Contractor: Hueber Breuer Construction Co.

PROJECT AREA

Project Element	Units, Beds or Clients	New GSF	Renovated GSF	Total Gross Area	Total on Site or Served by Project
Apartments (units)					11
Senior living/assisted living/ personal care (units)	18				18
Continuing care retirement communities					50
Special care for persons with dementia	25				25
Skilled nursing care (beds)	132				
Common social areas (people)					132
Elder day care (clients)					25
Retail space (shops, restaurants, etc.)	2				2

ASSISTED LIVING FACILITIES
General Social/Residential Assisted Living Models

Project Element	New Construction		Renovations	
	No. Units	Typical Size GSF	No. Units	Typical Size GSF
Studio units			2	495
One-bedroom units			16	685
Total, all units:			18	11,215
Residents' social areas (lounges, dining, and recreation spaces)				1,270
Medical, health care, therapies, and activities spaces				372
Administrative, public, and ancillary support services				3,475
Service, maintenance, and mechanical areas				1,006
Total gross area				17,338

Dementia-Specific Assisted Living Models

Project Element	New Construction		Renovations	
	No. Units	Typical Size GSF	No. Units	Typical Size GSF
Studio units			25	323
Total, all units:			25	8,018
Residents' social areas (lounges, dining, and recreation spaces)				2,377
Medical, health care, therapies, and activities spaces				670
Administrative, public, and ancillary support services				7,246
Service, maintenance, and mechanical areas				708
Total gross area				16,642

NURSING FACILITIES
Skilled Nursing Facilities

Project Element	New Construction		Renovations	
	No. Beds	Typical Size GSF	No. Beds	Typical Size GSF
Residents in one-bed/single rooms	42	334		
Residents in two-bed/double rooms	90	500		
Total no. of rooms/residents:				
Rooms: 87 Beds:	132	36,875		
Social areas (lounges, dining, and recreation spaces)				23,174
Medical, health care, therapies, and activities spaces				7,207
Administrative, public, and ancillary support services				6,705
Service, maintenance, and mechanical areas				8,437
Total gross area				82,398

OTHER FACILITIES

Project Element	New Construction		Renovations	
	No.	Size GSF	No.	Size GSF
Meditation room	1	764	1	367
Children's playroom			1	318
Boutique			1	292
Social areas (lounges, dining, and recreation spaces)				2,666
Administrative, public, and ancillary support services				6,179
Service, maintenance, and mechanical areas				6,494
Total gross area				17,080

CONSTRUCTION COSTS
The following information is based on bids received November 2000.

Building Costs
New construction	$9.12 M
Renovations	$3.49 M
Medical equipment costs	$855,000
Total building costs	$13.47 M

Site Costs
New	$828,800
Renovation	$54,000
Total site costs	$882,800

Total Project Costs $16 M

JONES-HARRISON RESIDENCE

Status of project: Completed July 2000
Facility administrator: Sharon Brenny
Owner: Jones-Harrison Residence
Architect: GLT Architects
Interior designer: BDH & Young
Structural engineer: Larson Engineering of Minnesota
Mechanical engineer: Lundquist Killeen Potvin & Bender, Inc.
Electrical engineer: Lundquist Killeen Potvin & Bender, Inc.
Contractor: R.A. Morton & Associates, Inc.

PROJECT AREAS

	Units, Beds or Clients	Renovated GSF
Senior living/assisted living/ personal care (units)	57	
Special care for persons with dementia	78	
Skilled nursing care (beds)	85	
Retail space (shops, restaurants, etc.)		684
Fitness/rehab/wellness		6,4/4
Pool(s) and related areas		1,656

ASSISTED LIVING FACILITIES

General Social/Residential Assisted Living Models

	New Construction		Renovations	
	No. Units	Typical Size GSF	No. Units	Typical Size GSF
Studio units			37	295
One-bedroom units			18	666
Two-bedroom units			2	908
Total, all units			57	24,719
Residents' social areas (lounges, dining, and recreation spaces)				4,388
Administrative, public, and ancillary support services				9,333
Service, maintenance, and mechanical areas				1,910
Total gross area				40,350

Skilled Nursing Facilities (Dementia/Non-Dementia)

	New Construction		Renovations	
	No. Beds	Typical Room Size	No. Beds	Typical Room Size
Residents in one-bed/single rooms			14/23	266
Residents in two-bed/double rooms			64/62	342
Total, all units			163	31,388
Social areas (lounges, dining, and recreation spaces)				13,158
Medical, health care, therapies and activities spaces				9,014
Administrative, public and ancillary support services				36,564
Service, maintenance, and mechanical areas				35,432
Total gross area				125,556

CONSTRUCTION COSTS

The following is based on actual costs.

Building Costs
Renovation costs	$5.33 M
Total building costs	$5.33 M

Site Costs
Renovation site costs	$58,000
Total site costs	$58,000

Total Project Costs | $5.39 M

MADISON CENTER PROVIDENCE HOUSE

Status of project: Completed May 2001
Facility administrator: Kathy Sly
Owner: Madison Center
Architect: Mathews-Purucker-Anella, Inc.
Interior designer: Mathews-Purucker-Anella, Inc.
Structural engineer: Archistructure Keith Wishmeier, P.E.
Mechanical engineer: ECI Group, Inc., Jerry White, P.E.
Electrical engineer: ECI Group, Inc., Jerry White, P.E.
Contractor: Casteel Construction Corp.

PROJECT AREAS

Project Element	Included in this Project				
	Units, Beds or Clients	New GSF	Renovated GSF	Total Gross Area GSF	Total on Site or Served by Project
Special care for persons with dementia	55		42,203	42,203	

Dementia-Specific Assisted Living Models

Project Element	Renovations	
	No. Units	Typical Size GSF
Studio units	55	476
Total, all units	55	26,180
Residents' social areas (lounges, dining, and recreation spaces)		2,604
Medical, health care, therapy, and activity spaces		1,645
Administrative, public, and ancillary support services		6,730
Service, maintenance, and mechanical areas		5,044
Total gross area		42,203

CONSTRUCTION COSTS

The following information is based on actual costs.
Final construction cost as of May 2001
Financing sources: conventional (private), line of credit with local financial institution

Building Costs
Renovations	$972,637

Site Costs
Total site costs	$18,325

Total Project Costs | $990,962

MARY'S WOODS AT MARYLHURST

Status of project: Completed August 2001
Facility administrator: Diane Hilton
Owner: Mary's Woods at Marylhurst, Inc. (sponsored by the Society of Sisters of the Holy Names of Jesus and Mary)
Architect: Mithun
Interior designer: Stanzione Associates
Landscape architect: The Berger Partnership, S.E.
Structural engineer: Kramer Gehlen and Associates, Inc.
Mechanical engineer: MacDonald Miler Industries
Electrical engineer: Travis, Fitzmaurice and Associates
Civil engineer: WRG Design
Contractor: Andersen/Weitz

PROJECT AREAS

	Units, Beds or Clients	New GSF	Renovated GSF	Total Gross Area GSF
Apartments (units)	235	213,670	23,724	349,578
Cottages/villas (units)	33	63,144		63,144
Senior living/assisted living/ personal care (units)	40	19,198		19,198
Special care for persons with dementia	22	7,040		7,040
Skilled nursing care (beds)	23	5,389		5,389
Common social areas (people)	14,616	15,219		29,835
Kitchen (daily meals served)	363	2,242		2,605
Fitness/rehab/wellness (daily visits)	3,392			3,392
Pool(s) and related areas (users)	2,700			2,700

RESIDENTIAL FACILITIES

	Cottages		Apartments	
	No. Units	Typical Size GSF	No. Units	Typical Size GSF
Studio units			2	475
One-bedroom units			133	898
Two-bedroom units	18	1,903	51	1,106
Two-bedroom + den units			49	1,218
Three-bedroom and larger units	15	1,932		
Total, all units	33	63,144	235	340,588
Residents' social areas (lounges, dining, and recreation spaces)				18,426
Medical/health/fitness and activities areas				5,167
Administrative, public, and ancillary support services				4,156
Service, maintenance, and mechanical areas				15,471
Total gross area				383,808

ASSISTED LIVING FACILITIES
General Social/Residential Assisted Living Models

	New Construction		Renovations	
	No. Units	Typical Size GSF	No. Units	Typical Size GSF
Studio units	18	440		
One-bedroom units	12	520		
Two-bedroom units	10	704		
Total, all units	40	19,198		
Residents' social areas (lounges, dining, and recreation spaces)				4,749
Medical, health care, therapies, and activities spaces				195
Administrative, public, and ancillary support services				579
Service, maintenance, and mechanical areas				380
Total gross area				25,101

Dementia-Specific Assisted Living Models

	New Construction		Renovations	
	No. Units	Typical Size GSF	No. Units	Typical Size GSF
Studio units	22	320		
Total, all units	22	7,040		
Residents' social areas (lounges, dining, and recreation spaces)				3,897
Medical, health care, therapies and activities spaces				316
Administrative, public, and ancillary support services				353
Service, maintenance, and mechanical areas				405
Total gross area				12,011

NURSING FACILITIES
Skilled Nursing Facilities

	New Construction		Renovations	
	No. Rooms, Units, or Beds	Typical Room Size GSF	No. Beds	Typical Room Size GSF
Residents in one-bed/ single rooms	15	270		
Residents in two-bed/ double rooms	4	376		
Total, all units	19	5,389		
Social areas (lounges, dining, and recreation spaces)				2,763
Medical, health care, therapies, and activities spaces				1,315
Administrative, public, and ancillary support services				1,237
Service, maintenance, and mechanical areas				764
Total gross area				11,468

CONSTRUCTION COSTS
The following is based on actual costs.

Building Costs

Total building costs	$50.2 M

Site Costs

Total site costs	$7.0 M

Total Project Costs	**$57.2 M**

Masonic Homes of California

Status of project: Completed April 2001
Facility administrator: Don Nearhood
Owner: Masonic Home for Adults
Architect: Ratcliff
Interior designer: Ratcliff
Landscape architect: Royston, Hanamoto, Alley & Abey
Structural engineer: Kariotis & Associates
Mechanical engineer: Mazetti & Associates—Wollenberg and Adams buildings
McCracken & Woodman—Administration, North, and South building
Electrical engineer: Mazetti & Associates—Wollenberg and Adams buildings
WHM, Incorporated Engineers—Adminstration, North, and South buildings
Contractor: Tilden Coil Constructors, Inc.

RESIDENTIAL FACILITIES

The South building is the only project submitted that has independent living units.

	Cottages		Apartments	
	No. Units	Typical Size GSF	No. Units	Typical Size GSF
Studio units			4	450
One-bedroom units			28	650
Total, all units				
Residents' social areas (lounges, dining, and recreation spaces)				5,000
Medical/health/fitness and activities areas				1,200
Administrative, public, and ancillary support service areas				700
Service, maintenance, and mechanical areas				39,000
Total gross area				

ASSISTED LIVING FACILITIES

General Social/Residential Assisted Living Models

Note: This project includes the renovation of multiple buildings. Listed below are comprehensive assumptions for the submitted four building renovations. Those buildings are Wollenberg, Adams, North, and Administration.

	New Construction		Renovations	
	No. Units	Typical Size GSF	No. Units	Typical Size GSF
Studio units			99	450
One-bedroom units			32	600
Total, all units				63,750
Residents' social areas (lounges, dining, and recreation spaces)				6,000
Medical, health care, therapy, and activity spaces				2,500
Administrative, public, and ancillary support service areas				25,000
Service, maintenance, and mechanical areas				2,500
Total gross area				171,000

CONSTRUCTION COSTS

The following is based on actual costs.

Building Costs

Total building costs	$60 M

Total Project Costs	$60 M

Messiah Village

Status of project: Completed March 2000
Facility administrator: Dr. Emerson L. Lesher
Owner: Messiah Village
Architect: Reese, Lower, Patrick & Scott, Ltd.
Interior designer: Interiors 2000 (finish and furniture selections)
Structural engineer: Zug & Associates, Ltd.
Mechanical engineer: Moore Engineering Company
Electrical engineer: Reese Engineering, Inc.
Civil engineer: Pennoni Associates, Inc.
Contractor: R.S. Mowery & Sons, Inc.

PROJECT AREAS

Project Element	Included in this Project				
	Units, Beds, or Clients	New GSF	Renovated GSF	Total Gross Area GSF	Total on Site or Served by Project
Senior living/assisted living/ personal care (units)	100	1,284	7,594	67,986	100
Skilled nursing care (beds)	133	5,685	41,010	45,404	130

ASSISTED LIVING FACILITIES

General Social/Residential Assisted Living Models

Project Element	New Construction		Renovations	
	No. Units	Typical Size	No. Units	Typical Size GSF
Residents' social areas (lounges, dining, and recreation spaces)				4,628
Medical, health care, therapy, and activity spaces				1,873
Administrative, public, and ancillary support services				2,377
Service, maintenance, and mechanical areas				N/A
Total gross area, new construction and renovations				8,878

NURSING FACILITIES

Skilled Nursing Facilities

Project Element	Renovations	
	No. Beds	Typical Room Size GSF
Residents in one-bed/single rooms		293
Residents in two-bed/double rooms		293
Total no. of rooms/residents:		
Rooms: 68 Beds:	134	
66 2-bed rooms		
2 1-bed rooms		20,664
Social areas (lounges, dining, and recreation spaces)		5,820
Medical, health care, therapy, and activity spaces		8,203
Administrative, public, and ancillary support services		8,741
Service, maintenance, and mechanical areas		1,976
Total gross area		45,404

CONSTRUCTION COSTS

The following information is based on actual costs.
Final construction cost as of March 2000
Financing sources: conventional (private)

Building Costs

Total building costs	$4.15 M

Site Costs

Total site costs	$100,000

Total Project Costs	$4.25 M

MISSOURI VETERANS' HOME

Status of project: Completed October 2000
Facility administrator: Andrew Buffenbarger, Acting Director
Owner: State of Missouri, Veterans Commission
Architect: Rafael Architects, Inc.
Associate architect: Nelson-Tremain Partnership
Interior designer: Rafael Architects, Inc.
Landscape architect: Rafael Architects, Inc.
Structural engineer: Walter P. Moore Engineers—Consultants
Mechanical engineer: Olsson Associates
Electrical engineer: Olsson Associates
Civil engineer: Walter P. Moore Engineers—Consultants
Contractor: Midwest Titan

PROJECT AREAS

	Units, Beds or Clients	New GSF
Skilled nursing care (beds)	200	52,500
Common social areas (people)	24	24,000
Kitchen (daily meals served)	800	2,270

NURSING FACILITIES

	New Construction	
	No. Beds	Typical Room Size GSF
Residents in one-bed/single rooms	72	
Residents in two-bed/double rooms	128	
Total	200	252
Total resident rooms		52,500
Social areas (lounges, dining, and recreation spaces)		17,800
Medical, health care, therapies, and activities spaces		2,486
Administrative, public, and ancillary support services		14,560
Service, maintenance, and mechanical areas		8,345
Total gross area		131,697

CONSTRUCTION COSTS
The following is based on actual costs.

Building Costs

New construction	$16.2 M
Total building costs	$16.2 M

Site Costs

New	$1.4 M
Total site costs	$1.4 M

Total Project Costs	**$17.6 M**

MOTHER ANGELINE McCRORY MANOR

Status of project: Under construction
Facility administrator: Sr. Ann Brown
Owner: Carmelite Sisters for the Aged and Infirm
Architect: THW Design
Interior designer: THW Design
Landscape architect: THW Design
Structural engineer: Lantz, Jones, Nebraska
Mechanical engineer: McMullen Engineering Co., Inc.
Electrical engineer: McMullen Engineering Co., Inc.
Civil engineer: EMH&T Consulting Engineers
Preconstruction Services: Corna/Kokosing Construction

PROJECT AREAS

	Units, Beds or Clients	Total GSF
Special care for persons with dementia	21	11,945
Skilled nursing care (beds)	126	71,670
Common social areas (people)	147	4,500
Kitchen (daily meals served)	3	1,650
Fitness/rehab/wellness (daily visits)		2,115

NURSING FACILITIES
Skilled Nursing Facilities

	New Construction		Renovations	
	No. Beds	Typical Room Size GSF	No. Beds	Typical Room Size GSF
Residents in one-bed/single rooms	147	210		
Total, all units	147			
Social areas (lounges, dining, and recreation spaces)				7,500
Medical, health care, therapy, and activity spaces				2,115
Administrative, public, and ancillary support services				9,100
Service, maintenance, and mechanical areas				2,500
Total gross area				132,000

CONSTRUCTION COSTS
The following is based on contractor's estimates.

Building Costs

New construction	$15.0 M
Medical equipment costs	$75,000
Total building costs	$15.083 M

Site Costs

New site costs	$1.4 M
Total site costs	$1.4 M

Total Project Costs	**$18.7 M**

New Hampshire Veterans Home

Status of project: Estimated completion date: July 2003
Facility administrator: Barry Conway
Owner: Paul Hedstrom
Architect: MorrisSwitzer Environments for Health
Interior designer: Currier & Associates Inc.
Structural engineer: Durbrow Associates Inc.
Mechanical engineer: Allied Consulting Engineering Services
Electrical engineer: Allied Consulting Engineering Services
Civil engineer: Underwood Engineering Inc.
Contractor: Harvey Construction Corporation of NH

PROJECT AREAS

Project Element	Units, Beds or Clients	New GSF	Renovated GSF	Total Gross Area GSF	Total on Site or Served by Project
		Included in this Project			
Special care for persons with dementia	50	37,865		37,865	50
Skilled nursing care (beds)	50	37,865		37,865	200
Common social areas (people)	150	5,225		5,225	250
Fitness/rehab/wellness (daily visits)			1,100	1,100	55
Other	250		3,312	4,700	250

NURSING FACILITIES
Skilled Nursing Facilities

Project Element	New Construction		Renovations	
	No. Beds	Typical Room Size GSF	No. Beds	Typical Room Size GSF
Residents in One-Bed/ Single Rooms	100	268		
Dementia-specific skilled nursing care	50			
Total no. of rooms/residents:				
Rooms: 100 Beds:	100			26,800
Social areas (lounges, dining, and recreation spaces)				14,885
Medical, health care, therapy, and activity spaces				11,520
Administrative, public, and ancillary support services				10,685
Service, maintenance, and mechanical areas				11,840
Total gross area				75,730

OTHER FACILITIES

Project Element	New Construction		Renovations	
Main Street Concept	No.	Size GSF	No.	Size GSF
Rehabilitation/recreation				3,815
Chapel/library/bank/store				2,300
Service, maintenance, and mechanical areas				760
Total gross area				6,875

CONSTRUCTION COSTS

The following information is based on architect's estimates, May 2001 and November 2002.
Financing sources: 65 percent, U.S. Department of Veterans Affairs; 35 percent, state of New Hampshire

Building Costs

New construction	$9.29 M
Renovations	$257,820
Total building costs	$9.55 M

Site Costs

Total site costs	$944,313

Total Project Costs	$10.5 M

New Madonna Residence

Status of project: Completed July 2000
Facility administrator: Paula Lewis
Owner: St. Anthony Foundation
Architect of Record: Hardison Komatsu Ivelich & Tucker
Design Architect: John Stromwall, AIA
Landscape architect: Robert La Rocca & Associates
Interior designer: Hardison Komatsu Ivelich & Tucker
Structural engineer: H.D. Rueb Structural Engineer
Mechanical engineer: Fard Engineers, Inc.
Electrical engineer: Fard Engineers, Inc.
Civil engineer: Luk and Associates
Contractor: James E. Roberts/Obayashi Corp.

PROJECT AREAS

	Units, Beds or Clients	Total Gross Area GSF
Senior living/assisted living/ personal care (units)	51	19,074
Common social areas (people)	51	
Kitchen (daily meals served)	153	
Elder day care (clients)	50	
Elder outreach (clients)	50	

RESIDENTIAL FACILITIES

	Apartments	
	No. Units	Typical Size GSF
Studio units	51	374
Total, all units	51	19,134
Residents' social areas (lounges, dining, and recreation spaces)		5,934
Medical/health/fitness and activities areas: includes ADHC and social services		7,994
Administrative, public, and ancillary support service areas		2,500
Service, maintenance, and mechanical areas: includes corridors, driveway, and parking spaces under building		18,319
Total gross area		53,890

OTHER FACILITIES

	New Construction	
	No.	Size GSF
Adult day health care center	1	4,329
Social services	1	2,005
Multipurpose room	1	640
Drop-in center	1	1,020
Total gross area		7,994

CONSTRUCTION COSTS

The following is based on actual costs.

Building Costs

New construction	$6.7 M
Total building costs	$6.7 M

Total Project Costs	$6.7 M

Normandy Farms Estates

Status of project: Completed January 2000
Facility administrator: Stephen Eggles
Owner: ACTS Retirement-Life Communities, Inc.
Architect: Reese, Lower, Patrick & Scott, Ltd.
Interior designer: Reese, Lower, Patrick & Scott, Ltd.
Structural engineer: A.W. Lookup Corporation
Mechanical engineer: Moore Engineering Company
Electrical engineer: Reese Engineering, Inc.
Civil engineer: Chambers Associates, Inc.
Contractor: J.J. DeLuca Company, Inc.

PROJECT AREAS

Project Element	Units, Beds or Clients	New GSF	Renovated GSF	Total Gross Area GSF	Total on Site or Served by Project
		Included in this Project			
Special care for persons with dementia	50	42,919	1,200	44,119	

CONTINUING CARE RETIREMENT COMMUNITIES (CCRC)

Other Facilities

Project Element	New Construction		Renovations	
	No.	Size GSF	No.	Size GSF
Residents in one-bed/single rooms	42	309		
Residents in two-bed/double rooms	8	396		
Total number of rooms/residents:				
Rooms: 46 Beds:	50	14,562		
Social areas (lounges, dining, and recreation spaces)				13,579
Administrative, public, and ancillary support services				11,160
Service, maintenance, and mechanical areas				3,618
Total gross area				42,919

CONSTRUCTION COSTS

The following information is based on actual costs.
Final construction cost as of March 2001
Financing sources: non-taxable bond offering

Building Costs

New construction	$5.7 M
Renovations	$120,000
Total building costs	$5.8 M

Site Costs

Total site costs	$1.1 M

Total Project Costs	$6.9 M

Northpointe

Status of project: Completed August 1999
Owner: Lakeview Retirement Village, Inc.
Architect: Burns & McDonnell
Interior designer: Burns & McDonnell
Structural engineer: Burns & McDonnell
Mechanical engineer: Concept, Burns & McDonnell
Electrical engineer: Concept, Burns & McDonnell
Civil engineer: Burns & McDonnell
Contractor: Rau Construction

PROJECT AREAS

	Units, Beds or Clients	New GSF	Renovated GSF	Total Gross Area	Total on Site or Served by Project
Apartments (units)	96	101,680		101,680	96
Common social areas (people)	12	600		2,400	48
Kitchen (daily meals served)	90	2,700		2,700	90

RESIDENTIAL FACILITIES

Project Element	Apartments		
	No.	Typical Size GSF	Size Range GSF
One-bedroom units	34	760	760–849
Two-bedroom units	52	1,175	1,175–1,264
Three-bedroom and larger units	10	1,385	
Total, all units	96	101,680	101,680
Residents' social areas (lounges, dining, and recreation spaces)			7,300
Medical/health/fitness and activities areas			600
Administrative, public, and ancillary support service areas			15,500
Service, maintenance, and mechanical areas			33,920
Total gross area			159,000

CONSTRUCTION COSTS

The following information is based on actual costs.
Financing sources: conventional (private)

Building Costs

New construction	$15.2 M

Site Costs

Total site costs	$3 M

Total Project Costs	$18.2 M

North Shore Senior Center, Arthur C. Nielsen Jr. Campus

Status of project: Completed September 2000
Facility administrator: Sandi Johnson, Executive Director
Owner: North Shore Senior Center
Architect: OWP&P Architects
Interior designer: OWP&P Architects
Landscape architect: OWP&P Architects
Structural engineer: OWP&P Architects
Mechanical engineer: OWP&P Architects
Electrical engineer: OWP&P Architects
Civil engineer: Gary A. Wiss, Inc.
Contractor: Valenti Builders, Inc.

PROJECT AREAS
Other Facilities

	New Construction		Renovations	
	No.	Size GSF	No.	Size GSF
Continuing education				9,100
Fine arts				2,550
Volunteer				2,440
Wellness				2,080
Social areas (lounges, dining, and recreation spaces)				6,800
Administrative, public, and ancillary support services				7,480
Service, maintenance, and mechanical areas				5,450
Total gross area				40,000

CONSTRUCTION COSTS
The following is based on actual costs.

Building Costs
New construction	$5.5 M
Total building costs	$5.5 M

Site Costs
New	$500,000
Total site costs	$500,000

Total Project Costs — $10 M

Oak Creek

Status of project: Completed March 2001
Facility administrator: Scot Sinclair, Executive Director
Owner: O'Connor Woods
Architect: Hardison Komatsu Ivelich & Tucker
Interior designer: Corporate Interior Services
Landscape architect: Robert La Rocca & Associates
Structural engineer: H.D. Rueb Structural Engineer
Mechanical engineer: Fard Engineers, Inc.
Electrical engineer: Fard Engineers, Inc.
Civil engineer: Sigfried Engineering
Contractor: Huff Construction Co., Inc.

PROJECT AREAS

	Units, Beds or Clients	New GSF
Cottages/villas (units)	14	18,060
Senior living/assisted living/personal care (units)	40	36,860

RESIDENTIAL FACILITIES

	Cottages	
	No.	Typical Size GSF
Two-bedroom units	14	1,290
Total, all units	14	18,060
Total gross area		18,060

ASSISTED LIVING FACILITIES
General Social/Residential Assisted Living Models

	New Construction	
	No. Units	Typical Size GSF
Studio units	10	485
One-bedroom units	30	540
Total, all units	40	21,050
Residents' social areas (lounges, dining, and recreation spaces)		1,595
Medical, health care, therapies, and activities spaces		1,160
Administrative, public, and ancillary support services		11,700
Service, maintenance, and mechanical areas		1,355
Total gross area		36,860

CONSTRUCTION COSTS
The following is based on actual costs.

Building Costs
New construction	$6.88 M
Total building costs	$6.88 M

Total Project Costs — $6.88 M

PATHWAYS CENTER FOR ALZHEIMER'S CARE

Status of project: Completed March 2000
Owner: Ohio Masonic Home
Architect: Maddox NBD Architecture
Interior designer: Maddox NBD Architecture
Landscape architect: Maddox NBD Architecture
Structural engineer: Jezerinac-Geers & Associates
Mechanical engineer: McMullen Engineering Company, Inc.
Electrical engineer: McMullen Engineering Company, Inc.
Civil engineer: Bird & Bull
Contractor: Elford, Inc. (Construction Manager)

PROJECT AREAS

	Units, Beds or Clients	Total Gross Area GSF
Special care for persons with dementia	60	46,900

ASSISTED LIVING FACILITIES
Dementia-Specific Assisted Living Models

	New Construction		Renovations	
	No. Units	Typical Size GSF	No. Units	Typical Size GSF
One-bedroom units	60	275		
Total, all units		16,500		
Residents' social areas (lounges, dining, and recreation spaces)				18,800
Medical, health care, therapies, and activities spaces				4,000
Administrative, public, and ancillary support service				3,800
Service, maintenance, and mechanical areas				3,800
Total gross area				46,900

CONSTRUCTION COSTS
The following information is based on actual costs.

Building Costs
New construction	$5.03 M
Total building costs	$5.03 M

Site Costs
New	$462,750
Total site costs	$462,750

Total Project Costs	$6.87 M

PEABODY MANOR

Status of project: Completed October 2000
Facility administrator: Mary Wisnet
Owner: ThedaCare
Architect: Hoffman Corporation
Structural engineer: Hoffman Corporation
Mechanical engineer: Longberg & Associates
Electrical engineer: Lang Engineering
Civil engineer: Omni Engineers
Contractor: Boldt Construction

PROJECT AREAS

	Units, Beds or Clients	New GSF	Renovated GSF	Total Gross Area GSF
Senior living/assisted living/ personal care (units)	10	2,150		2,150
Skilled nursing care (beds)	48	11,540		11,540
Common social areas (people)		15,368		15,368
Kitchen (daily meals served)	300	2,841	1,525	4,366
Retail space (shops/restaurants etc.)		425		425
Fitness/rehab/wellness (daily visits)		400		
Hospice	10	2,150		2,150

NURSING FACILITIES
Skilled Nursing Facilities

	New Construction		Renovations	
	No. Beds	Typical Room Size GSF	No. Beds	Typical Room Size GSF
Residents in one-bed/single rooms	44	215		
Residents in two-bed/double rooms	4	370		
Total	48	10,940		
Social areas (lounges, dining, and recreation spaces)				15,368
Medical, health care, therapy, and activities spaces				400
Administrative, public, and ancillary support services				6,500
Service, maintenance, and mechanical areas				9,389
Total gross area				51,750

Hospice Care Facilities

	New Construction		Renovations	
	No. Beds	Typical Room Size GSF	No. Beds	Typical Room Size GSF
Residents in one-bed/single rooms	10	215		
Total	10			
Social areas (lounges, dining, and recreation spaces)				539
Medical, health care, therapy, and activity spaces				989
Administrative, public, and ancillary support services				200
Service, maintenance, and mechanical areas				200

CONSTRUCTION COSTS
The following is based on actual costs.

Building Costs
New construction	$7.55 M
Renovations	$200,000
Medical equipment costs	$445,000
Total building costs	$8.2 M

Site Costs
New	$720,000
Total site costs	$720,000

Total Project Costs	$9.4 M

PEABODY RETIREMENT COMMUNITY

Status of project: Completion expected December 2003
Facility administrator: James R. Ransomer
Owner: Peabody Retirement Community
Architect: Reese, Lower, Patrick & Scott, Ltd.
Interior designer: Carson Design Associates
Structural engineer: A.W. Lookup Corporation
Mechanical engineer: Reese Engineering, Inc.
Electrical engineer: Reese Engineering, Inc.
Civil engineer: Engineering Resources, Inc.
Contractor: Weigand Construction Company, Inc.

PROJECT AREAS

Project Element	Units, Beds or Clients	New GSF	Total Gross Area GSF	Total on Site or Served by Project
Special care for persons with dementia	48			48
Skilled nursing care (beds)	144	111,070	111,070	144
Common social areas (people)	250	4,645	4,645	
Kitchen (daily meals served)	1,000	8,500	8,500	
Children's day care (clients)	64	4,100	4,100	
Fitness/rehab/wellness (daily visits)		7,250	7,250	
Pool(s) and related areas (users)		5,230	5,230	
Administration and support		6,800	6,800	

ASSISTED LIVING FACILITIES
Dementia-Specific Assisted Living Models

Project Element	New Construction No. Units	New Construction Typical Size GSF	Renovations Typical Size GSF
Studio units	48	308	
Total, all units	48	308	14,784
Residents' social areas (lounges, dining, and recreation spaces)			3,404
Medical, health care, therapy, and activity spaces			1,887
Administrative, public, and ancillary support services			2,332
Service, maintenance, and mechanical areas			628
Total gross area			36,492

NURSING FACILITIES
Skilled Nursing Facilities

Project Element	New Construction No. Beds	New Construction Typical Room Size GSF	Renovations Typical Room Size GSF
Residents in one-bed/single rooms	108	331	
Residents in two-bed/double rooms	36	370	
Total no. of rooms/residents: Rooms: 126 Beds:	144		42,408
Social areas (lounges, dining, and recreation spaces)			10,188
Medical, health care, therapy, and activity spaces			7,539
Administrative, public, and ancillary support services			11,898
Service, maintenance, and mechanical areas			2,608
Total gross area			111,070

CONSTRUCTION COSTS
The following information is based on the contractor's estimate.
Financing sources: non-taxable bond offering, $45.9 M

Building Costs
New	$36 M
Renovations	$1.2 M
Total Building Costs	$37.2 M

Site Costs
Total site costs	$4.3 M

Total Project Costs	**$41.5 M**

PECONIC LANDING

Status of project: Completion 2002
Facility administrator: Peter McGuckian
Owner: Peconic Landing of Southold, Inc.
Architect: Ewing Cole Cherry Brott
Associate architect: O'Donnell & Naccarato
Associate architect: Barton & Associates, Inc.
Interior designer: Ewing Cole Cherry Brott and Mary Cook & Associates
Landscape architect: Ecoscientific Solutions, LLC
Structural engineer: O'Donnell & Naccarato
Mechanical engineer: Becker and Morgan
Electrical engineer: Becker and Morgan
Civil engineer: Young & Young
Contractor: E & F/Walsh Building Company

PROJECT AREAS

	Units, Beds or Clients	Total Gross Area (GSF)
Apartments (units)	139	162,262
Cottages/villas (units)	111	186,858
Senior living/assisted living/ personal care (units)	26	28,170
Skilled nursing care (beds)	44	28,660
Common social areas (people)	350	15,085
Kitchen (daily meals served)	850	2,885
Fitness/rehab/wellness (daily visits)		5,420
Pool(s) and related areas (users)	75	2,880

RESIDENTIAL FACILITIES

	Cottages No.	Cottages Typical Size GSF	Apartments No.	Apartments Typical Size GSF
One-bedroom units			20	800
One-bedroom + den units			35	1,006
Two-bedroom units	33	1,350	40	1,210
Two-bedroom + den units	32	1,450	26	1,315
Two-bedroom + den deluxe units	46	1,950	10	1,590
Three-bedroom and larger units			8	1,635
Total, all units	111		139	
Residents' social areas (lounges, dining, and recreation spaces)				3,660
Administrative, public, and ancillary support service areas				6,025
Service, maintenance, and mechanical areas				7,180
Total gross area				523,268

ASSISTED LIVING FACILITIES
General Social/Residential Assisted Living Models

	New Construction No. Units	New Construction Typical Size GSF
One-bedroom units	26	620
Total, all units	26	16,165
Residents' social areas (lounges, dining, and recreation spaces)		1,305
Medical, health care, therapies, and activities spaces		1,200
Administrative, public, and ancillary support service spaces		1,650
Service, maintenance, and mechanical areas		110
Total gross area		28,170

NURSING FACILITIES
Skilled Nursing Facilities

	New Construction No. Units	New Construction Typical Size GSF
Residents in one-bed/single rooms	28	280
Residents in two-bed/double rooms	16	480
Total, all units	44	15,520
Social areas (lounges, dining, and recreation spaces)		2,120
Medical, health care, therapies, and activities spaces		3,485
Administrative, public, and ancillary support service areas		810
Service, maintenance, and mechanical areas		110
Total gross area		28,660

continued

OTHER FACILITIES

	New Construction Size GSF
Community center	40,000
Wellness center	3,900
Fitness and aquatic center	4,400
Social areas (lounges, dining, and recreation spaces)	15,085
Administrative, public, and ancillary support services	3,130
Service, maintenance, and mechanical areas	4,570
Total gross area	38,865

CONSTRUCTION COSTS

The following is based on contractor's estimates.

Building Costs

New construction	$59 M
Total building costs	$59 M

Site Costs

New	$5 M
Total site costs	$5 M

Total Project Costs	**$124.5 M**

THE POINTE AT HAMILTON COMMUNITIES

Status of project: Completed February 2000
Facility administrator: Joseph Dzwonar, President
Owner: Hamilton Communities, Inc.
Architect: InterDesign
Interior designer: InterDesign
Structural engineer: Silver Creek Engineering
Mechanical engineer: InterDesign
Electrical engineer: InterDesign
Civil engineer: Palm Associates
Contractor: Verkler, Inc.

PROJECT AREAS

Project Element	Included in this Project				
	Units, Beds or Clients	New GSF	Renovated GSF	Total Gross Area GSF	Total on Site or Served by Project
Apartments (units)					102
Cottages/villas (units)					52
Senior living/assisted living/ personal care (units)	90	35,990			180
Special care for persons with dementia	15	6,590			25
Skilled nursing care (beds)	10	3,855			10
Common social areas (people)	17,645				
Kitchen (daily meals served)	4,600				
Retail space (shops, restaurants, etc.)	725				
Fitness/rehab/wellness (daily visits)	3,565				
Intermediate nursing care (beds)	60	13,190			134

ASSISTED LIVING FACILITIES
General Social/Residential Assisted Living Models

Project Element	New Construction		Renovations	
	No. Units	Typical Size GSF	No. Units	Typical Size GSF
Studio units	57	315		
One-bedroom units	33	515		
Two-bedroom units				
Total, all units	90	34,950		

NURSING FACILITIES
Skilled Nursing Facilities

Project Element	New Construction		Renovations	
	No. Beds	Typical room Size GSF	No. Beds	Typical room Size GSF
Residents in two-bed/ double rooms	10	410		
Total no. of rooms/residents: Rooms: 5 Beds:	10	2,050		
Social areas (lounges, dining, and recreation spaces)				980
Administrative, public, and ancillary support services				370
Service, maintenance, and mechanical areas				170
Total gross area				3,855

Nursing Homes and Intermediate Care Facilities

Project Element	New Construction		Renovations	
	No. Beds	Typical room Size GSF	No. Beds	Typical room Size GSF
Residents in one-bed/single rooms	29	230		
Residents in two-bed/double rooms	46	385		
Residents share multi-bed rooms/wards				
Total no. of rooms/residents: Rooms: 52 Beds:	75	15,525		
Social areas (lounges, dining, and recreation spaces)				7,895
Medical, health care, therapy, and activity spaces				1,670
Administrative, public, and ancillary support services				2,875
Service, maintenance, and mechanical areas				710
Total gross area				16,900

OTHER FACILITIES

Project Element	New Construction		Renovations	
	No.	Size	No.	Size GSF
Social areas (lounges, dining, and recreation spaces)				17,645
Administrative, public, and ancillary support services				36,975
Service, maintenance, and mechanical areas				7,525
Total gross area				125,980

CONSTRUCTION COSTS

The following information is based on actual costs.
Final construction cost as of February 2000
Financing sources: tax-exempt bonds through Health Facilities Council

Building Costs

Total building costs	$11.3 M

Site Costs

Total site costs	$700,000

Total Project Costs	**$12 M**

PROVIDENCE PLACE

Status of project: Completed September 2001
Facility administrator: Retirement Companies of America, LLC,
Charles Trammell, Jr.
Owner: Kirby Pines Retirement Community
Architect: McGehee, Nicholson, Burke Architects
Interior designer: IDA
Structural engineer: Askew Hargraves Harcourt
Mechanical engineer: Shappley Design Consultants, Inc.
Electrical engineer: Liles Engineering Design Consultants
Civil engineer: W.H. Porter & Company
Contractor: S. Webster Haining Company

PROJECT AREAS

ASSISTED LIVING FACILITIES
General Social/Residential Assisted Living Models

Project Element	New Construction		Renovations	
	No. Units	Typical Size GSF	No. Units	Typical Size GSF
Studio units (2 units, 569 GSF)	22	456		
Total, all units	24	11,170		
Residents' social areas (lounges, dining, and recreation spaces)				4,553
Medical, health care, therapy, and activity spaces				486
Administrative, public, and ancillary support services				400
Service, maintenance, and mechanical areas				521
Total gross area				17,121

CONSTRUCTION COSTS
The following information is based on actual costs.
Final construction cost as of September 2001
Financing souces: non-taxable bond offering, Zeigler Securities

Building Costs
New construction	$1.9 M
Medical equipment costs	$20,000
Total building costs	$1.92 M

Site Costs
Total site costs	$280,000

Total Project Costs $3 M

THE REBECCA RESIDENCE

Status of project: Completed August 1999
Facility administrator: Mary Wilson, NHA
Owner: The Rebecca Residence for Women
Architect: Perkins Eastman Architects, PC
Associate architect: WTW Architects
Interior designer: Chester LeMaistre, Inc.
Landscape architect: Pashek Associates
Structural engineer: Structural Engineering Corporation
Mechanical engineer: Elwood S. Tower Corporation
Electrical engineer: Elwood S. Tower Corporation
Civil engineer: Civil & Environmental Consultant
Contractor: BAC Construction, Inc.

PROJECT AREAS

	Units, Beds or Clients	New GSF	Total Gross Area GSF
Senior living/assisted living/ personal care (units)	58	21,750	38,600
Skilled nursing care (beds)	40	14,620	14,620
Common social areas (people)	139	10,825	10,825
Kitchen (daily meals served)	360+	3,000	3,000
Fitness/rehab/wellness (daily visits)	980	980	

ASSISTED LIVING FACILITIES
General Social/Residential Assisted Living Models

	New Construction		Renovations	
	No. Units	Typical Size GSF	No. Units	Typical Size GSF
Studio units	36	240–375		
One-bedroom units	20	200–495		
Two-bedroom units	2	237		
Total, all units	58			
Residents' social areas (lounges, dining, and recreation spaces)				6,910
Medical, health care, therapy, and activity spaces				980
Administrative, public, and ancillary support services (shared with Nursing)				2,250
Service, maintenance, and mechanical areas (shared with Nursing)				9,500

NURSING FACILITIES
Skilled Nursing Facilities

	New Construction		Renovations	
	No. Beds	Typical Room Size GSF	No. Beds	Typical Room Size GSF
Residents in one-bed/single rooms	20	275		
Residents in two-bed/double rooms	40	456		
Total	60			
Social areas (lounges, dining, and recreation spaces)				3,910
Medical, health care, therapy, and activity spaces				700
Administrative, public, and ancillary support services				2,250
Service, maintenance, and mechanical areas				9,500

CONSTRUCTION COSTS
The following is based on actual costs.

Building Costs
New construction	$10.4 M
Total building costs	$10.4 M

Site Costs
Total site costs	$1.1 M

Total Project Costs $14 M

THE RENAISSANCE

Status of project: Completed February 2001
Facility administrator: Sibley Memorial Hospital
Owner: Sibley Memorial Hospital
Architect: Oudens + Knoop Architects, PC
Interior designer: Design Innerphase
Structural engineer: SK&A Consulting Engineers
Mechanical engineer: Hankins & Anderson
Electrical engineer: Hankins & Anderson
Civil engineer: Hankins & Anderson
Contractor: Forrester Construction Company

PROJECT AREAS

Project Element	Included in this Project				
	Units, Beds or Clients	New GSF	Renovated GSF	Total Gross Area GSF	Total on Site or Served by Project
Senior living/assisted living/ personal care (units)					104
Skilled nursing care (beds)	94	103,786		103,786	94
Other					237

NURSING FACILITIES

Skilled Nursing Facilities

Project Element	New Construction		Renovations	
	No. Beds	Typical Room Size GSF	No. Beds	Typical Room Size GSF
Residents in one-bed/single rooms	94	450		
Total no. of rooms/residents:				
Rooms: 94 Beds:	94	42,300		
Social areas (lounges, dining, and recreation spaces)				12,000
Medical, health care, therapy, and activity spaces				23,800
Administrative, public, and ancillary support services				13,900
Service, maintenance, and mechanical areas				10,566
Total gross area				102,566

CONSTRUCTION COSTS

The following information is based on actual costs.
Final construction cost as of February 2001
Financing sources: non-taxable bond offering

Building Costs

New construction	$16.2 M
Medical equipment costs	$202,000
Total building costs	$16.4 M

Site Costs

Total site costs	$1.2 M
Furniture/Fees/Miscellaneous costs	$2 M
Total Project Costs	**$19.6 M**

RIDGEWOOD AT FRIENDSHIP VILLAGE OF COLUMBUS

Status of project: Completed May 2000
Facility administrator: Mick Feauto (Executive Director)
Owner: Friendship Village of Columbus
Architect: Maddox NBD Architecture
Interior designer: Maddox NBD Architecture
Landscape architect: Maddox NBD Architecture
Structural engineer: Jezerinac-Geers & Associates
Mechanical engineer: McMullen Engineering
Electrical engineer: McMullen Engineering
Civil engineer: Pomeroy & Associates
Contractor: Frank Messer Construction (CM)

PROJECT AREAS

	Units, Beds, or Clients	New GSF	Renovated GSF	Total Gross Area GSF
Senior living/assisted living/ personal care (units)	49	39,043		39,043
Special care for persons with dementia (10 units/14 clients)	10	9,841		9,841
Kitchen (daily meals served)	2,219	2,277		4,496
Retail space (shops, restaurants, etc.)	3,910			3,910
Fitness/rehab/wellness (daily visits)	1,651			1,651

ASSISTED LIVING FACILITIES

General Social/Residential Assisted Living Models

	New Construction	
	No. Units	Typical Size GSF
Studio units	43	329
One-bedroom units	6	595
Total, all units	49	17,254
Residents' social areas (lounges, dining, and recreation spaces)		29,888
Medical, health care, therapies, and activities spaces		3,159
Administrative, public, and ancillary support service areas		3,265
Service, maintenance, and mechanical areas		11,191
Total gross area		64,757

Dementia-Specific Assisted Living Models

	New Construction	
	No. Units	Typical Size GSF
Studio units	6	300
One-bedroom units	4	425
Total, all units	10	3,500
Residents' social areas (lounges, dining, and recreation spaces)		5,900
Administrative, public, and ancillary support service areas		441
Total gross area		9,841

CONSTRUCTION COSTS

The following is based on actual costs.

Building Costs

Total building costs	$8.2 M

Site Costs

Total site costs	$0.27 M
Total Project Costs	**$11.9 M**

RIVER TERRACE ESTATES

Status of project: Completion expected in 2003
Facility administrator: Warren Satelite
Owner: Caylor Nickel Medical Center
Architect: Collins Gordon Bostwick Architects
Structural engineer: Peller & Associates
Mechanical engineer: Bacik Karpinski & Associates
Electrical engineer: Bacik Karpinski & Associates
Contractor: James S. Jackson Co., Inc.

PROJECT AREAS

	Units, Beds or Clients	Total Gross Area GSF
Cottages/villas (units)	12	12,000
Senior living/assisted living/ personal care (units)	58	23,490
Skilled nursing care (beds)	30	5,540
Common social areas (people)		15,000
Kitchen (daily meals served)		1,788

RESIDENTIAL FACILITIES

	Cottages		Apartments	
	No. Units	Typical Size GSF	No. Units	Typical Size GSF
One-bedroom units			14	
Two-bedroom units	12	1,000	30	
Total, all units	12		44	37,225
Residents' social areas (lounges, dining, and recreation spaces)				3,150
Administrative, public, and ancillary support service areas				890
Service, maintenance, and mechanical areas				3,427
Total gross area				66,065

ASSISTED LIVING FACILITIES
Medical Assisted Living Models

	New Construction		Renovations	
	No. Units	Typical Size GSF	No. Units	Typical Size GSF
Shared/double units	29	425		
Single occupancy units	29	385		
Total, all units	58	23,490		
Social areas (lounges, dining, and recreation spaces)				3,373
Administrative, public, and ancillary support services				680
Service, maintenance, and mechanical areas				774
Total gross area				36,030

Nursing Homes and Intermediate Care Facilities

	New Construction		Renovations	
	No. Beds	Typical Room Size GSF	No. Beds	Typical Room Size GSF
Residents in one-bed/single rooms	8	280		
Residents in two-bed/double rooms	22	150		
Total	30	5,540		
Social areas (lounges, dining, and recreation spaces)				1,428
Medical, health care, therapies, and activities spaces				404
Administrative, public, and ancillary support services				865
Service, maintenance, and mechanical areas				1,620
Total gross area				12,223

CONSTRUCTION COSTS
The following is based on contractor's estimates.

Building Costs

Total building costs	$10.69 M

Site Costs

Total site costs	$900,000

Total Project Costs | $11.59 M

THE SUMMIT AT FIRST HILL

Status of project: Completed April 2001
Facility administrator: Dov Sugarman
Owner: Kline Galland Center
Architect: Mithun
Interior designer: Mithun
Landscape architect: John M. Bernhard, ASLA
Structural engineer: Skilling Ward Magnusson Barkshire
Mechanical engineer: McKinstry Co.
Electrical engineer: Travis Fitzmaurice and Associates
Civil engineer: Coughlin Porter Lundeen
Contractor: Sellen Construction

PROJECT AREAS

	Units, Beds or Clients	Total Gross Area GSF
Apartments (units)	102	83,088
Senior living/assisted living/ personal care (units)	10	4,815
Special care for persons with dementia	13	5,716
Skilled nursing care (beds)		485
Common social areas (people)		14,489
Kitchen (daily meals served)		2,084
Fitness/rehab/wellness (daily visits)		2,757
Mechanical and service space		6,934
Administrative, public, and ancillary support		3,179

RESIDENTIAL FACILITIES

	Cottages		Apartments	
	No. Units	Typical Size GSF	No. Units	Typical Size GSF
Studio units			2	607
One-bedroom units			56	677
Two-bedroom units			42	978
Two-bedroom + den units			2	1,448
Total, all units			102	83,088
Residents' social areas (lounges, dining, and recreation spaces)				7,528
Medical/health/fitness and activity areas				3,899
Administrative, public, and ancillary support service areas				2,224
Service, maintenance, and mechanical areas				4,999
Total gross area				101,738

ASSISTED LIVING FACILITIES
General Social/Residential Assisted Living Models

	New Construction		Renovations	
	No. Units	Typical Size GSF	No. Units	Typical Size GSF
Studio units	6	423		
One-bedroom units	4	568		
Total, all units	10	4,815		
Residents' social areas (lounges, dining, and recreation spaces)				971
Medical, health care, therapies, and activities spaces				935
Administrative, public, and ancillary support service areas				57
Service, maintenance, and mechanical areas				1,014
Total gross area				7,792

Dementia-specific assisted living models

	New Construction		Renovations	
	No. Units	Typical Size GSF	No. Units	Typical Size GSF
Studio units	12	423		
One-bedroom units	1	642		
Total, all units	13	5,716		
Residents' social areas (lounges, dining, and recreation spaces)				1,265
Medical, health care, therapies, and activities spaces				326
Administrative, public, and ancillary support service areas				57
Service, maintenance, and mechanical areas				904
Total gross area				8,268

CONSTRUCTION COSTS

Building Costs

New construction	$25.26 M
Total building costs	$25.26 M

Total Project Costs | $25.26 M

SUMNER ON RIDGEWOOD

Status of project: Completed September 2003
Facility administrator: Ted Pappas, CEO
Owner: Sumner on Merriman
Architect: Dorsky Hodgson + Partners
Interior designer: Dorsky Hodgson + Partners
Structural engineer: Hach & Ebersole
Mechanical engineer: Scheeser, Buckley, Mayfield, Inc.
Electrical engineer: Scheeser, Buckley, Mayfield, Inc.
Civil engineer: GBC Design, Inc.
Contractor: The Weitz Company

PROJECT AREAS

Project Element	Units, Beds or Clients	New GSF	Renovated GSF	Total Gross Area GSF	Total on Site or Served by Project
Apartments (units)	79	105,680		105,680	79
Cottages/villas (units)	22	42,167		42,167	22
Senior living/assisted living/ personal care (units)	40	38,202		38,202	40
Skilled nursing care (beds)	48	43,862		43,862	48
Common social areas (people)		28,899		28,899	
Kitchen (daily meals served)		3,132		3,132	
Retail space (shops, restaurants, etc.)	2	1,352		1,352	2
Fitness/rehab/wellness (daily visits)		478		478	
Pool(s) and related areas (users)	all	7,172		7,172	all

RESIDENTIAL FACILITIES

Project Element	No.	Cottages Typical Size GSF	Cottages Size Range GSF	No.	Apartments Typical Size GSF	Apartments Size Range GSF
One-bedroom units				12	800	
One-bedroom + den				19	1,026	
Two-bedroom units	22	1,816	1,756–1,887	21	1,167	1,167–1,500
Two-bedroom + den units				27	1,453	
Total, all units		42,167			94,945	
Residents' social areas (lounges, dining, and recreation spaces)					4,739	
Service, maintenance, and mechanical areas					5,996	
Total gross area					105,680	

ASSISTED LIVING FACILITIES
General Social/Residential Assisted Living Models

Project Element (In Two Buildings)	New Construction No. Units	New Construction Typical Size GSF	Renovations No. Units	Renovations Typical Size GSF
Studio units	24	526		
One-bedroom units	8	557		
Total, all units	40	21,328		
Residents' social areas (lounges, dining, and recreation spaces)				7,428
Medical, health care, therapy, and activity spaces				1,904
Administrative, public, and ancillary support services				2,242
Service, maintenance, and mechanical areas				1,562
Total gross area				34,464

Dementia-Specific Assisted Living Models

Project Element	New Construction No. Units	New Construction Typical Size GSF	Renovations No. Units	Renovations Typical Size GSF
Studio units	24	518		
Total, all units	24	12,432		
Residents' social areas (lounges, dining, and recreation spaces)				3,412
Medical, health care, therapy, and activity spaces				3,167
Administrative, public, and ancillary support services				1,570
Service, maintenance, and mechanical areas				843
Total gross area				21,424

NURSING FACILITIES
Skilled Nursing Facilities

Project Element	New Construction No. Units	New Construction Typical Room Size GSF	Renovations No. Units	Renovations Typical Room Size GSF
Residents in one-bed/single rooms	20	528		
Residents in two-bed/double rooms	4	711		
Total no. of rooms/residents: Rooms: 22 Beds:	24	11,574		
Social areas (lounges, dining, and recreation spaces)				4,523
Medical, health care, therapy, and activity spaces				3,455
Administrative, public, and ancillary support services				517
Service, maintenance, and mechanical areas				691
Total gross area				20,760

OTHER FACILITIES

Project Element Community Building	New Construction No.	New Construction Size GSF	Renovations No.	Renovations Size GSF
Wellness/pool/clinic		7,415		
Guest suite		564		
Laundry/kitchen/housekeeping		6,699		
Social areas (lounges, dining, and recreation spaces)				20,816
Administrative, public, and ancillary support services				2,614
Service, maintenance, and mechanical areas				2,925
Total gross area				41,033

CONSTRUCTION COSTS
The following information is based on contractor's estimate, April 2001.
Financing sources: non-taxable bond offering, Herbert J. Sims and Company

Building Costs

New construction	$27 M
Medical equipment costs	$250,000
Total building costs	$27.25 M

Site Costs

Total site costs	$3.9 M

Total Project Costs	$42 M

Sunrise Assisted Living (Pacific Palisades)

Status of project: Completed June 2001
Facility administrator: Geraland Lester, Executive Director
Owner: Sunrise Assisted Living
Architect: Hill Partnership Inc.
Interior designer: Martha Childs Interiors
Landscape architect: Ivy Landscape Architects, Inc.
Structural engineer: Myers Houghton Partners, Inc.
Mechanical engineer: F.T. Andrews, Inc.
Electrical engineer: DGM & Associates
Civil engineer: Wagner Halladay, Inc.
Contractor: Suffolk Construction Company, Inc.

PROJECT AREAS

	Units, Beds or Clients	Total Gross Area*
Apartments (units)	25	14,500
Special care for persons with dementia	15	8,700
Common social areas (people)		2,550
Kitchen (daily meals served)		1,000
Fitness/rehab/wellness (daily visits)		250
Roof terrace (number of people)	36	720

* includes general circulation

ASSISTED LIVING FACILITIES
General Social/Residential Assisted Living Models

	New Construction		
	No. Units	Typical Size GSF	Total Size GSF
Studio units	24	305	7,320
One-bedroom units	11	440	4,840
Two-bedroom units	5	552	2,760
Total, all units	40		14,920
Residents' social areas (lounges, dining, and recreation spaces)			2,600
Medical, health care, therapy, and activity spaces			250
Administrative, public, and ancillary support spaces			900
Service, maintenance, and mechanical areas			1,230
Total gross area (excluding garage)			27,000

Sunrise Assisted Living at Fair Oaks

Status of project: Completed January 2001
Facility administrator: Jim Harris
Owner: Inova Health System
Architect: Wilmot/Sanz, Inc.
Interior designer: Martha Child Interiors
Structural engineer: Ehlert/Bryan
Mechanical engineer: RMF Engineering, Inc.
Electrical engineer: RMF Engineering, Inc.
Civil engineer: Dewberry & Davis
Contractor: Glen Construction Company

PROJECT AREAS

Project Element	Included in this Project		
	Units, Beds or Clients	New GSF	Total Gross Area GSF
Senior living/assisted living/ personal care (units)	72 Beds	30,456	30,456
Continuing care retirement communities	88 Beds		
Special care for persons with dementia	20 Units 24 Beds	6,473	6,473
Common social areas (people)	112	11,608	11,608
Kitchen (daily meals served)	3/day	1,150	1,150
Fitness/rehab/wellness (daily visits)	1,095	1,095	

ASSISTED LIVING FACILITIES
General Social/Residential Assisted Living Models

Project Element	New Construction		Renovations
	No. Units	Typical Size GSF	Typical Size GSF
Studio units	29	335	
Two-bedroom units	31	505	
Total, all units	60	424	
Residents' social areas (lounges, dining, and recreation spaces)			3,675
Medical, health care, therapy, and activity spaces			1,095
Administrative, public, and ancillary support services			2,965
Service, maintenance, and mechanical areas			3,300
Total gross area			51,930

Dementia-Specific Assisted Living Models

Project Element	New Construction		Renovations
	No. Units	Typical Size GSF	Typical Size GSF
Studio units	16	285	
Two-bedroom units	4	485	
Total, all units	20	325	
Residents' social areas (lounges, dining, and recreation spaces)			2,015
Administrative, public, and ancillary support services			655
Service, maintenance, and mechanical areas			135
Total gross area			12,550

Medical Assisted Living Models

Project Element	New Construction		Renovations
	No. Units	Typical Size GSF	Typical Size GSF
Shared/double units	7	505	
Single-occupancy units	5	335	
Total, all units	12	424	
Residents' social areas (lounges, dining, and recreation spaces)			720
Administrative, public, and ancillary support services			350
Service, maintenance, and mechanical areas			150
Total gross area			8,515

CONSTRUCTION COSTS

The following information is based on actual costs.
Final construction cost as of January 2001
Financing sources: conventional (private) corporation financed

Building Costs
Total building costs $8.1 M

Site Costs
Total site costs $1.45 M

Total Project Costs $9.55 M

SUNRISE OF SAN MATEO

Status of project: Completed
Facility administrator: Joseph Sarto
Owner: Sunrise Assisted Living
Architect: Mithun, Inc., Seattle
Interior designer: Mithun, Inc.
Structural engineer: KPFF Consulting Engineers
Mechanical engineer: Interface Engineering Inc.
Electrical engineer: Interface Engineering Inc.
Civil engineer: Brian Kangus Faulk
Contractor: Suffolk Construction Co.

PROJECT AREAS

	New GSF
Senior living/assisted living/personal care (units)	18,295
Special care for persons with dementia	6,728
Common social areas	5,835
Kitchen	1,065

ASSISTED LIVING FACILITIES
General Social/Residential Assisted Living Models

	New construction	
	No.	Typical Size GSF
Studio units	40	300
Two-bedroom units	6	335
Total, all units	46	18,295
Residents' social areas (lounges, dining, and recreation spaces)		4,491
Medical, health care, therapies, and activities spaces		420
Administrative, public, and ancillary support services		1,075
Service, maintenance, and mechanical areas		1,449
Total gross area		7,435

Dementia-Specific Assisted Living Models

	New construction	
	No.	Typical Size GSF
Studio units	16	300
Two-bedroom units	2	3,535
Total, all units	18	6,728
Residents' social areas (lounges, dining, and recreation spaces)		1,344
Medical, health care, therapy, and activity spaces		114
Administrative, public, and ancillary support services		376
Service, maintenance, and mechanical areas		186
Total gross area		1,834

CONSTRUCTION COSTS

Building costs
Total building costs	$7.8 M

Site Costs
Total site costs	$1.2 M

Total Project Costs	$9.77 M

VERNON WOODS RETIREMENT COMMUNITY

Status of project: Completed September 2000
Facility administrator: Susan Burdick
Owner: West Georgia Health System, Inc.
Architect: Perkins & Will
Interior designer: Perkins & Will
Landscape architect: LaGrange Landscape
Structural engineer: Browder + LeGuizamon and Assoc., Inc.
Mechanical engineer: Collaborative Design Group, Ltd.
Electrical engineer: Collaborative Design Group, Ltd.
Civil engineer: Stothard Engineering
Contractor: Batson Cook Company

PROJECT AREAS

	Units, Beds or Clients	Total Gross Area
Senior living/assisted living/personal care (units)—independent living	50+	84,872
Assisted living (units)	42	
Common social areas (people)	100	17,161
Kitchen (daily meals served)	300	2,600
Fitness/rehab/wellness (daily visits)	60	2,919

RESIDENTIAL FACILITIES

	Apartments	
	No.	Typical Size GSF
One-bedroom units	42	805
Two-bedroom units	4	1,125
Two-bedroom + den units	4	1,000
Total, all units	50	53,251
Residents' social areas (lounges, dining, and recreation spaces)		11,096
Medical/health/fitness and activity areas		1,710
Administrative, public, and ancillary support service areas		2,091
Service, maintenance, and mechanical areas		8,944
Total gross area		77,092

ASSISTED LIVING FACILITIES
General Social/Residential Assisted Living Models

	New Construction		Renovations	
	No. Units	Typical Size GSF	No. Units	Typical Size GSF
Studio units	4	515		
One-bedroom units	38	655		
Total, all units	42	31,621		
Residents' social areas (lounges, dining, and recreation spaces)	6,065			
Medical, health care, therapy, and activity spaces	1,209			
Administrative, public, and ancillary support services	1,488			
Service, maintenance, and mechanical areas	2,603			
Total gross area	42,986			

CONSTRUCTION COSTS
The following is based on actual costs.

Building Costs
New construction	$11.26 M
Equipment costs	$141,500
Total building costs	$11.4 M

Site Costs
New	$2.74 M
Total site costs	$2.74 M

Total Project Costs	$14.14 M

THE VILLAGE AT ROBINWOOD

Status of project: Completed June 2001
Facility administrator: Garrett Falcone
Owner: Tressler Lutheran Services
Architect: Cochran, Stephenson & Donkervoet, Inc.
Interior designer: Cochran, Stephenson & Donkervoet, Inc.
Structural engineer: Faisant Associates
Mechanical engineer: SRBR, Inc.
Electrical engineer: SRBR, Inc.
Civil engineer: Frederick Seibert Associates
Contractor: Brechbill & Helman Construction Co.

PROJECT AREAS

	Units, Beds, or Clients	New GSF	Renovated GSF	Total Gross Area GSF	Served by Project
Cottages/villas (units)					70
Senior living/assisted living/ personal care (units)	58	31,780		31,780	58
Special care for persons with dementia	12	4,540		4,540	12
Common social areas (people)	168	12,125		12,125	168
Kitchen (daily meals served)	280	2,640		2,640	280
Pool(s) and related areas (users)	160	4,595		4,595	160

ASSISTED LIVING FACILITIES
General Social/Residential Assisted Living Models

	No. Units	Typical Size GSF	No. Units	Typical Size GSF
Studio units		360 & 380		
One-bedroom units	16	500		
Total, all units	58	31,780		
Residents' social areas (lounges, dining, and recreation spaces)				6,323
Administrative, public, and ancillary support services				2,625
Service, maintenance, and mechanical areas				8,684
Total gross area				57,590

Dementia-Specific Assisted Living Models

Project Element	New Construction		Renovations	
	No. Units	Typical Size GSF	No. Units	Typical Size GSF
Studio units	12	260/300 net		
Two-bedroom units		4,540		
Total, all units	12			
Residents' social areas (lounges, dining, and recreation spaces)				920
Medical, health care, therapy, and activity spaces				920
Service, maintenance, and mechanical areas				7,380

OTHER FACILITIES

Project Element	New Construction		Renovations	
	No.	Size GSF	No.	Size GSF
Community center for cottages		10,395		
Service, maintenance, and mechanical areas				4,400
Total gross area				10,395

CONSTRUCTION COSTS
The following information is based on actual costs.

Building Costs
Total building costs	$9.6 M

Site Costs
Total site costs	$1.4 M

Total Project Costs | $11 M

VILLAGE SHALOM

Status of project: Completed June 2000
Facility administrator: Daniel Ruth
Owner: Village Shalom, Inc.
Architect: Nelson-Tremain Partnership
Interior designer: Tranin Design, Inc.
Landscape architect: Ochsner, Hare & Hare
Structural engineer: Kerr Conrad Graham Associates
Mechanical engineer: Henthorn, Sandmeyer & Company
Electrical engineer: Henthorn, Sandmeyer & Company
Civil engineer: Kerr Conrad Graham Associates
Contractor: Turner Construction

PROJECT AREAS

	Units, Beds, or Clients	Total Area GSF
Cottages/villas (units)	64	
Senior living/assisted living/ personal care (units)	54	46,000
Special care for persons with dementia	24	30,800
Skilled nursing care (beds)	64	26,000
Kitchen (daily meals served)	500	3,650
Elder day care (clients)	38	4,680
Retail space (shops, restaurants, etc.)	4	3,500
Fitness/rehab/wellness (daily visits)	50	1,700
Pool(s) and related areas (users)	2	2,860

RESIDENTIAL FACILITIES

	Cottages	
	No. Units	Typical Size GSF
Two-bedroom units	64	1,675

ASSISTED LIVING FACILITIES
General Social/Residential Assisted Living Models

	New Construction	
	No. Units	Typical Size GSF
Studio units	3	350
One-bedroom units	48	500
Two-bedroom units	3	1,000
Total, all units	54	28,050

Dementia-Specific Assisted Living Models

	New Construction	
	No. Units	Typical Size GSF
Studio units	36	250
Total, all units	36	9,000
Residents' social areas (lounges, dining, and recreation spaces)		4,200
Administrative, public, and ancillary support services		2,700
Service, maintenance, and mechanical areas		300
Total gross area		23,800

NURSING FACILITIES
Skilled Nursing Facilities

	New Construction	
	No. Beds	Typical Room Size GSF
Residents in one-bed/single rooms	56	250
Residents in two-bed/double rooms	8	450
Total	64	14,600
Social areas (lounges, dining, and recreation spaces)		3,700
Administrative, public, and ancillary support services		3,700
Service, maintenance, and mechanical areas		200
Total gross area		24,775

continued

OTHER FACILITIES

	New Construction	
	No.	Size GSF
ElderSpa fitness center	1	4,500
Adult day care, frail	1	2,400
Adult day care, dementia	1	2,200
Art gallery	1	1,500
Respite room	1	350
Synagogue	1	600
Social hall	1	2,500
Bistro	1	2,200
Children's play room	1	300
Store	1	450
Physical therapy	1	1,900
Clinic	1	1,000
Total gross area		19,900

CONSTRUCTION COSTS

The following is based on actual costs.

Building Costs

New construction	$21.9 M
Medical equipment costs	$2.2 M
Total building costs	$24.1 M

Site Costs

New	$1.8 M
Total site costs	$1.8 M
Total Project Costs	**$25.9 M**

WELLNESS CENTER/TWIN TOWERS

Status of project: Completed August 2001
Facility administrator: Monica Smith
Owner: Twin Towers
Architect: PDT Architects
Interior designer: PDT Interiors Group
Structural engineer: Truman P. Young & Associates
Mechanical engineer: KLH
Electrical engineer: KLH
Civil engineer: Thomas Graham Associates
Contractor: Frucon Construction

PROJECT AREAS

Wellness Center

	New Construction		Renovations	
	No.	Size GSF	No.	Size GSF
Therapy room	1	188		
Multipurpose room	1	1,088		
Fitness room	1	1,400		
Pool	1	4,850		
Whirlpool	1	280		
Locker rooms/changing rooms	2	1,288		
Administrative, public, and ancillary support services				800
Service, maintenance, and mechanical areas				365
Total gross area				11,000

CONSTRUCTION COSTS

The following is based on actual costs.

Building Costs

Total building costs	$1.9 M

Site Costs

Total site costs	$40,000
Total Project Costs	**$1.94 M**

WESTMINSTER-CANTERBURY OF THE BLUE RIDGE, CATERED LIVING BUILDING

Status of project: Completed July 2000
Facility administrator: C. Henry Hinnant, III, President/CEO
Owner: Westminster-Canterbury of the Blue Ridge
Architect: SFCS Inc.
Interior designer: SFCS Inc.
Landscape architect: Van Yahres Associates
Structural engineer: SFCS Inc.
Mechanical engineer: SFCS Inc.
Electrical engineer: SFCS Inc.
Civil engineer: Gloeckner Engineering/Surveying
Contractor: R.E. Lee & Son, Inc.

PROJECT AREAS

	Units, Beds or Clients	New GSF	Renovated GSF	Total Gross Area GSF
Senior Living/Assisted Living/ Personal Care (units)	45	44,809	288	45,097

ASSISTED LIVING FACILITIES
General Social/Residential Assisted Living Models

	New Construction	
	No. Units	Typical Size GSF
Studio Units	21	346
One-Bedroom Units	18	448
	6	466
Total, All Units	45	18,126

CONSTRUCTION COSTS
The following is based on actual costs.

Building Costs

New construction	$6.01 M
Medical equipment costs	$24,000
Total building costs	$6.03 M

Site Costs

New	$409,632
Total site costs	$409,632
Total Project Costs	**$7.15 M**

WESTMINSTER TOWERS

Status of project: Completed August 2001
Facility administrator: Elaine Guyton
Owner: Westminster Towers, Inc.
Architect: FreemanWhite Senior Living
Design consultant: Nelson Tremain Partnership
Interior designer: GMK Associates
Structural engineer: Coggin Carrara
Mechanical engineer: FreemanWhite, Inc.
Electrical engineer: FreemanWhite, Inc.
Civil engineer: Burton Engineering Associates
Contractor: RW Allen

PROJECT AREAS

Project Element	Included in this Project				
	Units, Beds or Clients	New GSF	Renovated GSF	Total Gross Area GSF	Total on Site or Served by Project
Skilled nursing care (beds)	66			16,440	
Common social areas (people)	66			6,125	
Kitchen (daily meals served)	180				
Fitness/rehab/wellness (daily visits)	25				

NURSING FACILITIES
Skilled Nursing Facilities

Project Element	New Construction		Renovations	
	No. Beds	Typical Room Size GSF	No. Beds	Typical Room Size GSF
Residents in one-bed/single rooms	30	275		
Residents in two-bed/double rooms	36	455		
Total no. of rooms/residents: Beds:	66	16,440		
Social areas (lounges, dining, and recreation spaces)				6,125
Medical, health care, therapy, and activity spaces				5,802
Administrative, public, and ancillary support services				2,070
Service, maintenance, and mechanical areas				8,130
Total gross area				50,340

CONSTRUCTION COSTS
The following information is based on actual costs.
Final construction cost as of August 2001
Financing sources: non-taxable bond offering, Ziegler Securities

Building Costs

New construction	$5.85 M
Medical equipment costs	$200,000
Total building costs	$6.05 M

Site Costs

Total site costs	$452,000
Total Project Costs	**$6.5 M**

WESTMINSTER VILLAGE, ADDITION

Status of project: Completed April 2000
Facility administrator: Robert Kratz
Owner: Presbyterian Homes Inc.
Architect: Becker Morgan Group, Inc.
Interior designer: Becker Morgan Group, Inc.
Landscape architect: Landscape Architectural Services
Structural engineer: Baker, Ingram & Associates, Inc.
Mechanical engineer: Carew Associates, Inc.
Electrical engineer: Carew Associates, Inc.
Civil engineer: Becker Morgan Group, Inc.
Contractor: Wohlsen Dashiell, Inc.

PROJECT AREAS

	Units, Beds or Clients	Total Gross Area GSF
Senior living/assisted living/ personal care (units)	42	19,800
Special care for persons with dementia	17	6,600
Common social areas (people)	100	6,000
Kitchen (daily meals served)	180	900
Retail space (shops, restaurants, etc.)	1	150

ASSISTED LIVING FACILITIES
General Social/Residential Assisted Living Models

	New Construction		Renovations	
	No. Units	Typical Size GSF	No. Units	Typical Size GSF
Studio units	6	375		
One-bedroom units	30	475		
Two-bedroom units	6	575		
Total all units	42	19,800		
Residents' social areas (lounges, dining, and recreation spaces)			5,000	
Medical, health care, therapy, and activity spaces			1,160	
Administrative, public, and ancillary support services			6,800	
Service, maintenance, and mechanical areas			3,000	
Total gross area			35,760	

Dementia-Specific Assisted Living Models

	New Construction		Renovations	
	No. Units	Typical Size GSF	No. Units	Typical Size GSF
Studio units	13	300		
One-bedroom units	4	425		
Total, all units	17	6,600		
Residents' social areas (lounges, dining, and recreation spaces)			1,000	
Medical, health care, therapy, and activity spaces			300	
Administrative, public, and ancillary support services			1,800	
Service, maintenance, and mechanical areas			300	
Total gross area			10,000	

CONSTRUCTION COSTS
The following is based on actual costs.

Building Costs

New construction	$4.37 M
Total building costs	$4.37 M

Site Costs

New	$300,000
Renovation	$200,000
Total site costs	$500,000

Total Project Costs	**$4.87 M**

WILLIAM BREMAN JEWISH HOME

Status of project: Completed July 2000
Facility administrator: Deborah Beards, Executive Director (during design and construction) Steve Gold, Executive Director (current)
Owner: The William Breman Jewish Home
Architect: Stevens & Wilkinson of Georgia, Inc.
Interior designer: Arthur Shuster, Inc.
Structural engineer: Stevens & Wilkinson of Georgia, Inc.
Mechanical engineer: Stevens & Wilkinson of Georgia, Inc.
Electrical engineer: Stevens & Wilkinson of Georgia, Inc.
Civil engineer: LRE Engineering
Contractor: Batson-Cook Company

PROJECT AREAS

	Units, Beds or Clients	New GSF	Renovated GSF	Total Gross Area GSF
Senior living/assisted living/ personal care (units)	60		45,324	45,324
Skilled nursing care (beds)	96	23,880		23,880
Common social areas (people)	400	22,116	15,815	37,931
Kitchen (daily meals served)	500	6,359		6,359
Retail space (shops, restaurants, etc.)	4	622		622
Fitness/rehab/wellness (daily visits)	25	12,070		12,070
Administrative		6,518	3,833	10,351

ASSISTED LIVING FACILITIES
General Social/Residential Assisted Living Models

	New Construction		Renovations	
	No. Units	Typical Size GSF	No. Units	Typical Size GSF
Studio units			24	597
One-bedroom units			36	861
Total, all units			60	45,324
Residents' social areas (lounges, dining, and recreation spaces)			15,815	
Administrative, public, and ancillary support services			3,833	
Service, maintenance, and mechanical areas			25,170	
Total gross area			90,142	

NURSING FACILITIES
Skilled Nursing Facilities

	New Construction		Renovations	
	No. Beds	Typical Room Size GSF	No. Beds	Typical Room Size GSF
Residents in one-bed/single rooms	48	260		
Residents in two-bed/double rooms	48	475		
Total	96	23,880		
Social areas (lounges, dining, and recreation spaces)			29,097	
Medical, health care, therapy, and activity spaces			12,070	
Administrative, public, and ancillary support services			6,518	
Service, maintenance, and mechanical areas			7,155	
Total gross area			78,720	

CONSTRUCTION COSTS
The following is based on actual costs.

Building Costs

New construction	$9.9 M
Renovations	$6.4 M
Medical equipment and furnishings costs	$1.25 M
Total building costs	$17.6 M

Site Costs

Total site costs	$540,173

Total Project Costs	**$18.1 M**

THE WINDROWS AT PRINCETON,
FORRESTAL APARTMENT BUILDING

Status of project: Completed August 2000
Facility administrator: Christine Dwyer
Owner: Windrows at Princeton Forrestal, Inc.
Architect: Wilmot/Sanz, Inc.
Interior designer: Louis Tyler Creative Services
Structural engineer: Cagley & Associates
Mechanical engineer: Schlenger/Pitz Associates, Inc.
Electrical engineer: Schlenger/Pitz Associates, Inc.
Civil engineer: Van-Note Harvey Associates
Contractor: Suffolk Construction Co.

PROJECT AREAS

Project Element	Units, Beds or Clients	New GSF	Renovated GSF	Total Gross Area GSF	Total on Site or Served by Project
Apartments (units)	192	217,000			217,000
Cottages/villas (units)	102	230,662			230,662
Senior living/assisted living/ personal care (units)	86	62,470			62,470
Skilled nursing care (beds)	190	105,870			105,870
Common social areas (people)	800	13,355		13,355	13,355
Kitchen (daily meals served)	1/day/ resident	2,700		2,700	2,700
Retail space (shops/restaurants, etc.)		800		800	800
Fitness/rehab/wellness (daily visits)		870		870	870
Pool(s) and related areas (users)		1,600		1,600	1,600

RESIDENTIAL FACILITIES

Project Element	Cottages No.	Cottages Typical Size GSF	Cottages Size Range GSF	Apartments No.	Apartments Typical Size GSF	Apartments Size Range GSF
Studio units				15	620	620–880
One-bedroom units				96	840	790–1,200
Two-bedroom units				35	1,210	1,210–1,295
Two-bedroom + den units				46	1,450	1,415–1,575
Total, all units				192	209,500	
Residents' social areas (lounges, dining, and spaces)					13,355	
Medical/health/fitness and activities areas					870	
Service, maintenance, and mechanical areas					118,845	
Total gross area					342,780	

OTHER FACILITIES

Project Element	New Construction No.	New Construction Size GSF	Renovations No.	Renovations Size GSF
Community Center	1	42,000		
Social areas (lounges, dining, and recreation spaces)				17,000
Administrative, public, and ancillary support services (serves community)				15,000
Service, maintenance, and mechanical areas (serves apartment building)				10,000
Total gross area				42,000

CONSTRUCTION COSTS

The following information is based on actual costs.
Final construction cost as of August 2000
Financing sources: conventional (private) corporation financed

Building Costs
Total building costs $48.6 M

Site Costs
Total site costs $7 M

Total Project Costs $55.6 M

WOON EN ZORG H. HART

Status of project: Completed July 2001 (phase 1)
Facility administrator: Wino Baecklandt, General Manager
Owner: V.Z.W. Woon en Zorg H. Hart
Architect: Van Kerckhove B.V.B.A
Interior designer: Van Kerckhove B.V.B.A.
Structural engineer: Studium N.V.
Mechanical engineer: Van Kerckhove B.V.B.A.
Electrical engineer: Van Kerckhove B.V.B.A.
Civil engineer: Studium N.V.
Contractor: N.V. Cordeel

PROJECT AREAS

Project Element	Units, Beds or Clients	New GSF	Renovated GSF	Total Gross Area GSF	Total on Site or Served by Project
Apartments (units)	90				
Special care for persons with dementia	50				
Skilled nursing care (beds)	155				
Kitchen (daily meals served)	250				
Elder day care (clients)	30				
Elder outreach (clients)	50				
Children's day care (clients)	91				
Fitness/rehab/wellness (daily visits)	50				
Children's night care (children's hotel)	23				

ASSISTED LIVING FACILITIES
Dementia-Specific Assisted Living Models

Project Element	New Construction No. Units	New Construction Typical Size GSF	Renovations No. Units	Renovations Typical Size GSF
One-bedroom units	50	20m²		
Total, all units	50	1,000m²		
Residents' social areas (lounges, dining, and recreation spaces)				738m²
Medical, health care, therapy, and activity spaces				338m²
Administrative, public, and ancillary support services				1,079m²
Service, maintenance, and mechanical areas				431m²
Total gross area				3,944m²

NURSING FACILITIES
Nursing Homes and Intermediate Care Facilities

Project Element	New Construction No. Beds	New Construction Typical Room Size GSF	Renovations No. Beds	Renovations Typical Room Size GSF
Residents in one-bed/single rooms	105	20m²		
Total no. of rooms/residents: Rooms: Beds:		2,100m²		
Social areas (lounges, dining, and recreation spaces)				1,550m²
Medical, health care, therapy, and activity spaces				709m²
Administrative, public, and ancillary support services				2,266m²
Service, maintenance, and mechanical areas				904m²
Total gross area				7,171m²

CONSTRUCTION COSTS

The following information is based on actual costs.
Final construction cost as of July 2001
Financing sources: bank loan, public-private sector subsidies

Building Costs
Total building costs $12.3 M

Site Costs
Total site costs $250,000

Total Project Costs $14.2 M

INDEX OF PROJECTS

The information and illustrations in this publication have
been prepared and supplied by the entrants. While all
reasonable efforts have been made to ensure accuracy,
the publishers do not, under any circumstances, accept
responsibility for errors, omissions and representations
express or implied.